THYME

Leaves of plant of mint family. Fairly aromatic so use with care for best flavor results.

Available in leaf or powdered form.

Use in meat, poultry and fish dishes, stuffings, chowders, bouquets garnis and combine with butter for vegetables.

SAGE

Leaf of plant of mint family. Very strong flavor. Use with care.

Available in dried leaf, rubbed and ground forms.

Use in stuffings for poultry or meat, pork dishes, cheese dishes, herb breads, tomato dishes.

...ARY

Leaves from shrub of mint family. Very fragrant and pleasing flavor. Use with care.

Available in leaf form.

Use for lamb and chicken dishes, seafood, vegetables, game, herb breads.

OREGANO

Leaves of plant of mint family — related to marjoram but stronger in flavor. Use with care.

Use in all tomato dishes, pasta sauces, pizza, vegetable and beef broths, stuffings for meat, poultry or fish, fish sauces, egg and cheese dishes.

BASIL

Leaf of plant of mint family. Savory yet delicate flavor.

Available in leaf or powdered form.

Use in tomato recipes, with other vegetables (eggplant, green beans, zucchini, peas, carrots, spinach), salads, meat dishes, fish and seafood, eggs, pizza, spaghetti sauce, macaroni.

MARJORAM

Leaves of plant of mint family. Fairly delicate but aromatic flavor.

Available in leaf form and ground.

Use in almost any dish except sweet foods. Good with all meats, game, poultry, fish, shellfish. Excellent addition to most vegetables, salads, stuffings, salad dressings, soups, egg dishes, herb breads.

MINT

Leaf of spearmint plant.

Available dried and fresh.

Use in sauce for lamb, jelly, punches, tea, garnish for beverages or salads or desserts, in sugar syrup to sweeten fruits, vegetables.

SAVORY

Leaves of plant of mint family. Fairly potent flavor.

Available ground.

Use with green beans, meats, meat stuffings, egg dishes, salads, sauces, ground beef dishes and blend with other herbs.

SAFFRON

Tips of pistils of blossoms of a species of purple crocus.

Extremely strong flavor—use very sparingly.

Available whole or powdered.

Use in Spanish and South American dishes — arroz con pollo, paella, risotto, and in yeast breads, rice, chicken, soups, seafood.

HERBS

TARRAGON

Leaves of shrub. Very aromatic with a touch of licorice flavor. Adds delightful flavor if used with care.

Available as dried leaves.

Use to flavor vinegar, pickles, salads, fish sauces, mayonnaise, game, lamb, veal, chicken.

CHERVIL

Fern-like leaves of plant of parsley family — more delicate but more aromatic than parsley.

Available in leaf form.

Use in soups, salads, sauces, eggs, cheese dishes, and in bouquets garnis and fines herbes combinations.

BAY LEAF

Leaf of evergreen laurel tree. Distinct, strong flavor so use carefully. (1 medium leaf enough for 6 portions — use a piece of leaf if in doubt.)

Use for soups, stews, stocks, pickles, cooking fish and shellfish, marinades, aspics, pot roasts.

THYME

Leaves of plant of mint family. Fairly aromatic so use with care for best flavor results.

Available in leaf or powdered form.

Use in meat, poultry and fish dishes, stuffings, chowders, bouquets garnis and combine with butter for vegetables.

SAGE

Leaf of plant of mint family. Very strong flavor. Use with care.

Available in dried leaf, rubbed and ground forms.

Use in stuffings for poultry or meat, pork dishes, cheese dishes, herb breads, tomato dishes.

ROSEMARY

Leaves from shrub of mint family. Very fragrant and pleasing flavor. Use with care.

Available in leaf form.

Use for lamb and chicken dishes, seafood, vegetables, game, herb breads.

BASIL

Leaf of plant of mint family. Savory yet delicate flavor.

Available in leaf or powdered form.

Use in tomato recipes, with other vegetables (eggplant, green beans, zucchini, peas, carrots, spinach), salads, meat dishes, fish and seafood, eggs, pizza, spaghetti sauce, macaroni.

MARJORAM

Leaves of plant of mint family. Fairly delicate but aromatic flavor.

Available in leaf form and ground.

Use in almost any dish except sweet foods. Good with all meats, game, poultry, fish, shellfish. Excellent addition to most vegetables, salads, stuffings, salad dressings, soups, egg dishes, herb breads.

OREGANO

Leaves of plant of mint family — related to marjoram but stronger in flavor. Use with care.

Use in all tomato dishes, pasta sauces, pizza, vegetable and beef broths, stuffings for meat, poultry or fish, fish sauces, egg and cheese dishes.

MARGO OLIVER'S

Weekend Magazine

COOK BOOK

Planning and design:
MAX NEWTON

Color Photography:
CHARLIE KING

Drawings and end papers:
PATRICIA DEWES

Type:
OPTIMA

Copyright ©, 1967

*By The Montreal Standard
Publishing Company Limited*

Printed and bound in Canada
1st printing October 1967
2nd printing July 1970
3rd printing June 1973
4th printing August 1974

PREFACE

I've often wished I were a mind reader. But never more than when I started this book.

I found I was talking to myself. Asking questions such as "If I were one of my readers what would I expect to find in Margo Oliver's cook book?" and "What do I expect to find in any cook book?"

To answer these questions I decided to see what my readers have told me in their letters to Weekend Magazine. And this book is the result of what I found.

Most requests for a cook book have come from readers who admit they are compulsive recipe clippers. But they tell me obviously there is a limit — that no matter how much they may like the looks of my recipes there is a point where there just isn't any more room for clippings. They ask for recipes in a book.

These letters sent me to the readers who ask for specific recipes. They often include a line to say that what they need most is ideas — help in planning daily meals. And help in planning entertaining meals too.

All of these letters told me I should make this a book of my most popular recipes. So I searched the mail again. And the recipes here are the result — the most requested of all my recipes, plus a few of my own favorites.

They are idea recipes — not basic ones. Most of us have a cook book to tell us "how to." I want this book to do something else. I want it to be useful daily. If it only suggests a soup, a salad, a main dish or a dessert to make your meal planning easier, I'll be happy.

For those who are looking for entertaining ideas, every recipe both my readers and I have found successful for a special menu is marked with this symbol ✻ in the contents.

So here it is — a cook book of ideas that my readers have found most useful, a book where entertaining ideas are specially marked, a book I hope you'll use often.

Margo Oliver

Contents

✻ *Symbol indicates recipes of special interest for entertaining.*

First Things First

What is a nicer invitation to a meal than a steaming bowl of hot soup — or an icy cup of cold soup? And what follows the soup, to add piquancy and freshness, better than salad? And what adds color, texture and flavor as vegetables do? This section is filled with ideas for these important items so necessary to good eating.

You may want to serve big and hearty hot Lentil Soup almost as a meal in itself. Or tickle bored palates with delicate but peppery cold Watercress Soup. You'll find recipes for these soups and others here. Some are old favorites, others may be new to you.

Whether you follow the soup with salad or prefer it served with or after the main course, this is where you'll find plenty of salad ideas. There are jellied salads filled with vegetables, fish or fruit, tossed green salads, fruit salads, potato salads and others. And there are dressings to go with them all.

If vegetables are a duty — rather than a pleasure — to eat you'll like these easy but slightly different approaches that add "zing" to most of the usual vegetables.

I hope these ideas will help give each of these foods its deserved and special place in your meal plans.

Minestrone — *recipe on page 8*

Soups

ASPARAGUS SOUP

2 lb. fresh asparagus
$1/4$ cup chopped green onions
  (with tops)
1 cup boiling water
2 tbsp. butter
2 tbsp. flour
$1^1/2$ tsp. salt
$1/4$ tsp. pepper
2 cups light cream
$1/2$ cup milk
$1/4$ tsp. dried mint leaves
  OR chopped fresh mint
2 tsp. lemon juice

Wash asparagus and cut in $1/2$-inch pieces. Combine with onions in a saucepan and add boiling water. Cover and cook until asparagus is very tender.

Force vegetables and cooking water through a sieve or buzz in blender until smooth.

Melt butter in saucepan. Sprinkle in flour, salt and pepper and let bubble up together. Remove from heat and add cream and milk all at once, stir to blend and return to moderate heat. Cook, stirring constantly, just until it comes to the boiling point.

Add mint and asparagus purée. Heat thoroughly but do not boil. Stir in lemon juice just before serving. (Serves 6.)

AUTUMN SOUP

1 lb. ground beef
1 tbsp. cooking (salad) oil
1 cup chopped onions
4 cups hot water
1 cup cut-up carrots
1 cup cut-up celery
1 cup cut-up potato
2 tsp. salt
$1/2$ tsp. pepper
1 tsp. meat extract
1 bay leaf
Pinch of basil
6 whole fresh tomatoes

Brown beef slowly in oil in heavy kettle. Add onions and cook 5 minutes, stirring constantly. Add remaining ingredients, except tomatoes. Bring to boil, cover and simmer 20 minutes.

Add tomatoes and simmer 10 minutes more. When serving, put a whole tomato in each bowl and surround with soup. (Serves 6.)

CHEESE SOUP

$1/4$ cup butter
$1/2$ cup finely-chopped onion
$1/2$ cup chopped celery
$1/4$ cup flour
1 tsp. dry mustard
Dash cayenne
Dash nutmeg
1 tsp. salt
$1/8$ tsp. pepper
$10^1/4$-oz. can beef bouillon
1 cup water
4 cups milk
1 tsp. Worcestershire sauce
2 cups grated sharp
  Cheddar cheese
1 lb. wieners, sliced
1 tbsp. butter
11-oz. pkg. frozen mixed
  vegetables, cooked
1 cup cubed cooked potatoes
Chopped parsley

Heat $1/4$ cup butter in large heavy saucepan. Add onion and celery and cook gently until onion is yellow. Stir in flour, mustard, cayenne, nutmeg, salt and pepper and let bubble up well.

Remove from heat and add bouillon, water and milk all at once. Stir to blend, return to moderate heat and cook, stirring, until mixture comes to boiling point. Stir in Worcestershire sauce and cheese, and heat, stirring, until cheese is melted. Do not boil.

Brown wieners in 1 tbsp. butter. Add to soup along with vegetables and potatoes. Heat well.

Serve hot sprinkled with chopped parsley. (Serves 12.)

CORN CHOWDER

5 slices bacon
1 tbsp. butter
1 medium onion, sliced
2 cups fresh-cooked corn (cut
  off cobs)
1 cup diced cooked potatoes
10-oz. can cream of celery soup
1 cup milk
1 cup light cream
1 tsp. salt
Dash pepper
Butter

Cook bacon until crisp. Lift out of pan, drain, cool and crumble.

Drain all but 1 tbsp. drippings from pan. Add 1 tbsp. butter and heat. Add onion and corn and cook gently until very lightly browned.

Add potatoes, soup, milk, cream, salt and pepper and bring to a boil. Cover and simmer 2 minutes. Pour into serving bowls, sprinkle with bacon and top with a small piece of butter. (Serves 4 to 6.)

BROWN POTATO SOUP

3 cups diced peeled potatoes
1 cup diced celery
1 medium onion, thinly sliced
2 cups boiling water
3 tsp. salt
$1/2$ tsp. pepper
2 cups light cream
2 cups milk
2 tbsp. butter
$1/2$ cup flour

Combine vegetables, water, salt, and pepper in saucepan and cook, covered, until vegetables are just tender.

Add cream and milk and bring back to boiling point. Turn heat to low.

Combine butter and flour, first with fork then with fingers, until crumbly. Put in small heavy skillet and brown well over moderate heat, stirring constantly.

Sprinkle flour mixture a little at a time into simmering mixture, stirring constantly (be sure to add only a little at a time and stir well so it doesn't lump). Cover and simmer 5 minutes, lifting cover and stirring several times. Serve very hot. (Serves 6 generously.)

CREAM OF POTATO SOUP

1 medium onion, chopped
6 green onions, chopped
2 tbsp. butter
2 large potatoes, diced
1 tbsp. chopped chives
  (optional)
2 tbsp. chopped parsley
2 sprigs celery leaves
1 tsp. salt
$1/8$ tsp. pepper
$1/8$ tsp. paprika
1 cup boiling water
2 tbsp. butter
1 tbsp. flour
$1/2$ tsp. salt
$1/8$ tsp. pepper
1 cup light cream
1 cup milk
2 chicken bouillon cubes

Cook onion and green onions in 2 tbsp. butter in heavy saucepan until yellow.

Add potatoes, chives, parsley, celery leaves, 1 tsp. salt, $1/8$ tsp. pepper, paprika and boiling water. Bring to a boil. Reduce heat, cover tightly and simmer 30 minutes or until vegetables are tender. Purée mixture by pressing through a sieve into a bowl.

Melt 2 tbsp. butter in same saucepan. Sprinkle in flour, $1/2$ tsp. salt and $1/8$ tsp. pepper and let bubble up. Remove from heat.

Add cream, milk and bouillon cubes. Return to moderate heat and cook, stirring constantly, until thickened and smooth and bouillon cubes are dissolved. Stir in potato purée and heat. (Serves 6.)

Note: This soup may be served chilled sprinkled with chopped chives, if desired.

Hot for winter or cold for summer, soups are always super

LEMON-RICE SOUP

2 cups water
$1/2$ cup long-grain rice
Two 10-oz. cans cream of
  chicken soup
1 cup water
8 thin strips lemon peel
  (see note below)
1 cup light cream
2 egg yolks
2 tbsp. lemon juice
$3/4$ tsp. salt
Freshly-ground pepper
2 tbsp. butter

Heat 2 cups water to boiling in top of double boiler over direct heat. Add rice, cover tightly and cook gently until rice is tender, about 20 minutes. Remove from heat.

Add soup, remaining 1 cup water and lemon peel and set over boiling water in bottom of double boiler. Heat thoroughly.

Beat cream and egg yolks together lightly with a fork. Add about half of hot mixture to egg yolk mixture gradually, stirring constantly. Pour back into top of double boiler and cook over simmering water, stirring often, until slightly thickened (it will look like thin custard).

Stir in lemon juice, salt, pepper and butter just at serving time and serve very hot. (Serves 8.)

Note: Cut lemon peel the full length of the lemon with a vegetable peeler or sharp paring knife. Cut very thin, using yellow part of peel only.

LENTIL SOUP

1 cup dried lentils
6 cups beef stock (recipe p. 10)
Ham bone (with a little meat
  left on) OR 1 cup slivered
  cooked ham
1 large potato, diced
1 medium onion, diced
1 large carrot, diced
1 tbsp. butter
$1/2$ tsp. flour
Salt and pepper
4 wieners

Wash lentils. Drain and put in large kettle. Cover with cold water and let soak overnight. Drain,

cover with cold water again and bring to a boil. Boil 15 minutes and drain.

Add beef stock and ham bone. Bring back to a boil, turn down heat, cover tightly and let simmer until lentils are nearly tender, about 2 hours.

Lift out ham bone, remove any pieces of meat, cut them in strips and return to soup. Discard bone.

Add potato, onion and carrot to soup. Cream butter and flour together and add bit by bit, stirring constantly to blend. Bring to a boil, taste and season (this varies with saltiness of ham and seasoning of broth).

Slice wieners into rounds $1/4$ inch thick and add to soup. Cover and simmer until vegetables are tender, about 15 minutes. Serve very hot. (Serves 8.)

MEATBALL SOUP

Soup bone with some meat
12 cups water
4 slices stale bread
Water
1 lb. ground beef
1 egg, slightly beaten
$1/2$ tsp. salt
$1/8$ tsp. pepper
$1/2$ tsp. leaf thyme
$1/4$ tsp. leaf oregano
2 tbsp. butter
2 medium carrots, slivered
$1/2$ cup thinly-sliced green onions
1 large stalk celery, sliced thin
$1/2$ cup diced turnip
14-oz. can whole-kernel corn,
  chopped
28-oz. can tomatoes
3 tsp. salt
$1/4$ tsp. pepper
Grated Parmesan cheese

Put soup bone in large kettle. Add 12 cups water, bring to a boil, turn down heat and simmer 4 hours. Strain and chill broth well. Lift off fat. Return to heat, bring to boiling and boil hard 30 minutes to concentrate stock.

Cover bread slices with water and let them soak up as much as possible. Squeeze dry. Break up bread and combine with beef. Add egg, $1/2$ tsp. salt, $1/8$ tsp. pepper, thyme and oregano and mix well.

Recipe continued on next page

Make into small balls about 1 inch in diameter. Heat butter in heavy skillet. Brown meat balls lightly on all sides. Add to stock.

Add carrots, onions, celery, turnip, corn, tomatoes, 3 tsp. salt and ¼ tsp. pepper. Cover and simmer 30 minutes or until vegetables are tender.

Serve in flat soup dishes sprinkled with cheese. (Makes 3 qts.)

MINESTRONE

8 cups beef bouillon, prepared in advance (recipe follows)
1 cup dried yellow peas
3 tbsp. olive oil
½ cup chopped onion
1 clove garlic, crushed
1 cup drained canned tomatoes
1 cup chopped cabbage
1 cup chopped celery
1 cup chopped carrots
2 cups diced cooked meat (left from making bouillon)
½ cup uncooked macaroni (bow or elbow shape)
4 cups torn-up raw spinach, lightly packed
Grated Parmesan cheese

Heat bouillon to boiling in large saucepan. Add peas (see note below), bring back to a boil, turn down heat, cover and simmer 1 hour, stirring occasionally.

Heat oil in small skillet and add onion and garlic. Cook gently, stirring, 2 minutes. Add to peas along with tomatoes. Cover and simmer 30 minutes.

Add cabbage, celery and carrots, cover again and simmer until vegetables are tender, about 30 minutes.

Add meat and macaroni, cover and simmer until macaroni is beginning to get tender, about 5 minutes. Add spinach and continue simmering until macaroni is completely cooked, about 5 minutes.

Serve immediately in soup bowls sprinkled with cheese. (Serves 8.)

Note: Most dried peas we get do not require soaking. Check package to be sure. If soaking is required cover with cold water and let stand overnight, drain and rinse under cold water and continue cooking as directed above.

Beef Bouillon

2 lb. stewing beef (in one piece)
1 large beef soup bone (with some meat)
12 cups water
Large sprig parsley
Large sprig celery leaves
1 tbsp. salt
1 tsp. pepper
¼ tsp. thyme
¼ tsp. nutmeg
6 whole cloves
1 bay leaf
2 carrots, cut up
1 large stalk celery, cut up
1 medium onion, cut up

Put all ingredients in a large soup pot. Bring to a full boil over high heat. Skim off scum. Lift off heat to let boiling stop. Return to high heat and bring back to a full boil. Skim again.

Turn heat down to simmer, cover tightly and simmer about 3 hours or until meat is very tender.

Cool. Lift out meat. Save meat to add to soup. Store in refrigerator.

Strain stock and discard all vegetables and bones. Chill and lift off and discard any fat that collects on the top. Keep refrigerated until needed.

ONION SOUP

3 tbsp. butter
4 large onions, sliced thin
1 tbsp. flour
8 cups beef stock (recipe p. 10)
Salt and pepper
French bread, lightly toasted
Grated Parmesan cheese

Melt butter in heavy skillet. Add onions and cook gently until soft but not brown. Add flour and stir to blend.

Stir in beef stock and simmer 10 minutes. Taste and add salt and pepper if necessary (amount will depend on seasoning in stock).

Heat oven to 450 degrees.

Pour soup into individual oven-proof soup bowls or large casserole. Top with toast and sprinkle toast thickly with Parmesan cheese. Put in oven and heat until cheese is nicely browned. (Serves 6 to 8.)

Gazpacho — recipe on page 10

BEEF STOCK

4 lb. beef bones, cracked
2 lb. veal bones, cracked
1 carrot, sliced
1 onion, sliced
Water
3 stalks celery (with leaves),
    cut up
3 sprigs parsley
1 leek, cut up (optional)
1 onion, cut up
1 carrot, cut up
10 peppercorns
1 tbsp. salt
5 cloves
1 bay leaf, crumbled

Have butcher crack bones and ask him to leave a little meat on them.

Heat oven to 400 degrees. Spread bones in a large roasting pan and sprinkle with sliced carrot and onion. Heat until bones are well browned, about 30 minutes.

Put bones and vegetables in large soup kettle. Add a little hot water to roasting pan and loosen any browned bits from bottom. Add to kettle.

Add boiling water to almost cover bones. Add celery, parsley, leek, onion, carrot and seasonings. Bring to a boil and skim off scum. Cover and simmer about 4 hours.

Strain, discard bones and vegetables. Cool stock quickly. Store in jars in refrigerator. Lift off fat before using stock in soup or other recipes.

To make croutons, spread slices of dry bread with soft butter. Cut in 1/2-inch cubes; toast in single layer in a shallow flat pan at 350 degrees in oven until golden, stirring often.

CHILLED TOMATO SOUP

6 large tomatoes
1/4 tsp. sweet basil
1 cup water
2 tsp. salt
3 cups buttermilk
1 cup light cream
Chopped chives
Croutons

Wash tomatoes and chop into saucepan. Add sweet basil and water. Set over moderate heat and simmer 15 minutes or until tomatoes are broken up.

Press through sieve to form a purée (or use a blender). Add salt and stir until dissolved. Cool.

Add buttermilk and cream and chill thoroughly.

Serve very cold topped with chopped chives and croutons. (Serves 8.)

CUCUMBER SOUP

3 medium cucumbers, peeled
    and sliced thin
1/2 cup chopped green onions
1/2 tsp. salt
Pinch pepper
1 cup water
2 tbsp. flour
1/4 cup cold water
2 cups hot water
Pinch cayenne
1 tbsp. chopped mint
1/2 cup heavy cream
Sprigs of mint
1/4 cup grated cucumber

Put cucumbers, onions, salt and pepper in saucepan. Add 1 cup water and bring to a boil, reduce heat, cover and simmer until cucumbers are very tender (about 10 minutes).

Blend flour and cold water until smooth and add to cucumber mixture gradually, stirring constantly. Add hot water and stir to blend. Simmer another 10 minutes.

Add cayenne and strain through a fine sieve, pressing as much of cucumber pulp through the sieve as possible. Add chopped mint.

Set in ice water and stir until cold, then strain again, add cream and chill thoroughly.

Serve in well-chilled bowls, garnished with a sprig of mint and topped with a small spoonful of grated cucumber. (Serves 6.)

GAZPACHO

Salt
1 clove garlic
4 large very ripe tomatoes
1 medium onion
1 large cucumber
1 medium green pepper
1 cup fresh tomato purée
    (see note)
3 tbsp. olive oil
1 tbsp. wine vinegar
1 tbsp. lemon juice
Dash Tabasco
1 1/2 tsp. salt
Freshly-ground pepper
Ice cubes
Chopped parsley

Sprinkle a little salt in a glass or pottery bowl. Peel clove of garlic and cut in half. Dip cut edges in salt and rub bowl all over with garlic. Discard garlic pieces.

Peel tomatoes and onion and chop very finely. Peel and seed cucumber and chop very finely. Seed green pepper and chop very finely. Combine all chopped vegetables in prepared bowl. Add tomato purée, oil, vinegar, lemon juice, Tabasco, salt and pepper to taste. Blend, cover and chill very well.

Chill soup bowls. Put an ice cube in each bowl at serving time and ladle soup over. Sprinkle with parsley. (Serves 6.)

Note: To make fresh tomato purée press very ripe peeled tomatoes through a sieve or buzz in blender. You may use a blender to chop all vegetables if desired.

QUICK TOMATO VICHYSSOISE

2 2/3-oz. pkg. cream of leek
    soup mix
2 cups water
6 ripe tomatoes, peeled and
    chopped
2 cups buttermilk
Salt
Chopped fresh dill

Combine soup mix and water in heavy saucepan. Bring to a boil, stirring constantly. Add chopped tomatoes and cover tightly. Simmer 15 minutes or until tomatoes are broken up, stirring occasionally.

Remove from heat and press soup mixture through a sieve or food mill or buzz in a blender. Chill.

Add buttermilk and salt to taste. Serve in chilled bowls sprinkled with dill. (Serves 8.)

WATERCRESS SOUP

2 leeks
3 tbsp. butter
2 medium potatoes, sliced thin
2 cups chicken stock
2 cups watercress (packed)
2 tbsp. butter
2 tsp. sugar
1 tsp. salt
¼ tsp. pepper
2 cups light cream
1 cup milk
1 egg yolk
Crumbled crisp bacon (optional)
Sprigs of watercress

Trim green and roots from leeks and slice thin. Heat 3 tbsp. butter in large heavy saucepan. Add leeks and cook gently, stirring, 5 minutes.

Add potatoes and chicken stock and simmer until potatoes are tender, about 20 minutes.

Discard large stems of watercress and chop remainder. Heat 2 tbsp. butter in small skillet, add cress and cook gently 3 minutes, stirring constantly. Add to leek-potato mixture along with sugar, salt and pepper. Cover and simmer 10 minutes.

Press mixture through a sieve or food mill (or buzz in blender a little at a time) and return to saucepan.

Stir in cream. Beat milk and egg yolk together lightly with a fork and stir in. Heat just to scalding point but do not boil. Taste and add more salt and pepper if necessary. Cool and chill well before serving.

Serve in small bowls garnished with finely-crumbled bacon and sprigs of watercress. (Serves 8.)

Salads

ASPARAGUS MOULD

10-oz. pkg. frozen asparagus
    OR 1 lb. fresh asparagus
1 envelope (1 tbsp.) unflavored
    gelatin
1/4 cup cold water
3/4 cup boiling water
1 tsp. salt
1 tsp. onion juice
1/4 tsp. Worcestershire sauce
2 tbsp. lemon juice
1 tsp. horseradish
1 hard-cooked egg, sliced
1 cup chopped celery
10-oz. can consommé

Cook asparagus until tender, drain and cool. Set 8 stalks aside to decorate mould and cut up remaining stalks into 1/2-inch pieces.

Soften gelatin in cold water. Dissolve in boiling water.

Add salt, onion juice, Worcestershire sauce, lemon juice and horseradish. Chill until slightly thickened.

Support whole asparagus stalks on the sides of a 1 1/2-qt. mould and arrange egg slices in a pattern on bottom of mould. Spoon in carefully a shallow layer of gelatin mixture to anchor asparagus and egg slices. Chill until firm.

Add chopped asparagus, celery and consommé to remaining gelatin. Add to mould and chill until firm. (Serves 6 to 8.)

CUCUMBER-LIME RING

3-oz. pkg. lime gelatin
1 1/2 tsp. salt
1 cup boiling water
2 small cucmbers OR 1 very
    large
3 tbsp. white vinegar
1 1/2 tsp. grated onion
1/2 cup commercial sour cream
1/4 cup thick mayonnaise
1/4 cup paper-thin radish slices
Lettuce
Sliced cucumbers
Sliced radishes

Combine gelatin and salt and add boiling water. Stir until gelatin is dissolved.

Peel cucumbers and grate on fine grater into a bowl. Drain well, saving liquid. Measure out 1 1/2 cups of grated cucumber pulp and

1/4 cup of the liquid.

Add the cucumber liquid to the gelatin mixture along with the vinegar and onion. Chill until beginning to set.

Add sour cream and mayonnaise and beat well with rotary beater. Stir in grated cucumber and 1/4 cup radish slices. Pour into 9-inch ring mould and chill until firm. Unmould on lettuce and garnish with sliced cucumbers and radishes. (Serves 6.)

PARTY TOMATO SALAD

2 envelopes (2 tbsp.) unflavored
    gelatin
1/4 cup cold water
10-oz. can tomato soup
1/2 tsp. salt
1/8 tsp. pepper
8-oz. carton cream-style
    cottage cheese
1/2 cup diced green pepper
1 cup diced celery
1 cup thick mayonnaise

Soak gelatin in cold water 5 minutes.

Heat soup, salt and pepper to boiling point. Add gelatin and stir until dissolved.

Chill until mixture begins to thicken, then fold in remaining ingredients.

Pour into 9-inch ring mould and chill until set. (Serves 6 to 8.)

FISH SALAD

1 envelope (1 tbsp.) unflavored
    gelatin
3/4 cup tomato juice
1 tbsp. bottled steak sauce
1 cup tomato juice
1 envelope (1 tbsp.) unflavored
    gelatin
1/2 cup cold water
1 cup commercial sour cream
3/4 cup mayonnaise
1/2 cup diced celery
1/4 cup chopped green pepper
1/4 cup chopped green onions
1 tbsp. diced pimento
1 tsp. grated lemon rind
1 tsp. lemon juice
7 3/4-oz. can salmon, flaked
7-oz. can tuna, flaked
Lettuce

Add 1 envelope gelatin to 3/4

Salads of all sorts are always in demand whether you plan on elegant entertaining or just plain easy eating

cup tomato juice in saucepan. Let stand 5 minutes. Add steak sauce. Heat, stirring constantly, until gelatin is dissolved. Remove from heat and stir in remaining 1 cup tomato juice. Pour into 2-qt. mould and chill until set, but still a little sticky on surface.

Add remaining 1 envelope gelatin to cold water in saucepan and let stand 5 minutes. Heat, stirring constantly, until gelatin is dissolved. Remove from heat, cool and add all remaining ingredients except lettuce, stirring lightly to blend. Add to mould on top of firm tomato layer and chill again until set. Unmould on lettuce to serve. (Serves 6 to 8.)

SALMON MOUSSE

3 envelopes (3 tbsp.) unflavored
    gelatin
3/4 cup cold water
1/4 cup lemon juice
1/2 cup vinegar
1 tbsp. dry mustard
Three 1-lb. cans red salmon
3 cups finely-diced celery
3 tbsp. chopped sweet pickle
2 tbsp. minced parsley
2 tbsp. finely-grated onion
1 tsp. dill seeds, crushed
1/2 tsp. Worcestershire sauce
2 tsp. salt
1/4 tsp. pepper
1 1/2 cups whipping cream
Watercress OR parsley
Cucumber Sauce (recipe
    follows)

Recipe continued on page 14

Julius Szelei

Combine gelatin, water, lemon juice and vinegar in small dish. Let stand 5 minutes. Add dry mustard and stir to blend. Set dish in boiling water and stir until gelatin is dissolved. Cool (do not chill).

Flake salmon finely into large bowl. Add celery, pickle, parsley, onion, dill seeds, Worcestershire sauce, salt and pepper. Stir in dissolved gelatin mixture.

Whip cream until stiff and fold into salmon mixture. Pour into large mould (2½ to 3 qts.) or 2 small moulds and chill until set.

Unmould and garnish with watercress or parsley. Serve with Cucumber Sauce. (Serves 12 to 16.)

Cucumber Sauce

2 cups sour cream
1 cup seeded grated cucumber
1 tsp. salt
4 tsp. finely-chopped chives
½ tsp. black pepper

Combine all ingredients. Chill 1 to 2 hours.

TUNA SALAD IN CUCUMBER RING

2 envelopes (2 tbsp.) unflavored gelatin
½ cup cold water
2½ cups boiling water
2 tbsp. sugar
½ tsp. salt
¼ cup lemon juice
Green food coloring
2 cups diced cucumber
1 cup sliced radishes
¼ cup chopped green onions
Lettuce
Tuna Salad (recipe follows)
Mayonnaise

Soak gelatin in cold water for 5 minutes. Measure boiling water into bowl, add gelatin and stir until dissolved.

Add sugar, salt, lemon juice and coloring to tint a delicate green. Cool, then chill until beginning to set. Fold in vegetables except lettuce.

Pour into 9-inch ring mould. Chill.

Unmould on lettuce at serving time. Fill with Tuna Salad. Serve with mayonnaise. (Serves 12.)

Tuna Salad

Two 7-oz. cans tuna
1 cup cooked peas
2 cups shredded cabbage
2 tbsp. chopped pimento
2 tbsp. chopped green pepper
½ cup French dressing
1 tbsp. minced parsley
1 tbsp. minced watercress
2 tsp. minced chives

Drain and flake tuna. Combine with peas, cabbage, pimento and green pepper, tossing lightly.

Mix remaining ingredients. Pour over tuna mixture and toss lightly. Chill. Spoon into centre of cucumber ring at serving time.

CRANBERRY-ORANGE SALAD

4 cups fresh cranberries
1 tbsp. grated orange rind
½ cup sugar
1 cup water
1 cup orange juice
Two 3-oz. pkg. orange gelatin
2 cups diced unpeeled red apples
1 cup coarsely-chopped walnuts
Lettuce

Grind berries through the coarse blade of the food chopper. Add orange rind and sugar and let stand while preparing gelatin mixture, stirring occasionally.

Heat water and orange juice. Add to gelatin and stir until gelatin is dissolved. Chill until beginning to set.

Stir in cranberries, apples and walnuts. Pour into 2-qt. mould or individual moulds. Chill until set. Unmould and serve on lettuce. (Serves 8 to 10.)

CRUNCHY CITRUS SALAD

5-oz. pkg. grapefruit-pineapple gelatin
1¾ cups boiling water
15-oz. can orange and grapefruit sections
4-oz. pkg. cream cheese
⅓ cup finely-chopped walnuts
½ cup chopped celery

Dissolve gelatin in boiling water. Drain juice from orange and grapefruit sections, measure juice and add water to make 1 cup liquid. Add to gelatin and chill mixture until thickened but not set.

Divide cheese into 16 pieces, shape each into small ball. Roll in nuts.

Fold cheese balls, celery and fruit sections into gelatin.

Pour into 1-qt. mould which has been rinsed with cold water. Chill until firm. (Serves 6.)

ANCHOVY SALAD

Four 2-oz. cans anchovies
3 large tomatoes
3 green peppers
1 sweet red pepper
12 scallions OR shallots
18 ripe olives
½ cup olive oil
1 tbsp. vinegar
Freshly-ground pepper
3 qts. mixed greens (lettuce, romaine, chicory, curly endive, spinach, etc.)

Drain oil from cans of anchovies into large wooden salad bowl. Separate anchovy fillets, cut in large pieces and add to salad bowl.

Peel and seed tomatoes and cut into thin strips. Seed peppers and cut into thin strips.

Slice scallions or shallots thinly, and cut ripe olives from stones into thin crescent-shaped pieces.

Add vegetables and olives to salad bowl. Pour olive oil and vinegar over mixture in bowl, and sprinkle generously with freshly-ground pepper.

Toss together lightly and put in refrigerator for 1 hour.

Add a variety of greens torn into bite-sized pieces at serving time. Add just enough to take up the oil in the bowl. Toss lightly and serve immediately. (Serves 12.)

CAULIFLOWER SALAD

1 small cauliflower
1 cup thinly-sliced celery
3 green onions (with tops),
   sliced thin
½ cup chopped parsley
Salt
1 clove garlic
3 medium apples
¼ cup salad oil OR olive oil
½ tsp. salt
½ tsp. paprika
Freshly-ground pepper
¼ cup wine vinegar

Break cauliflower into flowerettes, wash and slice them very thin (you will have about 5 cups). Add celery, onions and parsley and chill well.

Sprinkle a little salt into a wooden salad bowl. Peel garlic, cut in half and rub bowl with cut sides.

Add vegetable mixture to bowl. Dice apples and add. Sprinkle with oil and toss lightly. Sprinkle in salt, paprika and pepper, add vinegar and toss again lightly. Serve immediately. (Serves 6 to 8.)

CHEF'S SALAD

1 head lettuce
½ head romaine
½ head chicory
¼ cup chopped green onion
½ cup thinly-sliced celery
1 cup thin strips Swiss cheese
1 cup thin strips ham OR tongue
1 cup thin strips chicken
½ cup mayonnaise
¼ cup French dressing
Asparagus Vinaigrette (recipe
   follows)
Strips of pimento
Devilled eggs
Radish slices
Ripe olive slices

Tear lettuce, romaine and chicory in bite-size pieces into a salad bowl. Add onion, celery and ¾ cup each of the cheese, ham or tongue and chicken and toss together lightly.

Combine mayonnaise and French dressing, pour over salad ingredients and toss lightly.

Garnish top of salad with remaining strips of cheese, ham or

tongue and chicken, Asparagus Vinaigrette, pimento strips, devilled eggs, radish slices and ripe olive slices. (Serve 6.)

Asparagus Vinaigrette

18 slender stalks fresh asparagus,
   cooked
1 clove garlic, minced very fine
½ tsp. salt
¼ tsp. pepper
1 tsp. oregano
¼ tsp. mustard
2½ tbsp. cider vinegar
½ cup olive oil

Lay asparagus in shallow glass pan. Combine remaining ingredients and pour over asparagus. Cover tightly with foil and put in refrigerator to marinate 2 to 3 hours. Baste occasionally.

Lift out of oil mixture and use to garnish salad as directed.

NIÇOISE SALAD

½ lb. green beans
2 tbsp. oil drained from tuna
¼ cup olive oil
2 tbsp. wine vinegar
1 tsp. salt
¼ tsp. black pepper
½ tsp. dried sweet basil
1 medium green pepper, slivered
½ Spanish onion, sliced paper
   thin
½ cup sliced radishes (paper thin)
4 tomatoes, peeled and quartered
1 head Boston lettuce OR 1 small
   head iceberg lettuce, torn up
7-oz. can tuna, broken up
8 anchovy fillets, cut up
2 hard-cooked eggs, quartered
½ cup pitted ripe olives OR slivers
   of ripe olives
1 tbsp. capers

Wash beans and cut in 1½-inch lengths on the diagonal. Cook in boiling salted water until tender, about 15 minutes. Drain and chill.

Combine tuna oil, olive oil, vinegar, salt, pepper and sweet basil and let stand 30 minutes.

Toss green beans, green pepper, onion, radishes, tomatoes and lettuce together lightly. Pour oil mixture over and toss again lightly. Top with chunks of tuna, pieces of anchovy, pieces of eggs, ripe olives and capers. Serve immediately. (Serves 6.)

SPINACH SALAD

8 slices bacon
1 lb. crisp young spinach
3 hard-cooked eggs, chopped
¾ cup Garlic French Dressing
   (recipe p. 18)

Fry bacon until crisp, pouring off fat as it cooks. Drain and crumble.

Tear spinach into a salad bowl. Sprinkle bacon and eggs on top.

Pour dressing over and toss lightly. Serve immediately. (Serves 6 to 8.)

WESTERN SALAD

2 small cloves garlic, cut in halves
¼ cup olive oil OR salad oil
2 cups small toasted bread cubes
6 cups mixed salad greens
¼ cup olive oil OR salad oil
1 tbsp. Worcestershire sauce
½ tsp. salt
¼ tsp. pepper (freshly ground
   if possible)
½ cup grated Parmesan cheese
¼ cup crumbled blue cheese
¼ cup lemon juice
1 egg

Add garlic to ¼ cup oil. Let stand several hours. Remove garlic and mix oil and bread cubes.

Tear greens into large salad bowl (use several different kinds such as head lettuce, leaf lettuce, spinach, romaine, chicory). Add remaining ¼ cup oil, Worcestershire sauce, salt, pepper, Parmesan cheese and blue cheese and toss lightly.

Pour lemon juice over salad, break egg on top and toss again lightly.

Add bread cubes and toss just to blend lightly. Serve immediately. (Serves 6.)

Don't cut salad greens. Break them into bite-size pieces for crisper, more attractive salads.

KIDNEY BEAN SALAD

15-oz. can kidney beans
1 cup diced celery
½ cup diced green pepper
½ cup raw sliced fresh
 mushrooms
½ cup diced sweet pickles
2 green onions with tops, sliced
 very thin
1 tsp. salt
¼ cup commercial chili sauce
⅓ cup mayonnaise
Lettuce

Pour beans into sieve and rinse under cold water to remove sauce. Take out any pieces of pork.

Combine beans, celery, green pepper, mushrooms, pickles, onions and salt in a bowl and toss together lightly.

Combine chili sauce and mayonnaise, pour over vegetables and toss again lightly. Chill well.

Line a bowl with lettuce and spoon in bean mixture. (Serves 6.)

MARINATED TOMATOES AND CUCUMBERS

3 large tomatoes, peeled and
 sliced thick
½ large cucumber, sliced thin
½ cup thinly-sliced green onions
¾ cup bottled French dressing
1 clove garlic, crushed
1 dill pickle, minced
3 large green olives, minced
1½ tsp. minced pimento
½ tsp. oregano
Lettuce
Minced chives

Arrange tomato slices and cucumber slices overlapping in a shallow glass dish. Sprinkle with onions.

Combine French dressing, garlic, dill pickle, olives, pimento and oregano in a jar with a tight lid. Shake together well to blend. Pour over vegetables. Cover and chill in refrigerator at least an hour before serving.

Lift vegetable slices out of marinade, lay on lettuce and sprinkle with chives to serve. Spoon a little of marinade over each serving if desired. (Serves 4 to 6.)

HOT POTATO SALAD

6 medium potatoes
1 tsp. salt
6 slices bacon, diced
1 medium onion, diced
1 chicken bouillon cube
½ cup boiling water
⅓ cup vinegar
2 tsp. sugar
2 tsp. salt
¼ tsp. pepper
1 egg, beaten
¼ cup minced parsley
Sliced radishes

Scrub potatoes. Drop potatoes (in jackets) into boiling water. Add 1 tsp. salt. Cook until potatoes are just tender. Peel and cut into thick slices.

Fry bacon until crisp. Add onion and cook gently until yellow.

Dissolve bouillon cube in boiling water and combine with vinegar, sugar, 2 tsp. salt and pepper. Add to bacon and onion mixture and bring to a boil. Add egg slowly, stirring briskly all the time. Cook, stirring, until slightly thickened.

Pour over potatoes while hot, add parsley and toss lightly.

Serve immediately garnished with radish slices. (Serves 6.)

HOT POTATO SALAD IN SHELLS

6 medium baking potatoes
6 strips bacon
¾ cup minced onion
1½ tsp. salt
¼ tsp. pepper
½ tsp. celery seeds
1 tbsp. sugar
¼ cup vinegar
½ cup minced green pepper
Butter

Heat oven to 400 degrees.

Bake potatoes about 1 hour or until done.

Cook bacon until crisp, drain and crumble.

Add onion to bacon drippings and cook gently until yellow. Add salt, pepper, celery seeds, sugar and vinegar. Heat.

Cut a thin slice from tops of baked potatoes and scoop out inside, being careful not to break the shells.

Blend potato with vinegar mixture, crumbled bacon and green pepper. Stuff back into shells and dot with butter.

Set in baking dish and slip under broiler to heat thoroughly and lightly brown tops. (Serves 6.)

POTATO SALAD WITH SOUR CREAM DRESSING

4 cups diced cooked potatoes
½ cup diced cucumber
½ cup thinly-sliced radishes
1 tbsp. finely-minced onion
1 tsp. celery salt
1½ tsp. salt
¼ tsp. pepper
3 hard-cooked eggs
1 cup commercial sour cream
½ cup mayonnaise
2 tbsp. sweet pickle juice
2 tbsp. lemon juice
½ tsp. dry mustard

Toss potatoes, cucumber, radishes, onion, celery salt, salt and pepper together lightly with a fork.

Cut eggs in half and remove and set aside yolks. Dice whites and add to potato mixture.

Mash egg yolks. Add cream, mayonnaise, pickle juice, lemon juice and mustard and mix well. Add to potato mixture and toss well. Cover and chill. (Serves 6 to 8.)

FRUIT SALAD

3 cups mixed melon balls
 (cantaloup, honeydew,
 watermelon, etc.)
1½ cups seedless green grapes
1 cup cubed fresh peaches
1 tbsp. finely-chopped
 fresh mint
4-oz. pkg. cream cheese
¼ cup Sweet Boiled Dressing
 (recipe p. 18)
Lettuce

Combine fruit and mint and chill well.

Mash cream cheese and blend in salad dressing until smooth. Combine with fruit. Serve on lettuce. (Serves 6.)

PEAR WALDORF SALAD

2 cups diced, peeled pears
1 cup diced celery
½ cup broken walnuts
½ cup red grapes, halved and
    seeded
1 tbsp. lemon juice
¼ cup Sweet Boiled Dressing
    (recipe p. 18)

Mix pears, celery, walnuts and grapes.

Sprinkle with lemon juice, and toss with salad dressing.

Serve immediately. (Serves 6.)

CHICKEN AND MELON SALAD

2 cups diced cooked chicken
1 orange, sectioned and cut up
½ cup seedless green grapes,
    halved
¼ cup coarsely-chopped toasted
    salted almonds
1 cup cantaloup balls or cubes
Lettuce
1 medium cantaloup
½ cup mayonnaise (approx.)
½ cup blueberries (optional)
Mint sprigs

Combine chicken, orange, grapes, almonds and cantaloup balls or cubes. Chill very well.

Put lettuce on 4 individual serving plates at serving time. Cut whole cantaloup to make 4 slices about 1 inch thick. Remove seeds and peel and place rings on lettuce.

Add mayonnaise to chicken mixture and toss lightly. Spoon this mixture into rings of cantaloup. Garnish each salad with a few blueberries and a sprig of mint. (Serves 4.)

CHICKEN AND ORANGE SALAD

Cold roast chicken
4 large oranges
1 cup seedless green grapes
2 cups shredded lettuce
½ medium avocado
½ cup buttermilk
1 tbsp. grated onion
2 tbsp. lime juice
½ tsp. salt
Dash pepper
Dash Tabasco
Romaine OR leaf lettuce
Orange slices

Cut enough thin slices of chicken to serve 6. Chill.

Peel oranges and dice into bowl. Add grapes and lettuce and chill.

Mash avocado and combine with buttermilk, onion, lime juice, salt, pepper and Tabasco. (Whirl in the blender if you have one.) Chill.

Cover 6 individual serving plates with romaine or leaf lettuce at serving time. Put slices of chicken on one side of plate. Spoon orange mixture on other side of plate. Top orange salad with some of avocado mixture. Garnish plate with orange slices. (Serves 6.)

FRESH PINEAPPLE SALAD

2 large whole chicken breasts
¼ cup butter
1 tbsp. finely-chopped candied
    ginger
¼ cup finely-chopped green
    onion
½ tsp. salt
2 cups diced fresh pineapple
½ cup commercial sour cream
2 egg yolks
½ tsp. curry powder
Grated rind of 1 lemon
Juice of 1 lemon
½ cup chopped salted mixed
    nuts
Lettuce
Green pepper rings

Have butcher cut chicken breasts in two to make 4 halves. Skin and bone and cut raw meat into 1-inch cubes.

Heat butter, ginger and onion in large heavy skillet and add chicken pieces. Sprinkle with salt. Cook over moderate heat, stirring constantly, until chicken pieces turn white and are tender (this only takes a few minutes).

Lift chicken pieces out of pan with slotted spoon or egg turner.

Add pineapple to drippings left in pan. (You may use a 20-oz. can of pineapple chunks drained and diced if fresh pineapple is not available.) Cook over high heat, stirring constantly, 2 minutes. Remove from heat and turn heat to low.

Beat cream, egg yolks, curry powder, lemon rind and juice together lightly with a fork. Add to pineapple along with chicken pieces. Return to low heat and cook, stirring constantly, until very hot but not boiling. Spoon into bowl, cool and chill.

Stir in nuts at serving time. Line salad bowl with lettuce and spoon chicken mixture into bowl. Garnish with green pepper rings. (Serves 6 to 8.)

If you must prepare salad ahead, put dressing in bottom of bowl and add wedges of tomato. Tear greens in on top but don't toss. Tomato will marinate nicely and raise greens out of dressing so they won't wilt. Toss salad just before serving.

TURKEY SALAD

2 cups diced cooked turkey
2 tbsp. currants
¼ cup coarsely-chopped
    walnuts
¼ cup chopped celery
½ tsp. curry powder
¼ tsp. ginger
⅛ tsp. nutmeg
3 tbsp. salad oil
1½ tbsp. lemon juice
1½ tbsp. mayonnaise
⅛ tsp. salt
    Dash Tabasco
2 medium apples, cored and
    diced
2 oranges, peeled and diced
    Lettuce cups

Combine turkey, currants, walnuts, celery, curry powder, ginger and nutmeg. Chill ½ hour.

Combine oil, lemon juice, mayonnaise, salt and Tabasco in small jar and shake to blend well. Pour over salad and toss lightly. Add diced apples and oranges and toss again. Serve in lettuce cups. (Serves 6.)

FRESH SALMON SALAD

2 lb. fresh salmon, in one piece
¼ cup chopped celery and leaves
1 tbsp. chopped onion
1½ tsp. salt
¼ tsp. pepper
    Small piece of bay leaf, crushed
    Lettuce
    Mayonnaise
2 hard-cooked egg yolks
2 tbsp. capers

Set piece of salmon on a piece of wet parchment or heavy-duty aluminum foil large enough to wrap it completely. Measure thickness of fish and make a note of it for calculation of cooking time.

Sprinkle fish with celery, onion, salt, pepper and bay leaf. Bring parchment up around fish and tie at top to make a pouch or wrap foil around fish securely, using double folds to make package water-tight.

Put in boiling water to cover in large saucepan. Boil 10 minutes per inch of thickness. Lift out of water immediately and check to

see if it is done (fish should flake with a fork but should be holding its shape well). Cool. Skin and bone fish and chill thoroughly.

Break salmon into large flakes at serving time. Line salad bowl with lettuce and pile salmon in middle. Top with mayonnaise. Press hard-cooked egg yolks through a sieve to garnish top. Sprinkle capers around outer edge. Serve immediately. (Serves 6.)

MANDARIN-SHRIMP SALAD

11-oz. can mandarin oranges
4¼-oz. can large cleaned shrimp
¼ cup French dressing
    Freshly-ground pepper
¼ cup coarsely-chopped parsley
4 cups broken-up lettuce

Drain oranges very well. Drain shrimp and rinse under cold water. Drain well again and combine with oranges. Add French dressing and a good grating of pepper. Chill well. Toss in parsley and lettuce at serving time. (Serves 4.)

CRAB-STUFFED AVOCADO

6½-oz. can crab meat
    (about 1½ cups flaked)
½ cup mayonnaise
½ cup minced celery
¼ cup minced pimento
¼ cup minced parsley
2 tsp. lemon juice
1 tsp. prepared mustard
    Dash Tabasco
    Dash Worcestershire sauce
    Watercress
2 ripe avocados
    Lemon juice
    Salt
    Cherry tomatoes
    Ripe olives

Drain crab meat and flake into a bowl. Chill well.

Combine mayonnaise, celery, pimento, parsley, 2 tsp. lemon juice, prepared mustard, Tabasco and Worcestershire sauce. Chill.

Cover salad plates with crisp watercress at serving time. Cut each avocado in half lengthwise, remove pit and peel. Dip cut sides

in lemon juice, sprinkle lightly with salt and set on top of watercress. Fill with chilled crab meat.

Spoon mayonnaise mixture generously over crab. Garnish plates with tomatoes and olives. Serve immediately. (Serves 4.)

BASIC FRENCH DRESSING

1 cup olive OR salad oil
¼ cup vinegar
¼ cup lemon juice
1 tsp. salt
½ tsp. dry mustard
½ tsp. paprika

Shake all ingredients together in a tightly covered jar. Keep in refrigerator. Shake before using. (Makes 1½ cups.)

VARIATIONS

Sweet French Dressing: Replace vinegar in above recipe with orange or pineapple juice. Add ¼ cup liquid honey and 1 tsp. celery seed.

Garlic French Dressing: Let 1 clove garlic, cut in half crosswise, stand in ¾ cup of Basic French Dressing at least 1 hour before using. When flavor is strong enough discard garlic pieces.

SWEET BOILED DRESSING

1 egg
⅓ cup sugar
1½ tbsp. flour
1½ tsp. dry mustard
½ tsp. salt
⅓ cup white vinegar
1 cup milk

Put egg, sugar, flour, mustard and salt in saucepan and beat with wooden spoon until smooth and blended. Stir in vinegar and milk.

Set over moderate heat and cook, stirring constantly, until boiling. Boil 1 minute, stirring constantly. Cool and store in refrigerator in covered jar. (Makes 1½ cups.)

Note: This dressing keeps very well for several weeks in refrigerator and if you use a large amount you may want to double the recipe. Use for fruit and lettuce salads.

HOME-MADE MAYONNAISE

2 egg yolks
½ tsp. salt
Dash white pepper
½ tsp. dry mustard
Dash cayenne
1 tsp. vinegar OR lemon juice
1 cup olive oil (or part olive oil and part salad oil)
2 tsp. vinegar OR lemon juice

Warm small mixing bowl by running it under hot water. Dry well. Put egg yolks in bowl and beat with rotary beater or electric mixer at medium speed until well broken up. Add salt, pepper, mustard, cayenne and 1 tsp. vinegar or lemon juice and continue beating to blend well.

Start adding oil drop by drop, beating steadily. When about ⅓ of the oil has been added this way or when the mayonnaise begins to thicken, add the oil a little faster in a thin steady stream, beating steadily. Stop adding the oil a few times and continue beating to be sure the mixture is well blended. Add remaining vinegar or lemon juice when all oil has been added. (Makes 1½ cups.)

QUICK THOUSAND ISLAND DRESSING

½ cup mayonnaise
1 tbsp. chili sauce
1 tbsp. chopped stuffed olives
1 tsp. minced chives
1 hard-cooked egg, chopped
¼ tsp. paprika
Salt and pepper

Combine all ingredients, seasoning to taste with salt and pepper. (Makes about ¾ cup.)

Vegetables

ASPARAGUS SPECIAL

1 lb. fresh asparagus
3 tbsp. salad oil
1/4 cup water
3 green onions (with tops), sliced
   very thin
1/2 tsp. salt
1/4 tsp. marjoram

Cut asparagus on the diagonal in 1/2-inch pieces. Put in large heavy skillet.

Add remaining ingredients. Cover tightly (use aluminum foil if your skillet has no lid). Set over high heat and cook rapidly 4 to 5 minutes, shaking the pan occasionally. (Check about half-way through the cooking to be sure liquid hasn't cooked away and add a few drops of water if necessary.)

Test with a fork, cooking only until tender-crisp. Serve immediately. (Serves 2.)

BROCCOLI ALMONDINE

Two 10-oz. pkg. frozen
   broccoli
1/4 cup butter
1/2 cup slivered almonds

Cook broccoli according to package directions. Drain and put in serving dish.

Melt butter in heavy skillet. Add almonds and cook gently several minutes until they are crisp and golden.

Pour over broccoli. (Serves 6.)

CABBAGE AND EGG

2 tbsp. butter
3 tbsp. boiling water
5 to 6 cups finely-shredded
   cabbage (1 medium)
1 tsp. salt
1/4 tsp. pepper
1 egg, beaten
1/2 cup commercial sour cream
1 tsp. caraway seeds (optional)

Melt butter in heavy skillet, add boiling water and cabbage and season with salt and pepper.

Cover and cook over low heat for 5 minutes.

Add egg and cook slowly for 3 minutes, covered, stirring occasionally.

Add sour cream and caraway seeds. Heat through and serve immediately. (Serves 6.)

> **Pity the poor vegetable — it's oft-neglected and much maligned. Yet with a little care it can be one of the stars at your table**

BUTTER-COOKED CARROTS

3 tbsp. butter
4 cups match-like strips raw
   carrots
1 tsp. sugar
1 tsp. salt
2 tbsp. finely-minced parsley
2 tbsp. water
1 tsp. flour
1 tsp. lemon juice
1/2 cup light cream
Pepper

Melt butter in heavy skillet. Add carrots, sugar, salt, parsley and water. Cover very tightly (use aluminum foil if pan doesn't have a tight cover) and cook rapidly about 5 minutes or just until carrots are tender-crisp (be sure not to over-cook — goodness of dish depends on texture of carrots).

Add flour and lemon juice to the cream and stir until blended. Stir into hot carrots and set over low heat, stirring just enough to keep the mixture from sticking. Cook only until cream is hot. Sprinkle with pepper and serve immediately. (Serves 4.)

GINGER CARROTS

8 medium carrots
2 tsp. lemon juice
1 tsp. salt
1/2 tsp. ginger
1/8 tsp. pepper
1 tbsp. butter

Heat oven to 400 degrees. Peel carrots and slice. Put in greased 1-qt. casserole.

Mix lemon juice, salt, ginger and pepper and pour over carrots. Dot with butter.

Cover tightly and bake 30 minutes. Stir with a fork, cover and bake until tender, about 15 minutes. (Serves 2 to 4.)

GLAZED SHREDDED CARROTS

3 cups finely-grated carrots
5 tbsp. water
1/2 tsp. salt
1/4 tsp. pepper
1/4 cup butter
1 tsp. grated onion
1/4 cup brown sugar
1 tsp. grated lemon rind
Juice of 1 lemon

Combine all ingredients in a saucepan. Bring to a boil, turn down heat, cover tightly and simmer until carrots are tender, 8 to 10 minutes.

Serve immediately with pan juices. (Serves 4 to 6.)

CARROTS AND TURNIPS

6 medium carrots, sliced
2 cups diced turnips
2 tbsp. butter
Salt and pepper

Cook vegetables separately in boiling salted water until tender.

Combine vegetables, butter and salt and pepper to taste, and mash together until light and fluffy. (Serves 4.)

CRISPY PARSNIPS

8 medium-size whole parsnips
1/2 tsp. salt
1/4 tsp. pepper
1 egg
1/2 cup fine cracker OR
   dry bread crumbs
1/4 cup butter

Cook whole parsnips in boiling water until almost tender. Drain.

Add salt and pepper to egg and beat slightly with fork.

Dip each parsnip in egg, then in crumbs, coating well.

Heat butter in heavy skillet, add parsnips and cook slowly until golden brown, turning often. (Serves 4.)

MEATY SCALLOPED POTATOES

2 tbsp. butter
4-oz. jar chipped beef
1/4 cup minced onion
2 tbsp. flour
1/4 tsp. pepper
4 cups milk
6 large potatoes
1/2 cup sliced stuffed olives
1/2 cup fine dry bread crumbs
1/4 cup melted butter

Heat oven to 350 degrees. Butter a 2-qt. casserole.

Heat butter in heavy saucepan. Snip beef into small pieces with kitchen shears and add to hot butter along with onion. Cook gently until onion is yellow.

Sprinkle in flour and pepper and let bubble up well. Remove from heat. Add milk all at once, stir to blend and return to moderate heat. Cook, stirring constantly, until boiling.

Peel potatoes and slice very thin into prepared casserole. Add olives to sauce and pour over potatoes, mixing sauce through potatoes lightly.

Combine bread crumbs and melted butter and sprinkle over all.

Bake about 1 1/2 hours or until potatoes are tender and have absorbed the sauce. (Serves 6.)

SHIRRED POTATOES

3 tbsp. butter
2 tbsp. flour
1 tsp. salt
1/4 tsp. pepper
3 cups milk
3 cups grated raw potatoes
1 medium onion, finely grated
1 tsp. salt
Freshly-ground pepper
2 tbsp. butter

Heat oven to 325 degrees.

Melt 3 tbsp. butter in saucepan. Sprinkle in flour, 1 tsp. salt and 1/4 tsp. pepper. Blend and let bubble up well.

Remove from heat, add milk all at once, and stir to blend. Return to moderate heat and cook, stirring constantly, until thickened slightly.

Add potatoes, onion, 1 tsp. salt and freshly-ground pepper.

Pour into large shallow baking dish, 13 x 9 1/2 x 2 inches. Dot with 2 tbsp. butter.

Bake uncovered 2 hours until brown and crunchy on top and potatoes are tender. (Serves 4 to 6.)

SWISS POTATOES

2 tbsp. soft butter
1 small clove garlic, crushed
2 lb. potatoes, peeled and sliced thin (4 large)
1 1/2 tsp. salt
1/4 tsp. pepper
Dash nutmeg
1/4 lb. Gruyère cheese, grated
2 cups light cream, scalded
1 egg, beaten
1/2 cup grated Parmesan cheese

Heat oven to 450 degrees.

Blend butter and garlic together and use part of mixture to grease a 2-qt. earthenware or glass casserole.

Mix potatoes, salt, pepper, nutmeg and Gruyère cheese together lightly. Put into prepared casserole.

Beat cream gradually into beaten egg with a fork. Pour over potatoes. Sprinkle top with Parmesan cheese. Dot with remaining garlic butter.

Bake 1 hour or until potatoes are tender. If top begins to get too brown reduce heat to 350 degrees. (Serves 6.)

QUICK SKILLET POTATOES

2 tbsp. butter
1/2 cup minced green onions
Two 20-oz. cans whole potatoes
1/2 tsp. salt
Dash pepper
1/4 cup light cream
1/4 cup grated Cheddar cheese
Chopped parsley

Heat butter in heavy skillet. Add onions and cook gently 2 minutes.

Slice potatoes and add to skillet and heat gently but do not brown. Sprinkle with salt and pepper. Add cream and cheese and heat gently. Sprinkle with chopped parsley and serve immediately. (Serves 4 or 5.)

FRIED ONION RINGS

Fat for deep frying
4 to 6 large onions
Milk
Flour
Salt

Heat fat to 375 degrees. Peel onions and slice 1/4 inch thick. Separate into rings. Dip rings into milk, then into flour. Drop into fat a few at a time and fry until golden.

Drain on paper towelling and sprinkle generously with salt. Serve immediately. (Serves 4 to 6.)

SPINACH PUFFS

1 cup finely-chopped cooked spinach (about 1 lb. uncooked)
1 tsp. salt
1/8 tsp. pepper
Dash nutmeg
1 tbsp. grated onion
1/2 tsp. leaf basil, crumbled
2 eggs, well beaten
2 tbsp. butter
1 1/4 cups milk
Egg Sauce (recipe follows)

Heat oven to 350 degrees.

Mix spinach, salt, pepper, nutmeg, onion and basil together lightly with a fork. Blend in eggs.

Heat butter and milk together until butter is melted. Add to spinach and blend well. Spoon into six 5-oz. greased custard cups. Set in pan of hot water.

Bake about 40 minutes or until puffed and set in the middle. Unmould and serve immediately with Egg Sauce. (Serves 6.)

Egg Sauce

2 tbsp. butter
2 tbsp. flour
1/2 tsp. salt
Dash pepper
1 cup milk
2 hard-cooked eggs, chopped
1 tsp. lemon juice

Melt butter in small saucepan. Sprinkle in flour, salt and pepper and let bubble up, stirring constantly. Remove from heat and add milk all at once, stirring to blend. Return to moderate heat and cook and stir until thick. Stir in eggs and lemon juice and heat well. Serve over Spinach Puffs.

OVEN-GLAZED SQUASH

2 acorn squash
¼ tsp. salt
½ cup butter
¾ cup finely-crushed salted
  soda biscuits
¾ cup brown sugar, packed
  Dash nutmeg

Heat oven to 400 degrees. Have ready a baking pan about 13 x 9½ x 2 inches.

Cut squash into halves. Scoop out seeds and discard. Cut each half into six, lengthwise, and peel pieces.

Heat a small amount of water to boiling in a large skillet. Add salt and pieces of squash, spreading them out so they are in a single layer. Cover tightly and cook until squash is beginning to get tender, about 10 minutes. Drain immediately.

Melt butter and pour into a shallow plate (a pie pan is just right). Combine soda biscuit crumbs, brown sugar and nutmeg in a second shallow plate.

Dip squash pieces into butter, then into crumb mixture and put in baking dish in a single layer.

Bake about 30 minutes or until squash is tender and golden. (Serves 6.)

BROILED TOMATOES

Cut peeled tomatoes (1 per person) in thick slices. Set slices on broiler pan. Sprinkle lightly with salt, pepper and sweet basil. Dot with butter. Broil 3 inches from heat for 3 to 5 minutes without turning.

Note: I like to put these on my broiler just as a steak is nearly cooked.

DUTCH TOMATOES

6 medium green tomatoes
¼ cup flour
½ tsp. salt
⅛ tsp. pepper
¼ cup butter
¼ cup brown sugar
1 cup heavy cream
  Chopped parsley

Wash green tomatoes and slice very thick. Combine flour, salt and pepper and dip tomato slices in this mixture.

Heat butter in large heavy skillet. Add tomato slices and sprinkle tops with half of brown sugar. Cook gently until lightly browned. Turn carefully and sprinkle with remaining sugar. Cook gently until lightly browned. Turn carefully.

Add the cream and heat gently but do not boil.

Lift tomato slices out of pan with egg turner and put on hot serving plate. Pour sauce over and sprinkle generously with chopped parsley. (Serves 4 to 6.)

Note: Firm ripe tomatoes may be done in the same way.

TURNIP FLUFF

1 medium turnip
3 medium potatoes
¼ cup melted butter
  Salt and pepper
⅛ tsp. allspice

Cut turnip and potatoes into pieces about the same size and cook together in boiling salted water until tender.

Drain and mash, adding remaining ingredients during mashing. (Serves 4.)

SAVORY TURNIPS

1 large turnip, peeled and
  cut in ½-inch cubes
  Boiling water
1 tsp. salt
½ tsp. caraway seeds
¼ cup butter
1 medium onion, sliced very thin
⅓ cup chopped parsley
1 tsp. lemon juice
  Salt and pepper

Cover turnip cubes with boiling water in saucepan. Add salt and caraway seeds, cover and cook about 20 minutes or until almost tender. Drain.

Melt butter in heavy skillet, add onion, cover and cook over low heat until onion is yellow but not browned. Stir occasionally.

Add parsley, lemon juice and cooked turnip. Cook, stirring gently, until turnip is coated with butter and lightly browned. Sprinkle lightly with salt and pepper. (Serves 6.)

TURNIP CUPS

4 cups hot mashed turnips
2 tbsp. butter
2 tbsp. wheat germ
2 tbsp. sugar
1 tsp. salt
⅛ tsp. pepper
⅛ tsp. nutmeg
¾ cup milk

Heat oven to 350 degrees. Butter six 6-oz. custard cups.

Combine all ingredients, blending well. Spoon into prepared custard cups.

Bake 30 minutes. Serve immediately. (Serves 6).

HOLLANDAISE SAUCE
(For vegetables, fish, shellfish, poultry and eggs)

2 egg yolks
3 tbsp. lemon juice
½ cup very cold butter

Put egg yolks and lemon juice in a small saucepan and stir together with a wooden spoon. Add half the butter.

Put over very low heat and stir until butter is melted.

Add remaining butter and continue stirring until butter is melted and sauce thickened. Be sure to cook very slowly.

Serve hot or at room temperature. (Makes 1 cup.)

When asparagus stalks are different sizes, split the larger ones half-way up for even cooking.

Add new Weekend Magazine Tested Recipes here

Add new Weekend Magazine Tested Recipes here

Add new Weekend Magazine Tested Recipes here

Add new Weekend Magazine Tested Recipes here

SECTION II

The Heart of the Matter

The heart of a meal is its main dish. It may be meat, poultry, fish or eggs. It may be a casserole. It may be pasta, cheese or any number of other things. No matter what it is it's all-important. It makes the meal a success or a failure.

Sometimes it's hard to feel inspired about this part of the meal. That's the reason this is an extra-large section of recipes.

To begin with, there is a selection of meat recipes. You'll find these are classified according to cut rather than kind of meat. The ground meat recipes are first, whether it's ground beef, pork, veal or lamb. In the same way all roast recipes are together, all steak, chops and ribs recipes and all stews.

The poultry recipes include some favorite stuffings. And I haven't forgotten fish and seafood, eggs and the odds and ends we all like so much, such as Pizza and Baked Beans.

The meat recipes vary from simple ground beef dishes to complicated but marvellous dishes like Pâté En Croûte. They also include some all-time readers' favorites — Savory Pot Roast, Fondue Bourguignonne, Lamb Chops With Dill, Burgundy Beef and Hawaiian Pork.

I can't begin to name my own favorites among the rest of the recipes. They vary from such simple but delicious dishes as Oven-Fried Chicken to rather impressive ones, such as Cornish Game Hens With Rice Stuffing. And from such basics as Crispy Fried Fish Fillets or Steamed Salmon to glamorous Island Shrimp or Shrimp Curry.

This selection of recipes should help with the planning of the most important part of your meal — the main dish.

Ground Meat

Ground beef is great. Give it a chance when you are trying to make the most of a meal

HAMBURGER STROGANOFF

1/2 cup minced onion
1 clove garlic, minced
1/4 cup butter
1 lb. ground beef
2 tbsp. flour
2 tsp. salt
1/4 tsp. pepper
10-oz. can mushrooms, sliced
10 1/4-oz. can cream of chicken soup, undiluted
1 cup commercial sour cream
2 tbsp. minced parsley OR fresh dill
Hot cooked rice

Cook onion and garlic in butter over medium heat 3 minutes. Add meat and brown well.

Sprinkle in flour, salt, pepper and stir in mushrooms. Cook gently 5 minutes.

Add soup, stir and simmer, uncovered, 10 minutes.

Stir in sour cream and heat but do not boil. Sprinkle with parsley or dill. Serve with cooked rice. (Serves 4 to 6.)

SOUTHERN BURGERS

2 tbsp. cooking oil
1 lb. ground beef
1 medium onion, diced
3 tbsp. ketchup
3 tbsp. prepared mustard
10-oz. can chicken-gumbo soup
Picnic Buns (recipe p. 148) OR hamburger buns

Heat oil in heavy skillet.

Add ground beef and onion and brown, stirring constantly.

Stir in ketchup, mustard and soup and simmer 15 minutes.

Spoon over Picnic Buns or hamburger buns to serve. (Serves 6.)

ELEGANT HAMBURGERS

1/3 cup soft butter
1 tbsp. chopped parsley
1 clove garlic, crushed
6 hamburger buns
1 1/2 lb. ground round steak
1 1/2 tsp. salt
3 tbsp. capers, rinsed
1/3 cup dry red table wine
1/2 tsp. monosodium glutamate (optional)
Freshly-ground pepper
Chili sauce, warmed
Thin sweet onion slices

Mix butter, parsley and garlic and spread on split hamburger buns.

Wrap buns in aluminum foil, and heat about 15 minutes in hot oven.

Mix steak, salt, capers, wine, monosodium glutamate and pepper lightly with a fork.

Shape into 6 patties, lay on broiler rack and broil, 4 inches from heat, 3 to 5 minutes on each side (they are best a little pink inside) or until cooked as you like them.

Spread buns with warmed chili sauce and serve hamburgers in buns with onion slices. (Makes 6.)

SWEDISH MEAT BALLS

1 lb. ground beef
1/2 lb. ground pork
1/2 cup minced onion
3/4 cup fine dry bread crumbs
1 tbsp. minced parsley
1 1/2 tsp. salt
1/8 tsp. pepper
1 tsp. Worcestershire sauce
1 egg
1/2 cup milk
1/4 cup cooking oil
1 tbsp. butter
1/4 cup flour
1 tsp. paprika
1/2 tsp. salt
1/8 tsp. pepper
2 cups boiling water
3/4 cup commercial sour cream

Mix beef, pork, onion, bread crumbs, parsley, 1 1/2 tsp. salt, 1/8 tsp. pepper, Worcestershire sauce, egg and milk together lightly. Shape mixture into small balls.

Heat oil in heavy skillet, add

meat balls and brown well on all sides. Lift out meat balls as they brown.

Add butter to drippings in pan when all meat balls have been removed. Sprinkle in flour, paprika, 1/2 tsp. salt and 1/8 tsp. pepper. Allow to bubble up together, stirring constantly.

Remove from heat. Add boiling water all at once and stir to blend. Return to heat and bring to boiling, stirring constantly. Return meat balls to pan and simmer gently 20 minutes.

Add cream, stir to blend and heat just to boiling but do not boil. Serve immediately. (Serves 6.)

MEAT BALLS AND NOODLES

1 lb. ground beef
1 lb. ground lean pork
1 lb. ground veal
1/4 cup chopped green onions
2 cloves garlic, mashed
2 tsp. dill seed (use chopped fresh dill if available)
2 tbsp. sugar
2 tsp. salt
1/4 tsp. pepper
1/8 tsp. cayenne
1 tsp. Worcestershire sauce
2 eggs, beaten
1/2 cup whipping cream, whipped
Flour
1/4 cup butter
3 tbsp. flour
3 cups light cream
Salt and pepper
Hot buttered noodles

Mix meat together lightly. Add onions, garlic, dill, sugar, salt, pepper, cayenne and Worcestershire sauce. Mix in eggs, then fold in whipped cream, blending well.

Make into small balls, 1 inch in diameter, with buttered hands. Roll balls in flour. Heat butter in heavy skillet and brown meat balls slowly on all sides. This will take about 20 minutes.

Heat oven to 350 degrees.

Remove meat balls as they brown, and place in extra-large flat baking dish in a single layer. When they are all browned measure out 1/4 cup of drippings left in pan and pour remaining drippings over meat balls. Put them in oven and cook 20 to 25 minutes more, or until cooked through.

Pour the saved ¼ cup drippings back into skillet and heat, scraping all browned bits up from the bottom of the pan. Stir in 3 tbsp. flour and let bubble up.

Remove from heat and add cream all at once, stirring constantly. Return to moderate heat and cook, stirring constantly, until slightly thickened and smooth.

Taste and season with salt and pepper. Pour over meat balls and serve over buttered noodles. (Serves 8 to 10.)

CHINESE MEAT BALLS

½ cup cooking oil
1 lb. ground beef
1 small clove garlic, crushed
1 tsp. salt
¼ tsp. pepper
2 eggs
¼ cup flour
1 tsp. salt
¼ tsp. pepper
½ cup chicken stock
2 large green peppers, cut in
   1-inch squares
1 cup canned pineapple chunks,
   drained
3 tbsp. cornstarch
½ cup sugar
½ cup pineapple juice (drained
   from chunks)
½ cup cider vinegar
3 tbsp. soy sauce
1 large tomato, peeled and
   chopped
Hot cooked rice

Heat oil in large heavy skillet. Combine beef, garlic, 1 tsp. salt and ¼ tsp. pepper and shape into 36 small meat balls.

Beat eggs, flour, 1 tsp. salt and ¼ tsp. pepper together to make a thin batter. Dip meat balls in batter with fingers, shake off excess and drop into hot oil. Cook slowly to brown on all sides. Lift out meat balls as they brown.

Discard all but 1 tbsp. of oil left in pan when all meat balls are browned. Add chicken stock, green peppers and pineapple chunks to pan. Cover and simmer 5 minutes. Return meat balls to

Meatballs will all be the same size if you pat meat mixture into oblong, then cut crosswise and lengthwise into small, even squares before shaping.

pan and simmer about 3 minutes more (green pepper should still be slightly crisp).

Mix cornstarch, sugar, pineapple juice, vinegar and soy sauce together until smooth. Add gradually to liquid in pan, stirring constantly. Continue cooking and stirring until thickened. Add tomato pieces just before serving and serve over hot cooked rice. (Serves 6.)

MEXICAN MEAT CAKES

1½ lb. ground beef
½ lb. ground pork
2 tsp. salt
½ tsp. pepper
1 egg, beaten
¼ cup cooking oil
½ cup finely-chopped onion
2 cloves garlic, minced
14-oz. can whole-kernel corn
20-oz. can tomatoes
7½-oz. can tomato sauce
1 cup slivered ripe olives
1 tsp. salt
1 tbsp. chili powder
Dash cayenne
¼ tsp. cumin seed

Combine ground beef, ground pork, 2 tsp. salt, pepper and egg. Shape mixture into small thin cakes (about 2½ inches in diameter by ¼ inch thick).

Heat oil in large heavy skillet. Add meat cakes and brown well, making sure they are cooked through. Lift meat cakes out of pan as they are done.

Drain all but 2 tbsp. of fat from pan when all meat cakes have been browned. Add onion and garlic to this fat and cook gently 2 minutes. Add corn (not drained) and remaining ingredients and cook gently a few minutes until sauce thickens a little. Return meat to sauce and simmer 10 minutes. Serve immediately. (Serves 6.)

MARITZA'S MEAT ROLL

2 lb. ground beef
3 eggs
2 medium onions, chopped
2 cloves garlic, minced
Small bunch of parsley, chopped
4 sprigs fresh mint, chopped OR
   2 tsp. dried mint
3/4 cup fine dry bread crumbs
1 tsp. oregano
1/2 tsp. thyme
1/4 tsp. basil
2 tsp. salt
1/4 tsp. pepper
2 tsp. cooking oil
2 wieners, sliced thin
4 slices bacon, cut up
3 hard-cooked eggs, coarsely
   chopped
10 stuffed olives, coarsely
   chopped
6 ripe olives, coarsely chopped
1 egg
1 cup fine dry bread crumbs
2 tbsp. cooking oil

Mix thoroughly with hands ground beef, 3 eggs, onions, garlic, parsley, mint, 3/4 cup bread crumbs, oregano, thyme, basil, salt and pepper.

Heat 2 tsp. oil in heavy skillet. Cook wiener slices and bacon until lightly browned. Take off heat. Add hard-cooked eggs and olives and mix lightly. This is the filling for the rolls.

Divide ground meat mixture into 2 portions. Pat out each part on a floured board into rounds about 10 inches in diameter. Put half of filling across the centre of each round and roll meat carefully around it, pressing firmly into a roll.

Beat 1 egg with a fork on a large flat dish or platter and roll each meat roll in it to coat all sides. Then roll in 1 cup fine bread crumbs.

Heat 2 tbsp. oil in large heavy skillet. Lift rolls carefully into pan and brown on all sides over low heat.

Heat oven to 300 degrees.

To Serve Hot: Put skillet into oven and bake rolls 45 minutes. Blend 1/4 cup cold water and 1 tbsp. flour. Stir into 6-oz. can tomato paste. Remove skillet from oven and stir tomato paste mixture into drippings in pan. Baste meat with mixture. Return to oven and bake another 15 minutes, basting several times.

To Serve Cold: Wrap browned rolls, while warm, in waxed paper and tie securely with string. Put in baking dish and bake 1 hour. Cool in paper.

BEEF ROLL

2 lb. ground beef
2 tsp. salt
1/8 tsp. pepper
1 tbsp. Worcestershire sauce
1 medium onion, minced
1 egg, slightly beaten
3 slices bacon
1/2 cup sliced mushrooms
3 cups warm mashed potatoes
Salt and pepper
1 cup 1/2-inch cubes sharp
   Cheddar cheese
1/2 cup fine cracker crumbs
1/2 cup chili sauce

Heat oven to 350 degrees.

Combine ground beef, 2 tsp. salt, 1/8 tsp. pepper, Worcestershire sauce, onion and egg. Put on waxed paper and pat into a rectangle, 14 x 10 inches (about 1/3 inch thick).

Fry bacon until crisp, remove from pan, cool and crumble. Pour most of fat out of pan, add sliced mushrooms and cook until tender. Season mashed potatoes with salt and pepper to taste. Blend in cheese cubes, mushrooms and crumbled bacon.

Pile down centre of meat in a mound. Bring edges of paper up to wrap meat around potatoes. Seal edges and ends by pressing meat together. Sprinkle with cracker crumbs and roll around on waxed paper until meat is coated with crumbs on all sides.

Roll meat carefully off waxed paper into lightly-greased long, shallow baking pan. Turn sealed side down. Spread with half of chili sauce.

Bake 1 hour. Heat remaining chili sauce and drizzle over. (Serves 6.)

Lasagna — recipe on page 34

BEEF AND PORK ROLL

1 lb. ground beef
1/2 lb. ground pork
1 1/2 cups soft bread crumbs
1 egg, lightly beaten
1/2 cup evaporated milk
1 1/2 tsp. salt
1/8 tsp. pepper
1 1/2 cups coarsely-grated apple
1 1/2 cups soft bread crumbs
1/4 cup chopped celery
2 tbsp. chopped parsley
1 tbsp. minced onion
3 tbsp. brown sugar
1/8 tsp. poultry seasoning
1/2 tsp. salt

Heat oven to 350 degrees. Grease a large shallow baking pan.

Mix beef, pork, 1 1/2 cups bread crumbs, egg, evaporated milk, 1 1/2 tsp. salt and pepper, blending thoroughly. Turn out on a large sheet of waxed paper and pat into a rectangle 12 x 8 inches (about 1/2 inch thick).

Combine remaining ingredients and spread over meat mixture. Roll up from one of wide sides, using the waxed paper to help turn the meat. Seal well by pressing meat mixture together.

Lift meat roll on paper to baking pan and roll it off the paper into the pan.

Bake 1 1/2 hrs. Slice 1 inch thick. (Serves 8.)

VEGETABLE-BEEF LOAF

1 1/2 lb. ground beef
1 medium onion, chopped fine
1/2 cup chopped green pepper
1/2 cup chopped celery
2 cups grated carrots (medium grater)
1 cup fine dry bread crumbs
1 1/2 tsp. salt
1/4 tsp. pepper
1/4 tsp. dry mustard
Dash cayenne
1/2 tsp. Worcestershire sauce
10 1/4-oz. can vegetable soup

Heat oven to 375 degrees. Grease a 9 x 5 x 3-inch loaf pan.

Combine all ingredients, blending thoroughly. Pack in prepared pan.

Bake 1 hour. (Serves 8.)

MOUSAKA

2 tbsp. cooking oil
1 medium onion, chopped fine
1 lb. ground beef
6-oz. can tomato paste
3/4 cup water
2 tsp. salt
1/8 tsp. pepper
Pinch of cinnamon
Pinch of nutmeg
Pinch of cloves
1/8 tsp. thyme
1 tsp. oregano
1/2 cup dry red table wine
1/2 cup canned mushrooms (optional)
1 medium eggplant
Salt
2 tbsp. butter
2 tbsp. flour
1/4 tsp. salt
1/8 tsp. pepper
1 cup milk
1 egg, lightly beaten

Heat oven to 300 degrees.

Heat oil in heavy skillet. Add onion and cook gently until yellow. Add meat and brown. Add tomato paste and water and simmer 5 minutes.

Mix in seasonings, wine and mushrooms and simmer again gently until sauce is thick.

Slice eggplant (do not peel) 1/2-inch thick. Put in saucepan and pour boiling water over slices. Cover and heat just until water returns to the boil. Drain.

Layer meat mixture and eggplant in a 2-qt. casserole, ending with a layer of eggplant. Sprinkle each layer of eggplant lightly with salt.

Melt butter in a small saucepan. Add flour, 1/4 tsp. salt and 1/8 tsp. pepper and let bubble up together. Remove from heat and add milk all at once. Stir to blend and return to moderate heat and cook, stirring constantly, until thickened. Stir at least half of the mixture gradually into egg then stir back into remaining sauce. Cook 1 minute over moderate heat, stirring constantly. Pour over top of layers in casserole.

Bake 40 to 45 minutes or until mixture bubbles up well and top browns lightly. (Serves 6.)

Note: In Greece this dish is highly seasoned and you may find you want to add more of the spices.

LASAGNA

2 slices bacon
1/4 cup olive oil
2 tbsp. butter
2 cloves garlic, cut in halves
1 large onion, chopped
2 tbsp. finely-chopped carrot
2 tbsp. finely-chopped celery
1 1/2 lb. ground beef
1/2 lb. Italian salami, chopped
1/4 tsp. allspice
1/2 tsp. marjoram
2 tbsp. finely-chopped parsley
2 cups canned tomatoes
Two 6-oz. cans tomato paste
1/2 cup water
Salt and pepper
8 oz. ricotta or cottage cheese
1 egg
1/2 cup grated Parmesan cheese
1/2 tsp. salt
1/4 tsp. pepper
8 oz. lasagna noodles, cooked
1 cup finely-diced Mozzarella cheese

Cut up bacon and cook gently in large heavy skillet until pan is well greased. Add oil, butter, garlic pieces, onion, carrot and celery and cook gently 5 minutes. Lift out and discard garlic pieces.

Add beef, salami, allspice, marjoram and parsley to pan and cook, stirring constantly, until meat is browned.

Add tomatoes and break up large pieces with a spoon. Add tomato paste and water. Simmer, uncovered, 45 minutes or until very thick. Taste and add salt and pepper if desired.

Heat oven to 375 degrees. Butter a large shallow baking dish about 13 x 9 1/2 x 2 inches.

Combine ricotta or cottage cheese, egg, Parmesan cheese, 1/2 tsp. salt and 1/4 tsp. pepper.

Put a layer of the tomato sauce in the bottom of the prepared baking dish. Add a layer of noodles then a layer of ricotta or cottage cheese mixture. Sprinkle with some of Mozzarella cheese. Repeat layers, ending with some sauce and a final sprinkling of Mozzarella cheese.

Bake 30 minutes or until bubbling well. (Serves 6 to 8.)

SPAGHETTI SAUCE

2 tbsp. cooking oil
1 lb. ground beef
1 large onion, sliced
2 cloves garlic, minced
15-oz. can spaghetti sauce
    (without meat)
6-oz. can tomato paste
½ cup dry red table wine
1 cup water
1 bay leaf
1 tsp. oregano
4 peppercorns
1 tsp. salt

Heat oil in heavy kettle. Add beef, onion and garlic and cook, stirring, until beef is well browned.

Add remaining ingredients, heat to boiling, turn down heat, cover tightly and simmer gently 3 to 4 hours. If sauce becomes too thick, thin with red wine or water. (Serves 4.)

CHILI CON CARNE

6 strips bacon
2 medium onions, sliced thin
1 clove garlic, minced
2 lb. ground beef
Two 15-oz. cans kidney beans
3½ cups canned tomatoes
1 tbsp. chili powder
¼ tsp. crushed red peppers
¾ tsp. oregano
1 tsp. salt

Fry bacon until crisp in a heavy skillet. Remove, crumble and set aside.

Cook onions and garlic in bacon fat until onions are yellow. Add meat and cook until well browned, breaking apart with a wooden spoon.

Add remaining ingredients and crumbled bacon, cover tightly and simmer 30 minutes.

Serve very hot in deep bowls. (Serves 6 to 8.)

Note: Chili powder may be increased up to 3 tbsp. if you like a hotter chili.

For easy removal of meat loaf and speedy washing up, line bottom and ends of loaf pan with aluminum foil.

If some members of your family cannot eat onion, mix meat loaf without it and pack half in one end of pan. Add onion to rest of meat and pack into other end of pan, separating two parts with a "wall" of aluminum foil.

BARBECUED LIMA BEANS

1 lb. dried Lima beans
8 cups water
¼ lb. salt pork
¼ cup cooking oil
1 lb. ground beef
2 large onions, chopped
2 cloves garlic, minced
1½ tbsp. prepared mustard
2 tsp. Worcestershire sauce
1 tsp. chili powder
1 tsp. salt
⅓ cup white vinegar
15-oz. can tomato sauce

Rinse Lima beans under running water. Bring water to a boil and add beans slowly, stirring and keeping water at a boil. Turn down heat.

Dice pork into ½-inch cubes and add to beans. Cover and simmer until beans are tender, 1½ to 2 hours. Add more water if necessary. Drain, saving cooking water. Pour beans into a greased 2-qt. casserole.

Heat oven to 400 degrees.

Heat oil in heavy skillet. Add beef, onions and garlic and cook and stir until beef is well browned. Stir in remaining ingredients and 1½ cups of the water beans were cooked in. Simmer 5 minutes.

Pour over beans and mix in lightly.

Bake 1 hour. (Serves 6 to 8.)

Note: If preferred, soak beans in cold water overnight, then simmer in soaking water until tender, 30 to 60 minutes.

LAMB BURGERS

Milk
1 slice day-old bread
1 lb. ground lean lamb
2 tbsp. finely-grated onion
1 egg, lightly beaten
1 tsp. salt
½ tsp. pepper
½ tsp. cinnamon
½ tsp. oregano
¼ tsp. garlic salt
Fine dry bread crumbs
2 tbsp. cooking oil
2 tbsp. butter

Pour a little milk over the slice of bread, let it absorb as much as possible then squeeze it gently to remove excess milk. Break in small pieces.

Combine lamb, bread pieces, onion, egg, salt, pepper, cinnamon, oregano (crushed between fingers) and garlic salt with a fork until well blended. Shape lightly into 4 large patties. Dip in bread crumbs to coat all sides.

Heat oil and butter in heavy skillet. Add meat patties and cook slowly until well browned and cooked through. (Serves 4.)

LAMB CAKES

2 large carrots
1 large potato
1 medium onion
1 small clove garlic
1 lb. shoulder of lamb, ground
1½ tsp. salt
¼ tsp. rosemary
¼ tsp. pepper
1 egg, beaten
Flour
2 tbsp. cooking oil
¼ cup chicken stock OR
  1 chicken bouillon cube and
  ¼ cup hot water
¾ cup chicken stock (optional)

Heat oven to 350 degrees.

Grind carrots, potato, onion and garlic through the fine blade of the food chopper. Add to ground lamb along with salt, rosemary, pepper and egg and blend. Shape mixture into 8 large thick cakes. Dip cakes into flour to coat all sides.

Heat oil in large heavy skillet

that can go in the oven. Brown lamb cakes slowly in oil. Drain off all fat when cakes are well browned. Add ¼ cup chicken stock to skillet.

Cover tightly and put in oven for 45 minutes, turning once.

Serve with remaining ¾ cup stock thickened slightly for gravy, if desired. (Serves 4 or 8.)

PÂTÉ EN CROÛTE

1 lb. lean veal
1 lb. uncooked ham
1 cup wine vinegar
¼ cup cooking oil
1 medium onion, sliced
½ clove garlic
6 peppercorns
1 small bay leaf
¼ tsp. thyme
2 tsp. salt
Pinch poultry seasoning
Lard Pastry (recipe follows)
1 strip bacon, cut up
1 small onion, chopped
1¼ lb. ground pork
½ tsp. ground marjoram
¼ tsp. nutmeg
2 tbsp. chopped green onions
1 tbsp. chopped parsley
1 egg
3 tbsp. heavy cream
2 tbsp. butter
1 cup sliced fresh mushrooms
2 strips bacon
1 egg yolk
1 tbsp. cold water
1 envelope (1 tbsp.) unflavored gelatin
2 tbsp. cold water
2 chicken bouillon cubes
1 cup boiling water

Have ready two 8 x 4¼ x 2¼-inch aluminum foil loaf pans (see note at end of recipe).

Cut veal and ham into thin strips about 4 inches long and 1 inch wide, removing all fat and connective tissue. Put meat strips into shallow dish. Combine vinegar, oil, sliced onion, garlic, peppercorns, bay leaf, thyme, salt and poultry seasoning. Pour over meat. Let marinate several hours in the refrigerator, stirring often and pressing meat down into the marinade.

Prepare Lard Pastry as directed in recipe following and put in refrigerator to chill.

Fry 1 strip bacon in heavy skillet until pan is greased. Add chopped onion and cook gently until yellow. Put ground pork in a bowl and add bacon bits and onion. Add marjoram, nutmeg, green onions, parsley, egg and cream. Mix and blend very well. Chill.

Heat butter in skillet. Add sliced mushrooms and cook gently 2 minutes. Cool.

Lift veal and ham strips out of marinade with a slotted spoon. Discard any bits of onion or seasoning clinging to strips and dry them well on paper towelling.

Divide chilled Lard Pastry into 3 equal parts. Roll 1 part into an oblong about 13 x 9 inches. Put carefully into one of loaf pans, fitting it into the corners and being careful not to stretch. Trim pastry so that it hangs about ½ inch over the sides of the pan. Repeat this step to line the second pan with pastry.

Chop strips of bacon and sprinkle them over the pastry in the bottom of the pans.

Put a ¼-inch layer of the chilled ground pork mixture in the bottom of each pastry-lined pan, spreading it evenly. Cover with a single layer of the ham strips, pressing them down well into the pork. Add a sprinkling of mushrooms. Top with a very thin layer of the pork mixture, then a single layer of the veal strips and a sprinkling of mushrooms. Top with another thin layer of pork mixture. Repeat these layers, pressing each down firmly, until each pan is filled, ending with a layer of the pork ¼ inch thick.

Divide remaining pastry in two and roll each piece slightly larger than the tops of the pans. Moisten edges of bottom pastry, lay pastry on top and seal together by pressing firmly. Trim top pastry to same size as lower pastry and roll edges under. Crimp.

Beat egg yolk and 1 tbsp. cold water together lightly with a fork and brush over top crust. Decorate with flowers and leaves cut from left-over pastry if desired. Cut a small round hole in the centre of the top crust so steam can escape.

Heat oven to 300 degrees. Bake 2½ hours. Cool to lukewarm in pan.

Soak gelatin in 2 tbsp. cold water 5 minutes. Dissolve bouillon cubes in boiling water. Add gelatin and stir until dissolved. Cool but do not chill. Pour mixture slowly into holes in tops of partly-cooled *pâtés* to fill up the spaces left by the meat shrinking. Completely cool *pâtés*, then chill very well.

Unmould on greens. Cut away end pastry and discard and cut in thick slices. (Serves 10 to 12.)

Lard Pastry

½ lb. lard
½ cup boiling water
2¾ cups sifted all-purpose flour
1 tsp. baking powder
1 tsp. salt
1 tsp. paprika

Cut lard up into bowl. Add boiling water and beat with rotary beater until cold and creamy.

Sift remaining ingredients together into lard mixture. Stir until smooth and dough leaves the sides of the bowl. Wrap in waxed paper and chill.

Note: The foil pans I use for the *pâté* are available quite inexpensively in supermarkets and department stores. The size marked on them is 8 x 4¼ x 2¼ inches but they are actually a little smaller than this, about 7¼ x 3½ x 2¼. It is important to use foil pans. With any other kind of pan you may have difficulty unmoulding the *pâté*. The foil pans are perfect because they can be bent enough to pull loose from the pastry.

Roasts

SAUERBRATEN

4- to 5-lb. rump roast of beef
1 tbsp. salt
½ tsp. pepper
1 tsp. grated lemon rind
½ tsp. allspice
¼ cup cooking oil
3 medium onions, chopped
2 large carrots, chopped
1 stalk celery, chopped
12 peppercorns
2 bay leaves
6 whole cloves
2 cups cider OR wine vinegar
1 cup water
¼ cup brown sugar
2 tbsp. cooking oil
4 cups liquid (see below)
1½ cups gingersnap crumbs
Salt
1 cup commercial sour cream
Potato Pancakes (recipe follows)

Rub outside of roast with a mixture of 1 tbsp. salt, ½ tsp. pepper, lemon rind and allspice. Put in large glass or porcelain bowl.

Heat ¼ cup oil in heavy saucepan and add onions, carrots and celery and cook gently until lightly browned. Add peppercorns, bay leaves, cloves, vinegar, water and sugar and heat to boiling. Pour over meat in bowl while hot. Let cool, cover tightly and put in refrigerator. Let meat marinate 3 days, turning several times.

Remove from marinade and dry with paper towels.

Heat 2 tbsp. oil in Dutch oven or other large heavy kettle. Add meat and brown quickly on all sides.

Strain liquid meat was marinated in over the meat. Cover tightly and simmer about 3 hours or until meat is very tender. Lift out meat and keep warm.

Strain liquid left in pan and measure, adding enough water to make 4 cups liquid (this is the 4 cups liquid called for in the ingredients).

Return liquid to pan and bring to boiling. Stir in gingersnap crumbs and cook and stir until thick. Taste and season with salt if necessary.

Stir a little of the hot mixture gradually into the sour cream, then stir this mixture back into pan and heat just to boiling (do not boil).

Serve some of gravy over thin slices of meat with Potato Pancakes.

Serve remaining gravy in gravy boat.

Potato Pancakes

¼ cup all-purpose flour
4 cups grated raw potatoes
   (use medium grater)
1 medium onion, grated
2 eggs, lightly beaten
2 tsp. salt
⅛ tsp. pepper
2 tbsp. melted butter

Grease a large heavy skillet lightly and heat well. Turn heat to medium.

Measure flour into bowl. Add remaining ingredients and stir together quickly. Drop by ⅓ cupfuls on hot skillet. Spread and flatten with bottom of cup.

Fry rather slowly until crisp and brown on both sides. Lift out and keep hot until all cakes are baked. Grease skillet before baking each batch. (Makes 12.)

SAVORY POT ROAST

2 tbsp. finely-chopped parsley
2 tbsp. finely-minced green
   onions
½ tsp. marjoram
4-lb. rump roast of beef
4 strips bacon
¼ cup cooking oil
2 tbsp. butter
1 clove garlic, minced
6 cloves
20-oz. can tomatoes
1 thick slice onion
2 bay leaves
¼ tsp. thyme
3 large sprigs celery leaves
2 tsp. salt
¼ tsp. pepper
1 cup dry red wine

Combine parsley, onions and marjoram. Cut holes with the point of a sharp knife all over the meat and stuff each hole with some of parsley mixture.

Wrap bacon slices around roast and tie on with string.

Heat oil and butter in heavy kettle and sear meat quickly on both sides. Lift out meat and set aside. Drain off all but 1 tbsp. of fat from kettle. Add garlic, cloves, tomatoes and onion and heat to boiling.

Return meat to kettle and add bay leaves, thyme, celery leaves, salt, pepper and wine.

To carve a standing rib roast, have ribs at left, insert fork between top two ribs and cut from the right.

Cover tightly, bring back to boil, turn down heat and simmer 2½ to 3 hours or until very tender.

Put roast on hot platter, removing strings and bacon. Keep warm.

Put pan juices through a sieve, pressing through as much of vegetables as possible. Return to heat and thicken gravy. Taste and season if necessary. Serve hot with roast.

Note: To thicken gravy, for each 2 cups of liquid, measure ½ cup cold water into a small jar with a tight lid. Add ¼ cup flour and shake until smooth. Stir into hot pan juices a little at a time. Cook, stirring constantly, 5 minutes.

ITALIAN POT ROAST

4-lb. beef pot roast
2 cloves garlic, slivered
1 tsp. salt
⅛ tsp. pepper
Pinch of thyme
Pinch of rosemary
4 strips bacon
2 tbsp. oil
2 onions, sliced
Strip of orange peel, 1 inch wide
Strip of lemon peel, 1 inch wide
Two 6-oz. cans tomato paste
1 cup consommé OR dry red
   wine
4 large carrots, cut in strips
1 large turnip, cut in strips

Cut small slits in top and bottom of roast. Slip slivers of garlic into slits. Mix salt, pepper, thyme and rosemary and rub into roast on all sides. Lay strips of bacon over meat and tie on with string.

Heat oil in heavy kettle and brown roast on all sides. Add onions, orange peel, lemon peel, tomato paste and consommé or wine.

Cover kettle and cook very slowly for about 3 hours, or until the meat is almost tender. The sauce will be thick.

Add carrots and turnip and continue cooking over low heat until they are tender (about 1 hour).

Serve vegetables separately or, if desired, combine them with sauce and purée the mixture by pressing through a sieve (or use a blender).

YANKEE POT ROAST

¼ cup cooking oil
2 medium onions, sliced
3-lb. rump roast of beef
1 tsp. salt
¼ tsp. pepper
2 beef bouillon cubes
1 cup hot water
1 cup canned tomatoes
⅛ tsp. ginger

Heat oil in heavy kettle. Add onions and sauté until yellow. Add meat and brown well on all sides. Season with salt and pepper.

Dissolve bouillon cubes in hot water, and add along with tomatoes and ginger.

Cover tightly and cook until tender over low heat (about 3 hours). Thicken juices for gravy.

ROAST BEEF AND YORKSHIRE PUDDING

¼ cup flour
6 tbsp. butter
1 tbsp. dry mustard
1 tsp. paprika
¼ tsp. pepper
3-rib standing rib roast (about
   6 lb.)
Beef drippings
2 eggs
1 cup milk
3 tbsp. beef drippings
1 cup sifted all-purpose flour
½ tsp. salt

Heat oven to 325 degrees.

Put ¼ cup flour in heavy skillet and set over moderate heat. Stir until lightly browned. Remove from heat.

Cream butter. Add browned flour, mustard, paprika and pep-

per and blend well. Spread mixture on surface of roast.

Set roast in roasting pan on bones (they will act as a rack). Do not cover or add water. Roast 15 minutes a pound plus an extra 15 minutes for rare (130 to 140 degrees on meat thermometer), 22 to 25 minutes a pound for medium (160 degrees).

Remove from oven and let stand while baking Yorkshire Pudding.

Increase oven temperature to 450 degrees. Grease six 6-oz. custard cups well with drippings from roast.

Beat eggs well. Beat in milk and 3 tbsp. drippings from roast. Add 1 cup flour and salt and beat until smooth with rotary beater.

Pour batter into prepared custard cups (they will be about half full).

Bake about 25 minutes or until well browned and firm to touch. Serve immediately with roast. Spoon pan juices over.

PIQUANT ROAST PORK

4- to 5-lb. pork butt
2 tsp. salt
¼ tsp. pepper
1 tsp. caraway seeds
¼ cup lemon juice
¼ cup water
Water
¼ cup water
2 tbsp. cornstarch

Brown roast on all sides in large heavy saucepan or Dutch oven. Sprinkle with salt, pepper and caraway seeds. Turn heat to low.

Add lemon juice and ¼ cup water. Cover tightly and simmer until meat is tender, about 2½ hours. Lift meat out on to hot platter.

Measure pan juices and add enough water to make 2 cups liquid. Return to saucepan and heat, stirring up any browned bits sticking to pan. Measure ¼ cup water and add cornstarch. Stir until smooth and blended. Add to hot pan juices gradually, stirring constantly. Cook, stirring until thickened and clear.

Slice meat and serve with gravy.

Men have written
poems about
roast beef and
it's easy to
understand why.
This is truly the
king of the table,
the most
magnificent main
course of all.
The one here is
Roast Beef And
Yorkshire Pudding
and you'll find
the recipe on
the preceding page

STUFFED PORK ROAST

4- to 5-lb. loin of pork
12 prunes
   Salt and pepper
1/4 cup butter
   2 cups bread crumbs (use day old bread)
   1 cup diced apple
   1 tbsp. minced onion
1/2 small clove garlic, crushed
1/2 tsp. grated lemon rind
1/2 tsp. salt
   Dash pepper
   Dash nutmeg
1/4 tsp. monosodium glutamate (optional)
   Gravy (recipe follows)

Have butcher remove bone from pork loin, leaving a pocket to hold the stuffing.

Cover prunes with cold water and let stand overnight.

Heat oven to 325 degrees.

Sprinkle cavity in meat generously with salt and pepper.

Melt butter in heavy skillet. Add crumbs and cook gently, stirring, until golden brown. Remove from heat.

Drain prunes, remove pits and cut in large pieces. Add to crumbs along with remaining ingredients *except* Gravy. Stuff into cavity in meat and tie closed (see black and white photos).

Put on rack in roasting pan, fat side up. Do not cover. Roast 35 to 40 minutes per pound or until meat thermometer registers 185 degrees. Let stand 20 minutes before slicing. Cut in thick slices and serve with Gravy.

Gravy

Drain fat and meat juice from pan. Skim fat off the top of the juice. For each cup of gravy measure 2 tbsp. fat back into pan, blend in 2 tbsp. flour and cook, stirring, until bubbling well. Remove from heat and stir in 1 cup liquid (meat juices plus water).

Return to heat and cook, stirring until thick. Scrape up all browned bits from bottom of pan. Season well with salt and pepper and simmer 5 minutes.

SAVORY LOIN OF PORK

   2 cloves garlic
   2 tsp. salt
   1 tsp. sage
1/2 tsp. poultry seasoning
1/2 tsp. cracked pepper
1/2 tsp. nutmeg
   4-lb. loin of pork
   4 large onions, chopped
   1 large carrot, chopped
   2 large sprigs parsley, coarsely chopped
1/2 cup red currant jelly
   1 tbsp. prepared mustard

Heat oven to 325 degrees.

Mince or put garlic through a press. Combine with salt, sage, poultry seasoning, pepper and nutmeg in a small dish. Rub mixture all over outside of pork roast.

Spread onions evenly over bottom of roasting pan. Sprinkle in carrot and parsley. Set roast, bone down, on top of vegetables. Roast 1 1/2 hours.

Mash jelly with a fork and combine it with mustard. Slash fat on roast and spread with jelly mixture. Continue the roasting until completely cooked, 1 to 1 1/2 hours.

BAKED BACK BACON

   3- to 4-lb. back bacon, in one piece
   1 cup brown sugar
   1 tsp. dry mustard
1/2 cup syrup from sweet spiced pickles OR pineapple juice

Heat oven to 350 degrees.

Remove casing from bacon if necessary. Score fat side. Put in shallow baking pan. Combine sugar, mustard and pickle syrup or pineapple juice and spread over meat.

Bake 20 to 25 minutes a pound, basting with glaze every 15 minutes. Serve hot or cold. (Serves 12.)

VEAL STUFFED WITH GREEN RICE

   5-lb. shoulder of veal
   2 tbsp. butter
   1 small clove garlic, crushed
   1 small onion, minced
1/4 cup finely-chopped spinach
   2 cups cooked rice
1/2 cup finely-chopped parsley
   2 tbsp. finely-chopped anchovies
1/4 tsp. pepper
1/8 tsp. nutmeg
1/4 cup milk
   1 egg
   4 strips bacon

Cut a long piece of heavy string. Tie loop of the string around one end of roast, pulling it tight and knotting it firmly. Loop string around roast about an inch further along. Thread string through loop as shown, pull tight and continue in this way until whole length of roast is securely tied. Then run the remaining string underneath the full length of the roast, tying it to the first loop.

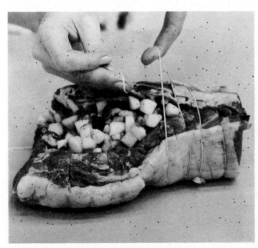

Have butcher bone shoulder of veal and leave a pocket where the bone is removed for stuffing.

Heat butter in heavy skillet. Add garlic, onion and spinach and cook gently 2 minutes, stirring constantly. Remove from heat.

Measure rice into a bowl. Add parsley, anchovies, pepper and nutmeg and blend lightly with a fork. Add spinach mixture and blend lightly again.

Measure milk, add egg and beat together lightly with a fork. Add to rice mixture and stir together with a fork. Stuff into prepared veal shoulder and tie opening closed. Lay strips of bacon over roast.

Heat oven to 325 degrees.

Set roast on rack in shallow roasting pan. Put in oven and roast uncovered until meat thermometer registers 170 degrees or about 45 minutes per pound.

Note: If desired, ask butcher to cut veal shoulder open from point where bone is removed (or do it yourself) to make a flat piece of meat. Spread stuffing over meat, roll up like a jelly roll and tie securely. The roast is a little more difficult to handle this way but the result is attractive.

LEG OF LAMB WITH HERBS

5- to 6-lb. leg of lamb
2 tbsp. salad oil
1 tsp. rosemary
½ tsp. sweet basil
1 tbsp. paprika
1 clove garlic, crushed

Remove the thin paper-like covering from the roast if it has not been done. This can be removed by using a paring knife to cut and pull it from the top of the leg.

Combine oil, rosemary, basil, paprika and garlic. Rub the lamb thoroughly with this mixture. Let stand in the refrigerator at least 4 hours.

Heat oven to 325 degrees. Place roast, fat side up, on rack in roasting pan. Do not cover. Roast for about 3½ hours.

Steaks, Chops, Ribs

STUFFED STEAK ROLL

½ cup flour
1½ tsp. salt
¼ tsp. pepper
¼ tsp. paprika
3-lb. round steak, cut ½- to
  ¾-inch thick (may be 2 pieces)
¼ lb. mushrooms, sliced
1 large onion, sliced thin
½ cup butter
¼ cup chopped parsley
2 cups cooked rice
4-oz. jar pimento, cut in thin
  strips
1 tbsp. water
1 egg
12 stuffed olives
¼ cup butter
6 whole mushrooms
3 small onions
1 cup red wine OR consommé

Heat oven to 350 degrees.

Blend flour, salt, pepper and paprika, and pound into both sides of steak, making sure that the steak is no more than ½ inch thick when finished.

Cook mushrooms and onion gently in ½ cup butter until onion is yellow. Remove from heat and mix in parsley, rice and pimento.

Beat water and egg together with a fork and mix into rice mixture lightly. Spread over one side of steak. Arrange olives in a row down the length of the steak and roll up from the long side, tying firmly with string in several places.

Heat ¼ cup butter in deep roasting pan and brown the roll on all sides. Add whole mushrooms, small onions and wine or consommé.

Cover and roast about 2 hours, or until tender, basting occasionally and turning once. Garnish with cooked mushroom caps if desired. (Serves 6 to 8.)

STEAK AND KIDNEY PIE

1½-lb. round steak, cut
  ½-inch thick
2 beef kidneys
6 tbsp. flour
1 tsp. salt
¼ tsp. pepper
¼ cup butter
2 onions, sliced
2 tsp. salt
¼ tsp. pepper
2 cups boiling water
1 tbsp. steak sauce
Dash Tabasco
3 large sprigs parsley, chopped
1 large sprig celery leaves,
  chopped
1 small bay leaf
2 tbsp. butter
2 tbsp. flour
2 tbsp. butter (optional)
½ lb. mushrooms, sliced
  (optional)
Pastry for 2-crust 8-inch pie
1 egg yolk
1 tbsp. cold water

Trim fat from steak and cut into ½-inch cubes. Skin kidneys, split lengthwise and remove all fat and veins. Drop into cold water and let stand 30 minutes. Drain and cut into small cubes. Dry well.

Combine 6 tbsp. flour, 1 tsp. salt and ¼ tsp. pepper in flat dish and dredge pieces of steak and kidney in this mixture.

Heat ¼ cup butter in large heavy pan. Add onions and cook gently until lightly browned. Add meat. Cook and stir until browned. Sprinkle with 2 tsp. salt and ¼ tsp. pepper.

Add water, steak sauce, Tabasco, parsley, celery and bay leaf. Bring to a boil, turn down heat, cover and simmer 1½ hours or until tender.

Cream 2 tbsp. butter and 2 tbsp. flour together until well blended. Add to boiling mixture a little at a time. Cook and stir until thickened.

Heat 2 tbsp. butter in skillet and cook mushrooms 2 minutes. Add to meat mixture.

Heat oven to 450 degrees.

Put steak and kidney mixture into 2-qt. casserole. Let cool slightly.

Roll pastry a little thicker than usual for a pie and 1 inch larger than the top of the casserole. Lay it on top of meat mixture, turn under edge and seal well to sides of casserole.

Beat egg yolk and cold water together with a fork and brush over pastry. Cut a large slash in the centre of the pastry to let the steam escape. Bake about 20 minutes or until pastry is well browned and meat mixture is bubbling. (Serves 6 to 8.)

BEEF AND ASPARAGUS CHINESE STYLE

1½-lb. round steak
1½ tbsp. soy sauce
1 tbsp. sherry
1 tsp. sugar
2 tbsp. cooking oil
1 lb. fresh asparagus
1 tsp. salt
1 tbsp. soy sauce

Cut fat from meat and cut into thin slices across the grain, then into thin shreds the other way. (The shreds should measure about 1 inch long by 1/16 inch by 1/16 inch.)

Add 1½ tbsp. soy sauce, sherry, sugar and oil to meat and let stand 30 minutes. Stir occasionally.

Wash asparagus and break off tough bottoms. Cut remaining into pieces a little larger than the meat shreds. Put in saucepan, add salt and cover with boiling water. Boil 30 seconds and drain immediately. Rinse under cold water.

Heat large heavy skillet. Add meat and cook quickly, stirring constantly, 1 minute. Add asparagus pieces and 1 tbsp. soy sauce and continue cooking and stirring 3 minutes more. Meat should be tender and asparagus tender-crisp.

Serve immediately with rice if desired. (Serves 4 to 6.)

SUKIYAKI

1 lb. sirloin steak
1 clove garlic, chopped very fine
1 small slice fresh ginger OR
  dried ginger root
3 tbsp. brown sugar

½ tsp. monosodium glutamate
⅓ cup soy sauce
1 chicken bouillon cube dissolved in ½ cup hot water
2 tbsp. cooking oil
½ lb. mushrooms, sliced thin
6 green onions, cut in 1-inch pieces
3 stalks celery, sliced thin
2 large onions, sliced thin
1 green pepper, slivered
3 cups raw spinach
Hot cooked rice

Slice steak into very thin slices (about ⅛ inch thick), removing all excess fat.

Mix garlic, ginger, brown sugar, monosodium glutamate, soy sauce and chicken bouillon mixture.

Place in flat dish and add sliced meat. Let meat marinate 2 hours, turning occasionally.

Heat oil in heavy saucepan or skillet. Remove meat from marinade, shaking off excess moisture. Save mixture meat was marinated in.

Add pieces of meat to hot oil and cook over moderate heat, stirring constantly, for 5 minutes.

Add mixture meat was marinated in and all other ingredients *except* spinach and rice. Cook, covered, over low heat, for 7 minutes.

Add spinach and cook 5 minutes more. Vegetables should be tender-crisp. Serve with rice. (Serves 4 to 6.)

Fondue Bourguignonne — *recipe on page 47*

PEPPER STEAK

1½-lb. sirloin steak, 1 inch thick
2 tbsp. cooking oil
½ cup chopped onion
1 clove garlic, halved
10¼-oz. can consommé
1 tsp. salt
⅛ tsp. pepper
2 tbsp. soy sauce
2 large green peppers, slivered
½ cup chopped celery
6 medium tomatoes, peeled and cut in eighths
¼ cup cold water
2 tbsp. cornstarch
Hot cooked rice

Heat oven to 350 degrees.

Cut steak into serving-size pieces, removing any excess fat.

Heat oil in heavy skillet (use one that can go into the oven), add meat and brown well on both sides. Shove meat to one side and add onion and garlic at other side. Cook gently until onion is tender. Remove and discard garlic pieces. Remove from heat. Spread meat over onion.

Combine consommé, salt, pepper and soy sauce and pour over meat. Sprinkle with peppers and celery. Cover tightly and bake 1½ hours or until meat is tender, basting occasionally.

Remove from oven, uncover and add tomato pieces. Return to oven and cook 15 minutes more.

Remove from oven and set over moderate heat on top of stove. Lift out meat and vegetables with a slotted spoon, putting in deep platter.

Measure cold water into small jar with tight top, add cornstarch and shake together until well blended. Add mixture gradually to hot liquid in skillet, stirring constantly. Cook and stir until thickened and clear. Pour over meat and vegetables. Serve immediately with rice. (Serves 6.)

BLUE CHEESE STEAK

½ lb. blue cheese (room
 temperature)
2 tbsp. cream
1 clove garlic
4-lb. sirloin steak,
 1½ inches thick

Cream cheese and cream together until a smooth paste is formed. Crush garlic and add. Blend well.

Slash fat on edge of steak at 1-inch intervals.

Broil steak on one side (for rare have top surface 3 inches from heat, for well-done 5 inches). Allow 18 to 25 minutes *total* cooking time, depending on how you like your steak cooked.

Remove steak from oven after half of cooking time has elapsed and turn it. Spread uncooked side with blue cheese mixture. Return to broiler and cook until it's the way you like it. (If you aren't sure it's done enough, make a small incision in the thickest part to see what color the meat is inside.)

SPAGHETTI AND MEAT ROLLS

1½ cups seedless raisins
 ½ cup blanched almonds
 2 tbsp. cooking oil
 ½ cup chopped celery
 ½ cup chopped onion
 ¼ cup grated Parmesan cheese
 1 egg, lightly beaten
 ½ tsp. salt
 8 minute steaks
 ¼ cup flour
 ½ tsp. salt
 ¼ tsp. pepper
 ¼ tsp. paprika
 ¼ cup cooking oil
 ½ cup chopped onion
 1 clove garlic, crushed
28-oz. can tomatoes
7½-oz. can tomato sauce
 1 tsp. salt
 ¼ tsp. pepper
 ½ tsp. sweet basil
 Hot cooked spaghetti
 (to serve 8)
 Grated Parmesan cheese

Grind raisins and almonds together through fine blade of the food chopper.

Heat 2 tbsp. oil in heavy skillet. Add celery and ½ cup chopped onion and cook gently, stirring often, 5 minutes. Add raisins and nuts, cover and cook gently 2 or 3 minutes more. Remove from heat and cool.

Stir ¼ cup Parmesan cheese, egg and ½ tsp. salt into raisin mixture and blend well. Lay minute steaks on table and divide raisin mixture up evenly among them. Spread mixture to within ¼ inch of the edge of the steaks and roll them up like a jelly roll, tying each with string.

Combine flour, ½ tsp. salt, ¼ tsp. pepper and paprika and roll each steak roll in mixture.

Heat ¼ cup cooking oil in large heavy skillet. Brown steaks on all sides. Remove steaks as they brown and set aside.

Add ½ cup chopped onion and garlic to drippings in pan. Cook gently 5 minutes. Add tomatoes, tomato sauce, 1 tsp. salt, ¼ tsp. pepper and sweet basil and simmer 5 minutes.

Return meat rolls to pan, cover and simmer about 1 hour or until meat is tender, turning rolls often.

Lift meat rolls out of sauce and remove strings. Put in centre of large serving plate. Surround meat with hot cooked spaghetti. Pour sauce over all. Serve with grated Parmesan cheese. (Serves 8.)

INDIVIDUAL STEAK ROASTS

6 minute steaks
6 thin slices cooked ham
1½-lb. veal steak, ¼ inch thick
 Salt and pepper
 ½ cup chopped parsley
 ½ cup grated Parmesan cheese
 6 small green onions
 ¼ cup flour
 1 tsp. salt
 ¼ tsp. pepper
 ¼ tsp. paprika
 ¼ cup cooking oil
 ½ cup water
 2 beef bouillon cubes
 2 tbsp. lemon juice
 1 cup sliced celery
 1 medium onion, sliced
 2 whole cloves
 Dash nutmeg
 1 tsp. salt
 ¼ tsp. pepper
 2 tbsp. cold water
 1 tbsp. cornstarch

Lay all meat out on table. Trim ham slices so they are the same size and shape as steaks. Cut veal steak into pieces the same size and shape as steaks. Sprinkle veal and beef lightly with salt and pepper. Sprinkle all pieces of meat with a little of the parsley and cheese.

Top each minute steak with a slice of ham, then with a piece of veal. Trim green onions so they are just the width of each stack of

To sauté canned mushrooms, add them, liquid and all, to hot butter in a heavy skillet. Cook rapidly until all liquid disappears and mushrooms are browned.

meat and roll each stack of meat up tightly around the onion. Tie securely with string.

Combine flour, 1 tsp. salt, 1/4 tsp. pepper and paprika in a flat dish. Roll each steak "roast" in this mixture.

Heat oil in Dutch oven or other heavy saucepan that can be put in the oven. Brown meat on all sides in hot oil.

Heat oven to 325 degrees.

Add water, bouillon cubes, lemon juice, celery, sliced onion, cloves, nutmeg, 1 tsp. salt and 1/4 tsp. pepper to Dutch oven. Cover tightly and put in oven to cook until tender, 1 1/2 to 2 hours. Turn meat occasionally.

Lift individual "roasts" out of pan, cut off strings and put on hot platter. Keep hot.

Strain drippings and return to Dutch oven. Set over moderate heat and bring to a boil. Measure cold water into small dish and stir in cornstarch to blend. Add to boiling mixture gradually, stirring constantly. Cook until slightly thickened. Taste and season if necessary.

Serve "roasts" cut in thick slices or whole with gravy spooned over. (Serves 6.)

BEEF STROGANOFF

2-lb. fillet of beef
1/2 cup flour
1 1/2 tsp. salt
1/4 tsp. pepper
6 tbsp. butter
2 large onions, sliced thin
1/2 lb. fresh mushrooms, sliced
2 small cloves garlic, crushed
3 tbsp. flour
1 1/2 cups canned consommé
1 pt. commercial sour cream
1 tsp. paprika
1 tbsp. Worcestershire sauce
Dill seeds (optional)
Brown Rice (recipe follows)

Cut any fat from beef and cut meat into 2-inch strips about as big around as a pencil. Combine 1/2 cup flour, salt and pepper in a flat dish and roll the beef strips in the mixture to coat all sides.

Heat butter in large heavy skillet. Add onions, mushrooms and garlic and cook gently until onions are yellow, stirring constantly.

Add beef strips and cook and stir constantly over high heat 2 to 3 minutes. (This should just brown beef but leave the inside pink.) Remove pan from heat and lift out meat and vegetables with a slotted spoon or egg turner.

Measure drippings left in pan and return 3 tbsp. to pan (or add butter to make 3 tbsp. in pan if fat has cooked away). Return to heat, sprinkle in 3 tbsp. flour and cook and stir until bubbling well. Remove from heat and add consommé all at once, stirring to blend.

Return to heat and cook and stir until thick and smooth.

Turn heat to very low and stir in cream gradually. Heat but do not boil or cream will curdle. Stir in paprika and Worcestershire sauce. Taste and add salt and pepper to taste.

Stir in beef and vegetables and heat but do not boil. Serve as soon as hot with Brown Rice. Crumble dill seeds over meat mixture, if desired. (Serves 6 to 8.)

Brown Rice

2 tbsp. butter
1 small onion, chopped
1 1/2 cups long-grain rice
3 1/2 cups liquid (consommé plus water — see note below)

Heat butter in heavy saucepan. Add onion and cook gently until yellow. Add rice and cook and stir until golden brown. Add liquid and cover tightly. Simmer 20 minutes without lifting cover. Then stir lightly with a fork and cook a few minutes longer, uncovered, to dry rice a little if desired.

Note: Use at least one 10 1/4-oz. can consommé for the liquid. When I make this rice with the Beef Stroganoff I use a full can, the part can left over from the Stroganoff plus water to make the 3 1/2 cups liquid.

FONDUE BOURGUIGNONNE

2-lb. fillet of beef
Salad oil
Sauces and condiments (see suggestions at end of recipe)

Trim all fat from fillet of beef and cut it into small cubes, about 1/2 inch.

Have ready in centre of table fondue pan, chafing dish or electric skillet with at least 1 inch of hot oil in it. Have long-handled forks available for each person at table. Have oil in pan bubbling slightly (if you are using a chafing dish or fondue pan you may want to heat the oil to bubbling on the stove, then transfer it to cooking pan and set over flame).

Have small dishes with three or more of the sauces and condiments suggested for each person at the table.

Spear cubes of beef on forks (everyone does his own) and dip them in hot oil to cook as desired (this will only take a few seconds). Dip meat in any or all of sauces and condiments. (Serves 4 to 6.)

CONDIMENTS

Finely-minced garlic
Finely-chopped parsley and capers (equal amounts chopped together)
Garlic butter (add crushed garlic to soft butter to taste)
Anchovy butter (add mashed anchovies or anchovy paste to soft butter to taste)

Béarnaise Sauce

3 green onions (with tops), cut up
1 large sprig parsley, chopped
1/2 tsp. dry tarragon leaves
1/2 tsp. dry chervil leaves
1/4 cup wine vinegar
2 tbsp. water
4 egg yolks
1/4 cup soft butter
1/4 tsp. salt
Dash cayenne

Combine onions, parsley, tarragon, chervil, vinegar and water in small saucepan. Set over low heat and simmer 5 minutes. Strain, saving liquid and discarding remainder.

Recipe continued on next page

Put egg yolks in top of double boiler. Add vinegar mixture to yolks a little at a time, beating constantly with a wire whip or rotary beater. Set over *simmering* (it must not be boiling) water and cook, stirring constantly, until mixture thickens.

Add butter a little at a time, stirring until butter is blended after each addition. (Mixture should look like mayonnaise.) Season with salt and cayenne. Serve slightly warm.

Note: The secret of success with this sauce is not to let it get too hot (water should be simmering in bottom of double boiler — not boiling) and to stir well after each addition of butter. If sauce should separate, a few drops of cold water should put it back together again. Traditionally Béarnaise Sauce is served lukewarm. It is usually made with fresh herbs but I find this one very satisfactory when fresh herbs are not available.

Blue Cheese Mayonnaise

1/4 cup crumbled blue cheese
1/4 cup ketchup
Dash garlic salt
Pinch tarragon
1 cup mayonnaise

Add cheese to ketchup and mash with a fork until smooth. Add remaining and blend well.

Tomato Sauce

2 cups milk
1/2 small bay leaf
1/4 cup butter
1/2 small onion, minced
1 medium stalk celery, minced
1/4 cup flour
1 tsp. salt
1/8 tsp. pepper
Dash nutmeg
1/4 cup canned tomato paste
1 tsp. paprika
1 tbsp. butter

Heat milk and bay leaf to scalding.

Heat butter and add onion and celery. Cook over moderate heat until tender but not brown.

Sprinkle in flour, salt, pepper and nutmeg and let bubble up. Add hot milk gradually, stirring constantly. Turn heat to low and

simmer 15 minutes, stirring often. Strain. Return to saucepan and set over low heat again.

Add tomato paste, paprika and butter and heat and stir until blended.

Mustard Sauce

Make as for Tomato Sauce, *except* instead of tomato paste and paprika add 2 tsp. dry mustard mixed with 2 tbsp. water and 1/2 tsp. Worcestershire sauce.

Horseradish Sauce

Make as for Tomato Sauce, *except* instead of tomato paste and paprika add 1 1/2 tbsp. drained prepared horseradish and 1/4 tsp. dry mustard.

STUFFED PORK CHOPS

4 double pork chops
2 tbsp. butter
2 tbsp. finely-chopped onion
1 cup chopped celery, with leaves
1/2 tsp. salt
1/2 tsp. poultry seasoning
1/8 tsp. pepper
2 cups soft bread crumbs
1/4 cup flour
1/2 tsp. salt
1/4 tsp. pepper
1/2 cup water
1 green pepper, cubed
6 carrots, sliced
4 medium potatoes, sliced
1 cup water

Have butcher cut pocket in chops for stuffing.

Melt butter in heavy skillet. Add onion, celery, 1/2 tsp. salt, poultry seasoning, 1/8 tsp. pepper and half of bread crumbs. Cook gently until onion is tender, stirring constantly. Add to remaining crumbs and toss lightly.

Cut excess fat from chops. Stuff with bread mixture and fasten openings securely with toothpicks. Combine flour, 1/2 tsp. salt and 1/4 tsp. pepper and dip chops into mixture to coat both sides.

Heat some of fat cut from chops in heavy skillet and brown chops well on both sides. Add 1/2 cup water, cover tightly and cook gently until chops are tender, about 1 hour. Turn occasionally and add

more water if necessary.

Add vegetables and remaining 1 cup water. Cover again and cook until vegetables are tender, about 20 minutes. (Serves 4.)

VEGETABLE-STUFFED PORK CHOPS

1/4 cup butter
1 cup finely-chopped onions
1 cup finely-chopped mushrooms
2 cups soft bread crumbs (day-old bread)
1 cup finely-grated carrots
1/2 cup chopped parsley
1 egg, lightly beaten
1 1/2 tbsp. lemon juice
2 tsp. salt
1/4 tsp. pepper
1/8 tsp. nutmeg
6 loin pork chops, 1 1/2 inches thick (see note)
1 clove garlic, cut in half
1 tsp. salt
1/4 tsp. thyme
1/4 tsp. sage
Cooking oil
1/4 cup water

Heat oven to 450 degrees. Have ready a large shallow baking pan, about 13 x 9 1/2 x 2 inches.

Heat butter in heavy skillet. Add onions and cook gently until transparent. Add mushrooms and continue cooking gently 1 minute. Add half of crumbs and cook and stir until crumbs are golden.

Combine remaining crumbs, carrots, parsley, egg, lemon juice, 2 tsp. salt, pepper and nutmeg in bowl. Add onion-mushroom mixture and toss together lightly.

Trim excess fat from chops. Rub on both sides with cut sides of garlic. Combine 1 tsp. salt, thyme and sage and rub a little of this mixture on each chop.

Stuff pockets in chops with prepared bread-vegetable mixture (do not pack). Fasten pockets closed with toothpicks.

Sprinkle any left over bread-vegetable mixture in bottom of baking pan. Lay stuffed chops on top in a single layer. Brush with oil.

Bake, uncovered, 30 minutes at 450 degrees or until lightly browned on both sides.

Reduce oven temperature to 350 degrees. Add ¼ cup water to pan, cover tightly (use aluminum foil) and cook about 1 hour or until very tender. (Serves 6.)

Note: Have butcher cut pockets in chops to hold stuffing when you buy them.

PORK CHOP DINNER

 4 pork chops, 1 inch thick
¼ cup flour
½ tsp. salt
¼ tsp. pepper
¼ tsp. paprika
 2 tbsp. cooking oil
 1 clove garlic, minced
 1 cup long-grain rice
 2 large onions, sliced
28-oz. can tomatoes
 2 tsp. salt
¼ tsp. pepper
½ tsp. dry mustard
½ tsp. sweet basil

Heat oven to 350 degrees.

Cut excess fat from chops. Combine flour, ½ tsp. salt, ¼ tsp. pepper and paprika and dip chops in mixture to coat both sides.

Heat oil in heavy skillet and brown chops well on both sides. Add garlic for last few minutes of browning. Lift chops out and set aside.

Add rice to drippings in pan and cook gently, stirring, until

Use tongs to turn steaks and chops so juices won't be lost from fork holes. If you don't have tongs be sure to stick fork in fat, not in meat.

golden.

Butter a 13 x 9½ x 2-inch baking dish and spread rice over bottom. Top with browned chops. Separate onion slices into rings and spread over chops.

Combine remaining ingredients and pour over. Cover tightly (use aluminum foil if dish has no cover).

Bake 1 hour covered and 20 to 30 minutes uncovered, or until the chops are tender and the rice has absorbed most of the liquid. (Serves 4.)

POLYNESIAN PORK CHOPS

 6 thick pork chops
 1 small onion, sliced thin
½ cup chopped celery
½ cup chopped green pepper
 1 clove garlic, minced
 1 tsp. salt
¼ tsp. pepper
20-oz. can pineapple tidbits
 2 cups liquid (pineapple juice
    plus water)
¼ cup cold water
 2 tbsp. cornstarch
⅓ cup vinegar
 2 tbsp. soy sauce
 1 tbsp. brown sugar
½ tsp. salt
 1 tbsp. chopped preserved
    ginger OR ½ tsp. ground
    ginger

Trim most of fat from chops. Heat some of fat in heavy skillet. Discard fat once the pan is well greased. Add chops to hot pan and brown well on both sides. Lift out as they brown.

Drain most of fat from skillet. Add onion, celery, green pepper and garlic to remaining fat and cook gently, stirring, 5 minutes. Return chops to pan. Sprinkle with 1 tsp. salt and pepper.

Drain pineapple well. Measure juice and add enough water to make 2 cups liquid. Add to skillet. Cover tightly and simmer about 1 hour or until chops are tender.

Push chops to one side of skillet. Combine cold water and cornstarch, blending until smooth. Stir gradually into hot liquid in skillet. Cook gently until thick and clear. Stir constantly.

Add pineapple, vinegar, soy sauce, brown sugar, ½ tsp. salt and ginger. Stir to blend and push chops back into mixture. Cover and simmer 10 minutes. Serve immediately. (Serves 6.)

GLAZED STUFFED SPARERIBS

 2 strips spareribs
    (about 4 lb.)
 2 tbsp. oil
 1 tsp. salt
⅓ cup butter
¼ cup minced onion
 4 cups bread crumbs
¼ cup chopped celery
 1 tsp. salt
¼ tsp. pepper
 1 tsp. thyme
½ tsp. sage
 1 cup chopped apple
 1 tsp. salt
 2 tbsp. vinegar
 2 tbsp. brown sugar
 1 tsp. dry mustard

Heat oven to 350 degrees.

Brown one side of each set of ribs in oil in roasting pan. Remove from heat. Sprinkle with 1 tsp. salt. Turn one set with brown side up.

Melt butter in heavy skillet, add onion and cook until yellow.

Add about half of bread crumbs

Recipe continued on next page

and heat, stirring, until crumbs are lightly browned. Turn into bowl and add remaining crumbs, celery, 1 tsp. salt, pepper, thyme, sage and apple.

Spread over set of ribs that was turned brown side up. Top with other set of ribs, brown side next to stuffing. Sprinkle with 1 tsp. salt.

Mix vinegar, sugar and mustard and pour over ribs.

Bake 1½ hours, adding a little water, if necessary, to prevent burning. (Serves 6.)

BAKED SWEET AND SOUR RIBS

3 lb. spareribs
2 tbsp. butter
¼ cup finely-chopped onion
½ small clove garlic, finely chopped
¼ cup finely-chopped celery
½ cup finely-chopped green pepper
¼ cup cold water
1 tbsp. cornstarch
1 cup pineapple juice
½ cup water
2 chicken bouillon cubes
¼ cup brown sugar
¼ cup vinegar
1½ tbsp. soy sauce

Heat oven to 450 degrees.

Cut ribs into serving-size pieces, about 3 ribs per piece. Lay in shallow roasting pan in a single layer and bake 30 minutes.

Prepare the following sweet-sour sauce while the ribs are cooking the first 30 minutes.

Melt butter in pan. Add onion, garlic, celery and green pepper and cook gently until almost tender.

Measure cold water, add cornstarch, stirring until completely blended and smooth. Blend into butter mixture gradually, stirring constantly.

Add pineapple juice, water and bouillon cubes and heat gently, stirring constantly, until boiling. Turn down heat and simmer 5 minutes. Stir in sugar, vinegar and soy sauce.

Remove pan of ribs from oven and pour off excess fat. Reduce oven temperature to 350 degrees.

Spread ribs with sweet-sour sauce. Cover loosely with aluminum foil. Return to oven and cook 30 minutes, basting occasionally. Remove foil and cook 30 minutes more or until meat is tender, basting occasionally. (Serves 4.)

RICH BROWN VEAL

1½-lb. veal steak, cut ¼ inch thick
¼ cup flour
½ tsp. salt
⅛ tsp. pepper
½ tsp. paprika
¼ cup butter
1 small clove garlic, minced
1 small green pepper, slivered
1 small onion, sliced thin and separated into rings
2 thin strips lemon rind
½ cup water
1½-oz. can dry cream of mushroom soup mix
¼ cup lemon juice
1 cup water
¼ cup cold water
2 tbsp. flour
1 cup commercial sour cream
Salt and pepper
Hot cooked rice (optional)

Cut meat into 4 serving-size pieces. Combine ¼ cup flour, ½ tsp. salt, ⅛ tsp. pepper and paprika in flat dish. Dip meat pieces into mixture to coat both sides.

Heat butter in heavy skillet. Add garlic and cook gently 3 minutes. Add meat and brown well on both sides. Lift out meat as it browns.

Add green pepper, onion rings, strips of lemon rind (cut them the length of the lemon with a vegetable peeler or paring knife, using only the yellow part), ½ cup water, soup mix and lemon juice to drippings in pan. Blend well and return meat to mixture. Cover tightly and simmer about 30 minutes or until meat is tender, turning occasionally and adding more water 1 tbsp. at a time if necessary to keep from sticking.

Remove meat from pan. Add 1 cup water to drippings and bring to a boil, scraping up browned bits from bottom of pan.

Combine ¼ cup cold water and 2 tbsp. flour (use any left over from dipping meat) and blend until smooth. Add to boiling mixture in pan gradually, stirring constantly. Boil 1 minute.

Turn heat to low and add sour cream gradually, stirring constantly. Heat to boiling point (do not boil). Taste and season with salt and pepper.

Return meat to pan and heat well. Serve immediately with hot cooked rice if desired. (Serves 4.)

Vegetable-Stuffed Pork Chops — *recipe on page 48*

VEAL AND LEMON

2-lb. veal steak, cut ¹/₂ inch thick
¹/₄ cup flour
1 tsp. salt
¹/₈ tsp. pepper
6 tbsp. butter
1 tbsp. paprika
¹/₂ tsp. marjoram
1 lemon, sliced thin
2 chicken bouillon cubes
¹/₂ cup boiling water
1 cup commercial sour cream
Salt and pepper
Hot buttered noodles

Cut steak into serving-size pieces. Combine flour, 1 tsp. salt and ¹/₈ tsp. pepper in a flat dish and dip meat in mixture to coat both sides.

Heat butter in heavy skillet, add meat and brown slowly until golden. Sprinkle in paprika and marjoram. Add lemon slices.

Dissolve bouillon cubes in boiling water and add. Cover tightly and simmer until meat is tender, 30 to 45 minutes. Lift meat out on to hot platter and keep hot.

Stir cream into drippings and heat. Do not boil. Taste and season. Pour over meat and serve immediately with buttered noodles. (Serves 6.)

VEAL PARMESAN

1½-lb. veal steak, cut very thin
  Salt
  Pepper
  Paprika
  ½ cup grated Parmesan cheese
  ¼ cup butter
  1 cup light cream
  Poppy Seed Noodles
    (recipe follows)

Cut steak into serving-size pieces and pound with edge of plate or mallet until no more than ¼ inch thick.

Sprinkle with salt, pepper and paprika and dip in grated Parmesan cheese to coat both sides.

Heat butter until golden brown, and cook steak in butter until lightly browned and tender (about 3 minutes on each side). Lift out and put on hot plate.

Add cream to drippings in pan. Heat, but do not boil, and pour over meat. Serve hot with Poppy Seed Noodles. (Serves 6.)

Poppy Seed Noodles

2 cups uncooked noodles
3 tbsp. butter
2 tsp. poppy seeds

Cook noodles according to package directions. Drain.

Add butter and poppy seeds, mixing lightly with fork.

SWISS VEAL

4 large mushrooms
1 tbsp. butter
1-lb. veal steak, sliced thin
Salt and pepper
4 thin slices Swiss cheese
1 egg
2 tsp. water
½ cup fine cracker crumbs
¼ cup butter

Slice mushrooms and cook gently in 1 tbsp. butter until tender.

Cut veal into 4 pieces. Pound with edge of plate until very thin (¼ inch thick). Sprinkle with salt and pepper.

Lay a thin slice of Swiss cheese on each piece of veal so that it covers half the piece. Top with mushroom slices. Fold meat over cheese and pinch edges together.

(I like to fasten them with toothpicks.)

Beat egg and water together with a fork. Dip veal in mixture, then in cracker crumbs.

Melt ¼ cup butter in heavy skillet. Cook veal in butter over moderate heat until golden brown on both sides. (Serves 4.)

VEAL SCALLOPINI

2-lb. veal steak, sliced
  ¼-inch thick
½ cup flour
1 tsp. salt
⅛ tsp. pepper
2 tsp. paprika
¼ cup butter
1 cup chicken broth OR canned
  chicken consommé
½ lb. fresh mushrooms, sliced
½ small green pepper, chopped
½ cup chopped celery
7½-oz. can tomato sauce
  Parmesan cheese
  Hot buttered noodles

Heat oven to 350 degrees.

Pound meat thoroughly with the edge of a heavy plate. Cut in serving-size pieces. Combine flour, salt, pepper and paprika and dip meat in mixture to coat both sides.

Heat butter in heavy skillet and add meat. Cook slowly until golden on both sides. Transfer to a 13 x 9½ x 2-inch baking dish as it browns. Pour chicken broth or consommé over meat and put in oven, uncovered, for 30 minutes.

Add mushrooms, green pepper and celery to drippings left in skillet, adding more butter if necessary. Cook gently until tender.

Add tomato sauce and simmer gently about 5 minutes, scraping up any browned bits from the bottom of pan. Remove from heat.

Pour sauce over meat when it has cooked 30 minutes. Baste well with chicken broth from bottom of pan. Return to oven and cook another 15 minutes or until meat is tender. Baste several times.

Sprinkle generously with Parmesan cheese and serve immediately with hot buttered noodles. (Serves 6.)

**Lamb and Veal
are two meats
that are too
good to ignore**

CURRIED LAMB CHOPS

8 loin lamb chops
3 tbsp. cooking oil
1 medium onion, sliced
1 medium tart apple, diced
1½ tbsp. curry powder
1½ tbsp. flour
1½ tsp. salt
1½ tsp. sugar
¼ tsp. dry mustard
2½ cups chicken broth
4 cups cooked rice
  Chutney

Trim all excess fat from chops, wrap meat at small end of each chop around wide end to form a round and tie with string.

Heat oil in heavy skillet and brown chops on both sides. Remove meat.

Add onion and apple to oil left in pan and cook until lightly browned. Sprinkle in curry powder and cook and stir for a few seconds. Sprinkle in flour, salt, sugar and mustard and stir to blend.

Add chicken broth, blend well and bring to a boil.

Return chops to pan, spoon sauce over, cover and simmer until chops are tender, about 30 minutes. Add a little water to curry mixture if it gets too thick.

Put rice around the outside edge of serving plate and chops in centre. Pour curry sauce over chops. Serve immediately with chutney. (Serves 4.)

LAMB CHOPS WITH DILL

1 tbsp. cooking oil
4 thick lamb chops
Salt and pepper
10-oz. can cream of celery soup
½ cup water
1 tsp. dill weed

Heat oven to 350 degrees. Have ready a baking dish just large enough to hold the chops in a single layer.

Heat oil in heavy skillet. Add chops and brown well on both sides. Lift out of pan and put in baking dish. Sprinkle with salt and pepper.

Combine soup, water and dill weed. Pour over chops. Cover baking dish (use aluminum foil if it has no cover) and bake 35 to 40 minutes or until chops are very tender. Turn chops occasionally during baking. (Serves 2.)

LAMB CHOPS AND VEGETABLES

2 tbsp. cooking oil
6 thick lamb chops
1 small clove garlic, crushed
3 medium onions, sliced
3 medium carrots, sliced
3 medium tomatoes, sliced
2 medium green peppers, seeded and cut in rings
2 tsp. salt
1/4 tsp. pepper
1 tsp. rosemary
1/4 tsp. cinnamon
1/4 cup cold water
2 tbsp. flour

Heat oven to 350 degrees.

Heat oil in Dutch oven or other heavy saucepan that can be put in the oven. Add chops and brown well on both sides. Lift out as they brown.

Add garlic to drippings in pan and cook gently 2 minutes. Remove pan from heat.

Put half of each kind of vegetable in pan. Sprinkle with half the seasonings and mix lightly. Lay chops in a single layer on top of vegetables. Cover chops with remaining vegetables and sprinkle with remaining seasonings.

Cover pan and bake about 1¹/₂ hours or until chops are very tender. Remove from oven and set over low heat on top of stove.

Measure water into small jar with a tight lid. Add flour, cover and shake well until blended. Stir mixture gradually into liquid in pan. Let come to a boil and boil 1 minute. (Serves 6.)

Stews

BURGUNDY BEEF

2½-lb. beef chuck
2 tbsp. butter
1 tbsp. oil
1 tbsp. flour
2 tsp. salt
¼ tsp. pepper
1 clove garlic, minced
2 cups red burgundy wine
Water
2 large sprigs celery leaves
2 large sprigs parsley
1 small bay leaf
Pinch of thyme
6 slices bacon, diced
12 small white onions
2 tbsp. butter
½ lb. fresh mushrooms, sliced
2 tsp. lemon juice
Chopped parsley

Heat oven to 350 degrees.

Cut beef into 1½-inch cubes, discarding excess fat.

Heat 2 tbsp. butter and oil in Dutch oven or heavy saucepan that can be put into the oven. Add cubes of meat and brown quickly, turning to brown all sides.

Sprinkle in flour and cook, stirring, until flour is golden brown. Add salt, pepper, garlic, wine and enough water to cover meat (about 1 cup). Bring to a boil.

Tie stems of celery leaves and parsley together with a piece of string or thread (so they can be removed later). Add to meat along with bay leaf and thyme. Cover tightly and put in oven for about 2 hours or until meat is tender.

Skim off fat if necessary and remove celery, parsley and bay leaf.

Put bacon in skillet and cook until crisp and brown. Add whole onions and cook gently, stirring until lightly browned. Lift onions and bacon bits out of pan with a slotted spoon and add to meat mixture (discard fat left in pan). Cover again and return to oven until onions are tender, about 15 minutes.

Heat 2 tbsp. butter in skillet, add sliced mushrooms and lemon juice and cook gently 2 minutes. Sprinkle mushrooms and parsley over beef and serve immediately. (Serves 6.)

CURRIED BEEF WITH RICE

2 lb. stewing beef, cut in large cubes
¼ cup cooking oil
1 medium onion, sliced thin
1 medium apple, chopped
1 tbsp. curry powder
1½ tsp. salt
½ tsp. pepper
½ tsp. ginger
28-oz. can tomatoes
6-oz. can tomato paste
2 tbsp. lemon juice
½ cup hot water
2 beef bouillon cubes
Hot cooked rice

Trim excess fat from stewing beef.

Heat oil in large heavy saucepan or Dutch oven. Add onion and apple and cook gently, stirring, until transparent. Sprinkle in curry powder and cook gently 3 minutes.

Lift out onion and apple with a slotted spoon and set aside. Drop beef cubes into drippings in pan and brown on all sides. Return onion and apple to pan. Add salt, pepper, ginger, tomatoes, tomato paste, lemon juice, hot water and bouillon cubes. Stir well. Cover tightly and simmer until meat is very tender, about 2 hours.

Serve over hot rice. (Serves 6.)

RICH BEEF STEW

¼ cup flour
1 tsp. salt
⅛ tsp. pepper
1 tbsp. paprika
2 lb. stewing beef, cubed
6 slices bacon, cut up
3 medium onions, chopped
3 tsp. salt
¼ tsp. pepper
⅛ tsp. marjoram
1 clove garlic, crushed
2 cups boiling water
2 beef bouillon cubes
6 medium potatoes, cut in 1-inch cubes
1 small turnip, cut in 1-inch cubes
6 carrots, cut in thick slices
1 pt. commercial sour cream

Combine flour, salt, pepper and paprika in a flat dish. Roll cubes of meat in mixture.

Put bacon pieces in large heavy saucepan or Dutch oven and cook until transparent. Add onions and cook and stir until onions are yellow and bacon browned.

Add meat and brown lightly on all sides, stirring constantly. Add salt, pepper, marjoram, garlic, water and bouillon cubes. Bring to a boil, turn down heat, cover tightly and simmer until meat is nearly tender, 1½ to 2 hours. Add more water if necessary to keep stew from sticking.

Add potatoes, turnip and carrots, cover and continue simmering until vegetables and meat are all tender.

Add cream gradually, stirring constantly, and heat but do not boil or cream will curdle. Serve immediately. (Serves 6 to 8.)

BRAISED SHORT RIBS

2 lb. beef short ribs
1 large clove garlic, cut in half
¼ cup flour
1 tsp. salt
¼ tsp. pepper
1 tsp. paprika
¼ cup cooking oil
20-oz. can tomatoes
1 cup hot water
1 large carrot, peeled and diced
1 medium onion, sliced
1 tsp. salt
¼ tsp. pepper
1 small bay leaf

Heat oven to 325 degrees.

Cut short ribs into pieces and trim off all excess fat. Rub all over with cut sides of garlic. Combine flour, 1 tsp. salt, ¼ tsp. pepper and paprika in flat dish and roll meat pieces in mixture to coat all sides.

Heat oil in Dutch oven or other heavy saucepan that can go in the oven. Add ribs and brown well on all sides. Lift out pieces as they brown.

Drain all except 2 tbsp. of the

Braised Short Ribs — *recipe on page 54*

fat from the pan. Sprinkle in any flour that was left from coating the pieces of meat and let bubble up, stirring constantly. Remove from heat and add tomatoes and hot water all at once, stirring to blend. Return to heat and bring to boil, stirring constantly. Add carrot, onion, 1 tsp. salt, ¼ tsp. pepper, bay leaf and short ribs. Cover tightly, put in oven and cook until tender, 2 to 2½ hours. (Serves 4.)

NEW ENGLAND BOILED DINNER

4-lb. corned brisket of beef
Cold water
6 small onions
6 small whole carrots
6 medium potatoes, halved
1 medium turnip, cut in
  1½-inch cubes
6 small whole parsnips
1 small green cabbage, cut in
  6 wedges

Wash corned beef. Cover with cold water in large heavy kettle. Cover tightly and simmer about 3½ hours, or until tender. Remove meat and keep warm.

Add onions, carrots, potatoes, turnip and parsnips to broth, and boil 30 minutes or until done.

Add cabbage for last 15 minutes of cooking.

Arrange vegetables around meat on hot platter. (Serves 6.)

55

PORK STEW

¼ cup flour
1 tsp. salt
¼ tsp. pepper
2-lb. pork shoulder, cubed
2 tbsp. cooking oil
1 large onion, chopped
6 green onions (with tops), chopped
2 large stalks celery, chopped
2 tbsp. flour
Water
3 sprigs parsley
1 small bay leaf
3 whole cloves
3 peppercorns
½ tsp. leaf thyme
1 clove garlic, minced
8 medium carrots, cut in large pieces
6 medium potatoes, cut in large pieces
Minced parsley

Combine ¼ cup flour, salt and pepper in flat dish. Roll cubes of pork in this mixture.

Heat oil in large heavy saucepan or Dutch oven. Add pork and brown well on all sides. Add onion, green onions and celery and cook gently 5 minutes. Sprinkle in 2 tbsp. flour, stirring constantly.

Remove from heat and add enough water to cover meat. Stir, return to heat and bring to a boil. Tie parsley, bay leaf, cloves, peppercorns and thyme in small cheesecloth bag and drop into stew. Add garlic, cover tightly, turn heat to low and simmer about 30 minutes or until meat is just beginning to get tender. Add carrots and potatoes, cover again and continue simmering until everything is tender, about 45 minutes.

Lift out bag of seasonings, sprinkle with minced parsley and serve. (Serves 6.)

HAWAIIAN PORK

1-lb. pork shoulder
2 eggs
¼ cup flour
1 tsp. salt
¼ tsp. pepper
½ cup cooking oil
3 green peppers
4 stalks celery

2 chicken bouillon cubes dissolved in 1 cup hot water
½ cup pineapple chunks, drained
½ cup pineapple juice
3 tbsp. cornstarch
½ cup sugar
3 tbsp. soy sauce
½ cup vinegar
Cooked rice

Cut pork into 1-inch cubes. Beat together eggs, flour, salt and pepper to make a batter.

Heat oil in heavy skillet. Dip pork cubes into batter and drop into hot oil. Fry slowly to brown. Drain off excess oil.

Cut peppers into 1-inch squares. Cut celery stalks diagonally into 1-inch pieces. Add vegetables to meat. Add ¼ cup of chicken bouillon-water mixture, pineapple and pineapple juice. Cover and simmer 10 to 15 minutes, until vegetables are tender-crisp.

Combine cornstarch and sugar in saucepan. Blend in soy sauce, vinegar and remaining ¾ cup chicken bouillon. Cook over medium heat, stirring constantly, until thick and clear. Pour over meat mixture, cover and simmer another 5 minutes.

Serve over hot cooked rice. (Serves 6.)

BROWN STEW

¼ cup flour
1 tsp. salt
¼ tsp. pepper
½ tsp. paprika
1-lb. boneless veal shoulder, cubed
2 tbsp. fat
1 cup water
1 tbsp. Worcestershire sauce
2 tbsp. ketchup
4 medium carrots, peeled and cut up
4 medium potatoes, peeled and cut up
4 small onions, peeled and cut up
4 stalks celery, cut in 1-inch pieces
½ pkg. frozen peas (optional)

Blend flour, salt, pepper and paprika. Roll meat in mixture.

Heat fat in heavy kettle and add meat. Brown well on all sides.

Nothing sharpens the appetite like the aroma of a stew simmering on the stove

Add water, Worcestershire sauce and ketchup. Cover and simmer 2 hours or until meat is tender.

Add cut-up vegetables (cut in pieces about the same size so they will cook in the same time).

Cook about 30 minutes or until vegetables are tender. At end of cooking time, add frozen peas. Allow to cook just until peas are thawed. (Serves 4.)

TURNIP STEW

3 tbsp. butter
1 lb. veal, cut in cubes
2 tbsp. flour
2 chicken bouillon cubes
1 cup boiling water
1 large onion, sliced thin
1 tsp. salt
¼ tsp. pepper
½ tsp. monosodium glutamate (optional)
6 whole cloves
2 tbsp. chopped parsley
⅛ tsp. thyme
⅛ tsp. marjoram
½ small bay leaf, crushed
1 medium turnip, cut in ½-inch cubes (about 3 cups)
2 tbsp. butter

Heat 3 tbsp. butter in heavy saucepan. Add veal and brown lightly on all sides. Sprinkle in flour and let brown, stirring constantly.

Dissolve bouillon cubes in boiling water and add to meat gradually, stirring constantly.

Add onion, salt, pepper, monosodium glutamate, cloves, parsley, thyme, marjoram and bay leaf. Cover and cook 1 hour over moderate heat.

Cover turnip with boiling water and boil 15 minutes. Drain.

Heat 2 tbsp. butter in heavy skillet. Add turnip cubes and fry gently until lightly browned. Add to stew and simmer until meat is fork-tender, about 30 minutes. (Serves 4.)

CURRIED LAMB

2-lb. boneless lamb shoulder, cubed
3 tbsp. flour
2 tsp. salt
2 tsp. paprika
¼ tsp. pepper
2 tbsp. fat
½ cup diced onion
1 cup diced celery
1 cup diced apple
¼ cup seedless raisins
1½ cups water
1 tbsp. curry powder
2 tbsp. flour
¼ cup cold water
1 tbsp. lemon juice
Hot cooked rice
Condiments (see note below)

Roll meat in a mixture of 3 tbsp. flour, salt, paprika and pepper.

Brown in fat in heavy skillet, and sprinkle any left-over flour mixture over meat.

Add onion, celery, apple, raisins and 1½ cups water.

Cover and simmer until meat is tender, about 1 hour. Add more water, if necessary, to prevent sticking.

Add curry powder and 2 tbsp. flour mixed to a smooth paste with ¼ cup water and lemon juice. Cook over low heat 10 to 15 minutes more.

Serve very hot with hot cooked rice. If you like a strong curry increase curry powder up to 2 tbsp. (Serves 6.)

Note: Condiments should include chutney and may include any or all of these: grated coconut, chopped parsley, sieved hard-cooked egg, chopped peanuts or other nuts, crumbled crisp bacon, raisins, chopped candied orange peel, sautéed bananas.

Poultry

CARIBBEAN CHICKEN

4 lb. chicken pieces (breasts
   and legs)
2 cups boiling water
1 tbsp. chili powder
2 tsp. salt
¼ tsp. pepper
¼ tsp. cinnamon
¼ cup minced onion
¼ cup butter
¼ cup cooking oil
Two 20-oz. cans pineapple
   chunks
1 cup seedless green grapes
2 bananas
1 large avocado
¼ cup cold water
2 tbsp. cornstarch

Put washed chicken pieces in
Dutch oven or other large heavy
kettle. Add boiling water, chili
powder, salt, pepper, cinnamon
and onion. Cover tightly and simmer until nearly tender, about 30
minutes. Drain chicken pieces and
dry well on paper towelling. Strain
stock and set aside for use later.

Heat butter and oil in large
heavy skillet. Add chicken pieces
and brown well on all sides. Put
pieces in large shallow baking dish
as they brown (have dish large
enough that the chicken can be in
a single layer).

Heat oven to 375 degrees.

Drain pineapple chunks. Combine pineapple juice with enough
chicken stock to make 4 cups
liquid (add a little water if necessary). Pour over chicken pieces.
Sprinkle pineapple chunks over all.
Bake 30 minutes, basting chicken
often with pan juices.

Lift chicken out on to hot platter. Spoon pineapple chunks over
and sprinkle with grapes. Garnish
edge of platter with slices of banana and avocado.

Combine water and cornstarch,
stirring until smooth. Stir into
liquid in cooking pan gradually.
Cook, stirring constantly, until
thickened and clear. Serve as gravy
with chicken and fruit. (Serves 8.)

Caribbean Chicken

OVEN–FRIED CHICKEN

1/2 cup butter
1 cup all-purpose flour OR
   biscuit mix
2 tsp. salt
1/4 tsp. pepper
2 tsp. paprika
1 cut-up frying chicken
1/2 cup milk
Juice of 1 lemon
Whole cloves
28-oz. can peach halves, drained

Heat oven to 400 degrees.

Melt butter in shallow baking dish (13 x 9 1/2 x 2 inches).

Mix flour or biscuit mix, salt, pepper and paprika in paper bag.

Shake chicken pieces (1 or 2 at a time) in bag with flour mixture, then dip in milk. Drop back in flour mixture and shake again.

Place, skin side down, in melted butter in baking dish. Sprinkle with lemon juice. Bake 1/2 hour. Turn chicken. Bake 15 minutes.

Stick a whole clove in each peach half and lay on top of chicken. Return to oven and bake 15 minutes. Serve hot. (Serves 4.)

CHICKEN ROSEMARY

1/4 cup butter
2 1/2- to 3-lb. frying chicken,
   quartered
Salt and pepper
1/2 cup chopped onion
1 small clove garlic, crushed
2 tbsp. flour
1 tsp. rosemary
3/4 cup dry white table wine
1 cup light cream

Heat oven to 300 degrees.

Heat butter in heavy skillet that can go in the oven.

Wash chicken pieces, dry on paper towelling and sprinkle lightly with salt and pepper. Brown well on both sides in hot butter. Remove from pan.

Add onion and garlic to drippings in pan and cook gently until onion is tender. Sprinkle in flour and rosemary and stir to blend. Remove from heat and stir in wine. Return chicken to pan, meaty side down. Cover tightly (use foil if pan has no cover) and bake about 45 minutes or until chicken is tender, turning pieces for last 15 minutes.

Remove pan from oven and put chicken pieces on hot platter or on serving plates. Add cream to juices in pan, heat just to boiling point and pour over chicken. (Serves 2 or 4.)

MARYLAND-STYLE CHICKEN

3/4 cup flour
1 1/2 tsp. salt
1/2 tsp. celery salt
1/2 tsp. paprika
1/8 tsp. garlic salt
1/4 tsp. pepper
3-lb. chicken, cut up
2 eggs
1/4 cup water
1 cup fine dry bread crumbs
1/2 cup cooking oil
3 tbsp. hot water
Cream Gravy (recipe follows)

Heat oven to 375 degrees.

Combine flour, salt, celery salt, paprika, garlic salt and pepper in a paper bag. Add chicken pieces, one or two at a time and shake bag to coat chicken well with flour mixture.

Beat eggs and 1/4 cup water together with a fork in a flat dish. Dip chicken pieces in mixture and shake to remove excess. Roll in crumbs.

Heat oil in large heavy skillet and add chicken pieces. Cook gently until golden on all sides. Transfer chicken pieces to a baking dish (about 13 x 9 1/2 x 2 inches) as they brown.

Add hot water to skillet, stir well, scraping up all browned bits and pour over chicken.

Bake uncovered about 45 minutes, or until chicken is very tender. Serve with Cream Gravy. (Serves 4.)

Cream Gravy

1/4 cup butter
1/4 cup seasoned flour (left from
   coating chicken)
1 1/2 cups chicken stock
1 cup light cream
Salt and pepper

Melt butter in heavy saucepan. Sprinkle in flour and let bubble up. Remove from heat and add chicken stock all at once. Stir in cream gradually. Return to moderate heat and cook and stir until thick and smooth. Taste and correct seasoning.

CHICKEN CACCIATORE

1/2 cup flour
1 tsp. salt
1/4 tsp. pepper
Two 3-lb. chickens, quartered
1/4 cup butter
1/4 cup cooking oil
1 clove garlic, minced
2 medium onions, sliced
1 large green pepper, chopped
2 cups canned tomatoes
7 1/2-oz. can tomato sauce
1/4 cup chopped parsley
1 1/2 tsp. salt
1/4 tsp. pepper
1/4 tsp. oregano
1/4 tsp. thyme
2 cups sliced mushrooms
   (optional)
Hot buttered noodles

Mix flour, salt and pepper together in a paper bag. Drop chicken pieces one at a time into the bag and shake to coat completely with flour mixture.

Heat butter and oil in large heavy skillet. Add garlic. Add chicken pieces and cook until browned on all sides.

Add onions, green pepper, tomatoes, tomato sauce, parsley, salt, pepper, oregano and thyme. Cover tightly and simmer 30 minutes, turning 2 or 3 times.

Add mushrooms, cover again and simmer another 30 minutes or until chicken is very tender.

Serve with hot buttered noodles. (Serves 8.)

For value and
variety chicken
is in a class
by itself.
And luckily for
us it has become
a splendid staple

CHICKEN STEW

¼ cup butter
3-lb. chicken, cut up
Salt and pepper
2 medium onions, sliced
1 cup chopped celery
½ cup chopped green pepper
28-oz. can tomatoes
2 cups chicken stock OR 4
    chicken bouillon cubes dis-
    solved in 2 cups boiling water
½ tsp. sweet basil
Pinch thyme
¼ tsp. Tabasco
½ tsp. monosodium glutamate
    (optional)
1½ tsp. salt
14-oz. can whole-kernel corn
¼ cup cold water
2 tbsp. flour

Heat butter in large heavy skillet. Add chicken pieces, sprinkle lightly with salt and pepper and brown well on all sides. Lift chicken pieces out of pan as they brown.

Add onions to drippings left in pan and cook gently until yellow.

Return chicken to pan and add celery, green pepper, tomatoes, stock, basil, thyme, Tabasco, monosodium glutamate and salt. Cover and simmer about 45 minutes or until chicken is tender. Lift chicken pieces out into a large serving dish.

Add corn to mixture remaining in skillet and bring to boiling. Combine water and flour and stir until smooth. Add to boiling mixture gradually, stirring constantly. Cook until thickened and smooth. Pour over chicken and serve. (Serves 6.)

ASPARAGUS AND CHICKEN

1½ lb. fresh asparagus
3 cups cut-up cooked chicken
¼ cup butter
¼ cup flour
1½ tsp. salt
¼ tsp. pepper
¼ tsp. dry mustard
¼ tsp. paprika
1 cup chicken stock
1 cup light cream
¼ cup chopped pimento
½ cup blanched slivered
    almonds

Heat oven to 375 degrees.

Wash asparagus and cut into 1-inch pieces, keeping the bottom ends separate from the tips. Cook bottom ends in boiling salted water until just starting to get tender, about 10 minutes. Add tips and cook 5 minutes more or until tender. Drain.

Butter a shallow baking pan about 13 x 9½ x 2 inches and spread cooked asparagus in bottom. Sprinkle with chicken pieces.

Melt butter in saucepan. Sprinkle in flour, salt, pepper, mustard and paprika and let bubble up together, stirring constantly. Remove from heat. Add chicken stock and cream all at once and stir to blend well.

Return to moderate heat and cook, stirring constantly, until boiling, thickened and smooth. Stir in pimento.

Pour over asparagus and chicken. Sprinkle with almonds.

Bake about 25 minutes or until bubbling well. (Serves 6.)

CHICKEN TETRAZZINI

5-lb. stewing chicken, cut up
¼ cup butter
1 cup chopped onion
2 cups diced celery
1 cup sliced mushrooms
1 cup chopped green pepper
½ cup slivered ripe olives
2 cups grated sharp Cheddar
    cheese
½ cup cut-up pimento
½ cup toasted slivered almonds
1 pkg. frozen peas, cooked
1 tsp. salt

¼ tsp. pepper
2 cups macaroni, cooked
½ cup chicken stock

Stew chicken (recipe p. 63). Cut chicken meat into bite-size pieces. Measure out ½ cup chicken stock. (Refrigerate remaining stock for use in other recipes.)

Heat butter in heavy skillet. Cook onion, celery, mushrooms and green pepper until tender.

Add olives, cheese, pimento, almonds, peas and the chicken. Sprinkle with salt and pepper.

Add hot drained macaroni and mix lightly. Add the chicken stock and heat. (Serves 8 to 10.)

Note: This recipe may be cut in half and reheats well.

CURRIED CHICKEN ALMOND

4- to 5-lb. stewing chicken,
    cut up
¼ cup butter (use part chicken
    fat if desired)
1 cup sliced fresh mushrooms
1 small clove garlic, crushed
¼ cup flour
2 tsp. curry powder
Pinch of saffron (optional)
2 cups chicken stock
1 cup sultana raisins
¼ cup sherry
Hot cooked rice
1 cup almonds, blanched,
    slivered and toasted

Stew chicken (recipe p. 63). Cut chicken meat in large pieces. Measure out 2 cups of chicken stock and set aside. (Store any remaining stock in refrigerator for use in other recipes.)

Melt butter in large heavy saucepan. Add mushrooms and garlic and cook gently 3 minutes. Stir in flour, curry powder and saffron and let bubble up together.

Remove from heat and add chicken stock all at once, stirring to blend. Stir in raisins and sherry. Return to moderate heat and cook, stirring constantly, until thick and boiling.

Add the chicken meat and heat well. Serve immediately with rice and topped with toasted almonds. (Serves 6.)

CREAMED CHICKEN ON TOAST

5-lb. stewing chicken, cut up
2 tbsp. chicken fat
1/2 lb. fresh mushrooms, sliced
2 green peppers, slivered
1/3 cup chopped pimento
6 tbsp. chicken fat
6 tbsp. flour
1 tsp. salt
1/4 tsp. pepper
2 cups chicken stock
1 cup light cream
2 egg yolks, lightly beaten
1/4 cup dry sherry (optional)
Buttered toast

Stew chicken (recipe p. 63). Cut chicken meat into bite-size pieces. Measure out 2 cups of the chicken stock. (Refrigerate any left-over stock to use in other recipes.)

Heat 2 tbsp. chicken fat in heavy skillet. Add mushrooms and green peppers and cook gently until mushrooms are tender. Stir in pimento. Turn off heat and stir in chicken.

Heat 6 tbsp. chicken fat in saucepan. Sprinkle in flour, salt and pepper and let bubble up well. Remove from heat. Add chicken stock and cream all at once, stirring to blend. Return to moderate heat and cook and stir until bubbling well and thick and smooth.

Add about half of the hot mixture to the egg yolks gradually,

stirring constantly. Return to saucepan and bring back to boil.

Add chicken mixture and sherry and heat well, stirring constantly. Serve on buttered toast. (Serves 8.)

CREAMED SWEETBREADS AND CHICKEN

1/4 cup butter
2 tbsp. finely-minced onion
1/4 cup flour
1 tsp. salt
1/4 tsp. pepper
1 cup liquid (see recipe for Braised Sweetbreads)
1 cup milk
1 cup thinly-sliced fresh mushrooms
2 tbsp. water
2 tsp. lemon juice
2 tbsp. butter
1 1/2 cups cubed cooked chicken
Braised Sweetbreads (recipe follows)
Patty shells

Melt 1/4 cup butter in saucepan. Add onion and cook gently 3 minutes (do not brown). Sprinkle in flour, salt and pepper and let bubble up.

Remove from heat and stir in 1 cup liquid and milk. Stir to blend. Return to moderate heat and cook and stir until boiling. Turn heat to low and simmer, stirring often, 15 minutes.

Put mushrooms, water and lemon juice in small saucepan. Cover and simmer 3 minutes. Add

mushrooms and liquid to sauce. Add 2 tbsp. butter and blend well. Add chicken and braised sweetbreads and heat well, stirring carefully so sweetbreads are not broken up.

Heat patty shells while making sauce and serve filled with creamed mixture. (Serves 6 to 8.)

Variation: Top toasted English muffin halves with a thin slice of ham and spoon creamed mixture over.

Braised Sweetbreads

3 pair sweetbreads
1/4 tsp. salt
Juice of 1 lemon
3 tbsp. butter
1 medium onion, sliced
1 carrot, sliced
Small piece bay leaf, crumbled
1/4 tsp. leaf thyme
2 tbsp. chopped parsley
1/2 tsp. salt
1/4 tsp. pepper
1 1/2 cups chicken stock

Cover sweetbreads with very cold water and let stand 1 hour. Drain. Cover with cold water and add 1/4 tsp. salt and juice of 1 lemon. Bring to a boil and boil gently 5 minutes. Drain and plunge immediately into cold water.

Remove membranes and tubes carefully when cold. Chill.

Heat oven to 375 degrees.

Cut sweetbreads into bite-size pieces. Heat butter in large skillet that can go in the oven. Add onion, carrot, bay leaf, thyme and parsley, and cook gently, stirring, 3 minutes. Lay sweetbread pieces on top of vegetables. Sprinkle with salt and pepper. Add chicken stock. Cover tightly (use foil if pan doesn't have a cover), put in heated oven. Cook about 45 minutes, or until sweetbreads are very tender, basting several times.

Lift pieces of sweetbreads carefully out of pan. Strain and save broth left in pan (it is the liquid called for in the recipe for Creamed Sweetbreads And Chicken).

Note: If desired, sweetbreads can be braised early in the day and chilled until they are added to the sauce at serving time.

It's a good idea to use a glass pan when cooking rice. This way you can see when all the water has been absorbed without lifting the lid.

SAVORY CHICKEN PIE

**4- to 5-lb. stewing chicken,
  cut up**
¼ cup chicken fat OR butter
1 cup sliced fresh mushrooms
¼ cup chopped green pepper
¼ cup flour
1½ tsp. salt
¼ tsp. pepper
2 cups chicken stock
1 cup light cream
1 cup cooked peas
1 cup cooked sliced carrots
**½ cup thinly-sliced
  cooked celery**
**6 slices back bacon, cut in
  large pieces and fried**
6 hard-cooked eggs, sliced
Savory Biscuits (recipe follows)
Milk

Stew chicken (recipe p. 63). Cut chicken meat in bite-size pieces. Set aside. Strain stock and measure out 2 cups. (Refrigerate remaining for use in other recipes.)

Heat oven to 425 degrees. Butter a 3-qt. casserole.

Melt chicken fat or butter in saucepan. Add mushrooms and green pepper and cook gently until tender.

Sprinkle in flour, salt and pepper and let bubble up together. Remove from heat and stir in chicken stock and cream all at once. Return to moderate heat and cook and stir until thickened and smooth.

Remove from heat and stir in cooked vegetables and the chicken pieces.

Put bacon in bottom of prepared casserole. Top with egg slices. Pour chicken mixture over.

Prepare Savory Biscuits and lay on top of mixture. Brush with milk. Bake about 20 minutes or until biscuit dough is browned and chicken filling is bubbling. (Serves 8 to 10.)

Savory Biscuits

2 cups sifted all-purpose flour
4 tsp. baking powder
1 tsp. salt
2 tsp. celery seeds
1 tsp. paprika
½ tsp. sage
¼ cup shortening
¾ cup milk (approx.)

Sift flour, baking powder and salt into mixing bowl. Add celery seeds, paprika and sage and mix lightly with fork. Add shortening and cut in finely.

Stir in enough milk with a fork to make a soft puffy dough that is easy to handle and roll.

Roll out ½ inch thick and cut with biscuit cutter or into wedges and use to top chicken pie as directed above.

CHICKEN-MACARONI BAKE

5-lb. stewing chicken, cut up
1 lb. fresh mushrooms, sliced
½ cup butter
8 oz. macaroni
1 cup slivered ripe olives
¼ cup chopped pimento
3 tbsp. flour
2 cups chicken stock
Salt and pepper
1 cup grated Cheddar cheese

Stew chicken (recipe p. 63). Cut meat in bite-size pieces. Measure out 2 cups stock. (Store rest, covered, in refrigerator to use in other recipes.)

Heat oven to 350 degrees. Butter a baking dish about 13 x 9½ x 2 inches.

Cook mushrooms in butter in heavy skillet until golden.

Cook macaroni as package directs. Drain.

Alternate layers of macaroni, chicken pieces, mushrooms, olives and pimento in prepared pan.

Combine flour with a little of the cold chicken stock, blending until smooth . Heat remaining chicken stock to boiling. Add flour mixture gradually, stirring constantly. Boil 1 minute. Season to taste with salt and pepper.

Pour stock over layers in baking dish. Sprinkle with cheese. Bake about 30 minutes or until bubbling and browned. (Serves 8.)

STEWED CHICKEN

5-lb. stewing chicken, cut up
Boiling water
1 large carrot, cut up
**1 large stalk celery (with leaves),
  cut up**
1 thick slice onion
4 sprigs parsley
6 peppercorns
6 whole cloves
1 small bay leaf
2 tsp. salt

Wash and put chicken in a large kettle. Add water to nearly cover. Add carrot, celery, onion, parsley, peppercorns, cloves, bay leaf and salt. Bring to a boil, turn down heat, cover and simmer until tender, 2 to 3 hours. Cool.

Lift out chicken pieces and remove meat in large pieces, discarding bones. Strain stock, chill and lift off fat. Keep meat, stock and fat refrigerated until needed. There should be about 4 cups chicken meat and 3 to 4 cups stock. Use chicken fat in place of butter in recipes if desired.

CHINESE CHICKEN

**2 cups fresh green beans, cut
  on diagonal**
¼ cup cooking oil
**2 cups slivered raw breast of
  chicken**
2 cups thinly-sliced celery
**Two 5-oz. cans bamboo shoots,
  drained**
**15-oz. can bean sprouts, drained
  and rinsed under cold water**
**½ cup toasted slivered
  blanched almonds**
¼ cup soy sauce
**1 tsp. monosodium glutamate
  (optional)**
3 cups chicken stock
6 tbsp. cold water
¼ cup cornstarch
Hot rice

Cook beans in a little salted water just until tender-crisp. Drain.

Heat oil in heavy skillet. Add slivers of raw chicken and cook until golden.

Add beans, celery, bamboo shoots, bean sprouts, almonds, soy sauce, monosodium glutamate and chicken stock. Mix gently, cover tightly and simmer 5 minutes.

Shake cold water and cornstarch together in a small jar with a tight lid until smooth. Add gradually to hot mixture, stirring to blend and cooking until thick and clear. Serve immediately with rice. (Serves 4.)

Fair is fowl and fowl is fair—be it plain or fancy

CHINESE-STYLE SHREDDED CHICKEN

3-lb. chicken
2 tbsp. cooking oil
1 cup celery, cut thin on diagonal
5-oz. can water chestnuts, sliced
1 cup sliced fresh mushrooms
1 cup chicken stock
3 tbsp. soy sauce
2 tbsp. cold water
1 tbsp. cornstarch
Hot Fried Noodles (recipe follows)
1 egg
Dash salt
Dash pepper
2 green onions, chopped

Cut all chicken meat (raw) from bones (use 2 large whole chicken breasts in place of whole chicken if you prefer). Cut meat in slivers.

Heat oil in large heavy skillet. Drop in chicken pieces and fry quickly until lightly browned. Add celery, water chestnuts, mushrooms and stock. Cover and cook gently 5 minutes.

Stir in soy sauce. Combine water and cornstarch and stir into sauce gradually. Bring to boiling.

Put Hot Fried Noodles on hot platter. Pour chicken mixture over and put in warm place.

Beat egg, salt and pepper quickly together with a fork and pour into same skillet chicken was cooked in. Cook like a thin pancake until golden on both sides. Lift out and quickly cut into thin strips. Sprinkle over chicken. Sprinkle green onions over all. Serve immediately. (Serves 4 to 6.)

Hot Fried Noodles

12 oz. noodles
1/2 cup cooking oil

Cook noodles until just tender in boiling salted water. Drain, rinse with cold water and drain very well. Dry by tossing in a dish towel.

Heat oil in large heavy skillet. Add noodles and cook, stirring often, until golden.

GLAZED CHICKEN BREASTS

3 whole chicken breasts
4 cups water
1 slice onion
1 stalk celery (with leaves)
1 small bay leaf
2 sprigs parsley
1 small carrot
1 1/2 tsp. salt
4 peppercorns
Pinch chervil
1 envelope (1 tbsp.) unflavored gelatin
1/4 cup cold water
1 cup commercial sour cream
Lettuce OR other salad greens
Cherry tomatoes OR tomato slices

Separate each chicken breast into 2 halves and put in a large saucepan in a single layer. Add water, onion, celery, bay leaf, parsley, carrot, salt, peppercorns and chervil. Bring to a boil. Turn down heat and simmer until chicken is just tender, about 30 minutes.

Lift chicken out of stock and cool. Carefully remove bones and skin, keeping meat whole. Chill very well.

Strain stock chicken was cooked in and return to saucepan. Boil hard until reduced to 1 1/2 cups. Chill and discard fat. Heat to boiling point.

Soak gelatin in cold water 5 minutes. Add to hot stock and stir until dissolved. Remove from heat and cool but do not chill. Stir into sour cream and set in ice water. Chill until like heavy cream but not set. Stir often while chilling.

Put chilled chicken breasts on cake rack over a pan and spoon the gelatin mixture over to coat on all sides. Spoon any of the gelatin mixture that runs off into the pan over the meat again until the chicken breasts are evenly coated. Chill on rack until set.

Put 1 or 2 glazed chicken breasts for each serving on lettuce or other salad greens. Garnish with tomatoes. (Serves 3 or 6.)

CHICKEN EN COCOTTE

4- to 5-lb. roasting chicken
1 onion, chopped fine
1/4 tsp. thyme
1 tbsp. butter
Salt and pepper
6 slices bacon
1 clove garlic
1 1/2 cups chicken stock OR 2 chicken bouillon cubes dissolved in 1 1/2 cups hot water
8 small onions
1/2 lb. whole fresh mushrooms
4 medium potatoes, quartered
8 small carrots, halved lengthwise
4 stalks celery, cut in 1-inch pieces
1 tsp. salt
1/4 cup melted butter
Parsley

Wash chicken thoroughly. Remove pin feathers and singe if necessary. Place chopped onion, thyme and 1 tbsp. butter inside chicken, and sprinkle inside with salt and pepper. Tuck wings under and tie legs as for roasting.

Fry bacon in large heavy deep pan or Dutch oven until crisp. Remove bacon, crumble and set aside. Drop clove of garlic, cut in half, into bacon fat. Brown and then remove it.

Brown chicken on all sides in bacon fat. When golden brown add chicken stock. Return bacon bits to pan, cover tightly and simmer 1 hour, turning chicken occasionally so cooking is even. Add small onions and mushrooms. Cover and cook 45 minutes longer.

Skim fat from top of liquid, add potatoes, carrots and celery. Sprinkle vegetables with 1 tsp. salt. Cover and cook 30 minutes more, or until vegetables are tender.

Pour melted butter over vegetables, garnish with parsley and bring pan to table to serve. This serves 4 generously, with chicken left over for another meal.

e it chicken, goose, Cornish game hen or pheasant

ROAST GOOSE

10- to 15-lb. goose
Salt and pepper
Apple Stuffing (recipe p. 68)
1 cup orange juice
Giblets
1 cup boiling water
1 tsp. salt
1/4 cup flour
Boiling water

Remove all fat from inside bird. Sprinkle inside generously with salt and pepper.

Stuff loosely with Apple Stuffing and truss.

Heat oven to 325 degrees.

Put goose on rack in roasting pan and roast 25 to 30 minutes a pound or until very tender. Prick the skin several places every half hour to let the fat run out and baste with a little of the orange juice each time. Pour or ladle off fat as it accumulates in pan.

Simmer giblets in boiling water and salt until tender. Drain, saving broth. Chop giblets finely.

Put goose on warm platter when it is done (drumstick moves easily). Drain almost all the fat from the pan. Stir in the flour and let it bubble up well and brown lightly. Remove from heat and add giblet broth all at once. Stir to blend. Return to moderate heat and cook and stir until boiling. Add enough boiling water gradually to make gravy the desired consistency. Stir in chopped giblets. Heat well, taste and season with salt and pepper to taste.

Note: Since there is a high proportion of fat and bone to meat in a goose, allow at least 1 lb. per person. If desired, the dressing may be cooked separately. Grease a large casserole with goose fat. Put dressing loosely in casserole and sprinkle 2 or 3 tbsp. goose fat over top. Bake about 1 1/2 hours at 350 degrees. If you do the stuffing this way, roast the goose with some apple quarters and orange slices inside.

CORNISH GAME HENS WITH RICE STUFFING

6 Cornish game hens
Salt and pepper
1/4 cup butter
1 cup long-grain rice
3 cups boiling water
1 tsp. salt
1/4 cup butter
1/2 cup finely-chopped onion
1/2 cup finely-chopped celery
1/2 cup finely-chopped carrot
1/4 cup finely-chopped parsley
1 tsp. salt
1/4 tsp. pepper
1 large onion
1 large carrot
1/2 cup melted butter
1 cup chicken stock
1 tsp. cornstarch
Parsley OR watercress

Prepare hens for stuffing as you would chickens. Sprinkle insides with salt and pepper.

Heat 1/4 cup butter in heavy saucepan that has a tight lid. Add rice to pan and cook gently, stirring, until rice is golden brown. Add water and 1 tsp. salt and bring to a boil. Cover tightly and cook 20 minutes without lifting lid. Take off lid and cool. Rice should be tender and quite moist.

Melt 1/4 cup butter in skillet. Add 1/2 cup onion, celery and 1/2 cup carrot and cook gently, stirring, until vegetables are lightly browned. Add to rice along with parsley, salt and pepper and blend lightly with fork.

Stuff rice mixture loosely into birds and skewer openings closed. Tuck wings under each bird and tie leg ends to tail.

Slice onion and carrot into shallow roasting pan. Set birds on top of vegetables and brush each with some of melted butter.

Heat oven to 450 degrees. Roast at this temperature for 15 minutes or until golden. Reduce heat to 350 degrees and continue roasting until tender, 30 to 45 minutes more. Baste occasionally.

Arrange in a circle on a hot platter.

Discard vegetables in roasting pan. Add 1 cup hot chicken stock to drippings in pan and boil hard 1 minute. Mix 1 tsp. cornstarch with a little cold water and stir in gradually. Continue cooking until clear. Pour over birds on platter. Garnish with parsley or watercress. (Serves 6.)

ROAST PHEASANTS

3 pheasants
Wild Rice Stuffing (recipe p. 69)
Salt and pepper
2 cups liquid (giblet broth plus water)
1/4 cup dry sherry
Melted butter
1/4 cup dry sherry (optional)

Thaw pheasants if they are frozen. Prepare Wild Rice Stuffing.

Wash giblets and cover with cold water in small saucepan. Simmer until tender. Drain and save broth.

Heat oven to 325 degrees.

Wash and prepare pheasants for roasting as you would chicken. Sprinkle inside of birds with salt and pepper. Stuff lightly with Wild Rice Stuffing and truss.

Set birds in roasting pan. Measure giblet broth and add enough water to make 2 cups liquid. Pour over birds along with 1/4 cup sherry.

Dip a large piece of cheesecloth in melted butter and lay double over the birds.

Roast about 1 hour or until tender, basting often with juices in bottom of pan. (Do not remove cheesecloth to baste. Just spoon juices over cloth.)

Remove cheesecloth and continue roasting until well browned and very tender, basting often.

Put birds on hot platter. Strain drippings in pan. Cut giblets into small pieces and add to drippings.

Recipe continued on next page

Julius Szelei

Heat to boiling and thicken with a little flour and water mixed together. Add ¼ cup dry sherry, if desired, and season to taste with salt and pepper. Serve hot with pheasants. (Serves 6.)

TURKEY AND RICE

¼ cup butter
¼ cup flour
1½ tsp. salt
  1 cup chicken OR turkey stock
2 cups light cream
2 tbsp. butter
1 cup sliced mushrooms
⅓ cup chopped green pepper
2 tbsp. chopped onion
2½ cups diced left-over turkey
3 cups cooked rice
¼ cup chopped pimento
½ cup slivered toasted almonds

Heat oven to 350 degrees.

Melt ¼ cup butter. Blend in flour and salt and let bubble up together. Remove from heat, add stock and cream, stir to blend.

Return to moderate heat and cook, stirring constantly, until thick and smooth.

Heat 2 tbsp. butter and cook mushrooms, green pepper and onion in it until tender. Add to sauce along with turkey, rice and pimento.

Pour into greased 13 x 9½ x 2-inch baking pan. Sprinkle with slivered almonds. Bake 30 minutes. (Serves 8.)

Turkey Pie

TURKEY PIE

8 small onions
4 medium potatoes, quartered
8 small carrots, cut in 1½-inch pieces
2 large stalks celery, cut in 1½-inch pieces
2 cups left-over turkey gravy
½ tsp. salt
¼ tsp. pepper
¼ tsp. oregano
3 cups cut-up left-over turkey
Pastry for 2-crust pie
1 egg yolk
1 tbsp. cold water

Heat oven to 400 degrees. Butter a 2½-qt. casserole.

Cook onions and potatoes separately in boiling salted water until just tender. Drain. Cook carrots and celery together in boiling salted water until just tender. Drain.

Heat gravy and stir in salt, pepper and oregano.

Combine drained vegetables, gravy and turkey and put in prepared casserole.

Roll pastry a little thicker than usual and about ½ inch larger than top of casserole. Lay over top of meat mixture. Turn edge of pastry under, crimp and seal well to sides of casserole. Cut slits in top to let steam escape.

Beat egg yolk and water together and brush over pastry.

Bake 25 to 30 minutes or until pastry is dark golden brown and filling is bubbling. (Serves 6.)

SHERRIED CHICKEN LIVERS

12 chicken livers
Seasoned flour
2 tbsp. butter
2 tbsp. chopped onion
1/2 cup chopped mushrooms
1 tsp. flour
1/2 cup cream
1/4 cup dry sherry
Salt and pepper
1/2 tsp. Worcestershire sauce
Scrambled eggs

Cut chicken livers in halves and roll in seasoned flour.

Melt butter in heavy saucepan. Cook onion and mushrooms until tender.

Add chicken livers and cook gently, stirring constantly, until lightly browned (about 3 minutes).

Stir in 1 tsp. flour and cream. When smooth and bubbling add sherry, salt, pepper and Worcestershire sauce. Cook 2 minutes over medium heat.

Serve immediately with scrambled eggs. (Serves 4.)

APPLE STUFFING

12 cups bread crumbs
   (use day-old bread)
1/2 cup butter
1 cup chopped onion
1 cup chopped celery
1/2 lb. fresh mushrooms, sliced
3 cups peeled coarsely-chopped
   apples
1 tbsp. salt
2 tsp. poultry seasoning
1 tsp. sage
Dash nutmeg

Put crumbs in large bowl and let stand several hours to dry, stirring often.

Melt butter. Add onion and celery and cook gently 5 minutes. Add mushrooms and cook 2 minutes more. Add half of crumbs and cook and stir until crumbs are lightly browned.

Add apples, salt and seasonings to crumbs remaining in bowl and toss lightly. Add browned crumb mixture and toss again. Cool. Use to stuff 12- to 15-lb. turkey or goose.

BEEF-BREAD STUFFING

1 lb. ground beef
1 tsp. salt
1/8 tsp. pepper
1/8 tsp. allspice
1/8 tsp. nutmeg
2 tbsp. cooking oil
1/4 cup butter
1 large onion, chopped
1 cup chopped celery (with
   leaves)
12 cups soft bread crumbs (use
   day-old bread)
3/4 cup melted butter
1 tsp. marjoram
1/2 tsp. rosemary
1 tsp. poultry seasoning
1 1/2 tbsp. salt
1/2 tsp. pepper

Mix beef, 1 tsp. salt, 1/8 tsp. pepper, allspice and nutmeg together lightly. Heat oil in large heavy skillet, add beef and brown lightly, breaking meat up with a fork. Put meat into a large bowl.

Heat 1/4 cup butter in same skillet meat was browned in. Add onion and celery and cook gently 3 minutes. Add half of bread crumbs and cook gently, stirring constantly, until they are golden.

Add remaining crumbs, melted butter, marjoram, rosemary, poultry seasoning, 1 1/2 tbsp. salt and 1/2 tsp. pepper to beef. Toss lightly. Add hot onion-celery mixture and toss again lightly. Cool. Use to stuff a 15-lb. turkey.

RAISIN-APPLE STUFFING

1 cup seedless raisins
Boiling water
1 cup butter
3/4 cup finely-chopped onion
1 1/2 cups chopped celery (with
   leaves)
3 medium tart apples, peeled
   and chopped
1 medium green pepper,
   chopped
12 cups soft bread crumbs (use
   day-old bread)
1 1/2 tbsp. salt
1 tsp. pepper
1 tsp. thyme
2 tsp. poultry seasoning
Dash nutmeg

Cover raisins with boiling water.

Let stand 5 minutes, drain and set aside.

Heat butter in large heavy skillet. Add onion and celery and cook gently 3 minutes. Add apples and green pepper and continue cooking 1 minute more. Add half of bread crumbs and cook, stirring constantly, until crumbs are golden. Remove from heat.

Put remaining bread crumbs in large bowl. Add raisins and seasonings and toss together lightly. Add hot apple mixture and toss again lightly. Cool. Use to stuff 12- to 15-lb. turkey.

SAUSAGE STUFFING

1 lb. bulk sausage meat
1/4 cup butter
1 large onion, chopped
1 1/2 cups chopped celery (with
   leaves)
1 large apple, chopped
12 cups soft bread crumbs (use
   day-old bread)
1 tbsp. salt
1 tsp. pepper
1 1/2 tsp. sage
1 1/2 tsp. thyme
1 tsp. poultry seasoning
1/4 tsp. nutmeg
1 cup raisins
1 1/2 cups chopped pecans

Brown sausage meat in skillet. Add butter, onion, celery and apple and cook gently until onion is yellow, stirring constantly.

Add half of bread crumbs and cook and stir until crumbs are golden.

Combine remaining crumbs, seasonings, raisins and nuts in large bowl. Add sausage meat mixture and blend well. Cool. Use to stuff a 12-lb. turkey.

SAVORY MUSHROOM STUFFING

¹/₂ cup butter
1 lb. finely-chopped mushrooms
¹/₂ cup finely-minced onion
12 cups soft bread crumbs
    (use day-old bread)
2 tbsp. salt
1 tsp. celery salt
1 tsp. pepper
¹/₄ tsp. cayenne
¹/₄ tsp. nutmeg
¹/₂ tsp. monosodium glutamate
    (optional)
¹/₂ cup chopped parsley
2 tsp. chopped chives
¹/₂ cup stock OR water

Melt butter in heavy saucepan. Add mushrooms and cook gently for 5 minutes.

Mix remaining ingredients in a large bowl. Add mushrooms and butter and mix lightly. Cool. Use to stuff a 12-lb. turkey.

WILD RICE STUFFING

1 cup wild rice
2¹/₂ cups boiling water
1 tsp. salt
¹/₄ cup butter
¹/₂ cup chopped onion
2 cups chopped mushrooms
¹/₂ cup chopped celery
1¹/₂ tsp. salt
¹/₂ tsp. marjoram
¹/₂ tsp. thyme

Wash rice well under cold running water. Cover with boiling water in a saucepan. Add 1 tsp. salt, cover and simmer over low heat until rice grains have split open and are tender, about 40 minutes. Check after 30 minutes and add a little more water if necessary. Fluff with fork when tender and cook, uncovered, 5 minutes. Drain if necessary.

Heat butter in heavy skillet. Add onion, mushrooms and celery and cook gently until tender. Mix lightly with rice and seasonings. Cool. Use to stuff pheasants or other birds.

Note: If there is any extra stuffing heat it in a covered casserole for 30 minutes.

Fish and Seafood

PICKEREL THERMIDOR

2 lb. pickerel fillets OR other
    white fish
2¼ cups milk
1½ tsp. salt
  ⅛ tsp. pepper
    Cayenne
  ½ cup butter
  ½ cup flour
1½ cups grated Cheddar cheese
  ½ cup lemon juice
    Paprika

Heat oven to 350 degrees.

Roll each fillet from narrow end (like a cinnamon roll), and set each roll on end in a 12 x 8 x 2-inch baking dish.

Pour milk over fish and sprinkle with salt, pepper and lightly with cayenne.

Bake 30 minutes or until fish flakes easily. Remove from oven. Drain milk off fish into a cup. Turn oven on to broil.

Melt butter in top of double boiler. Stir in flour. Add milk from fish and stir to blend. Cook over boiling water, stirring constantly, until thick. Add cheese and stir until melted. Add lemon juice.

Pour sauce over fish and sprinkle with paprika. Broil until sauce bubbles and is lightly browned. (Serves 6.)

OVEN-FRIED FISH

2 lb. pickerel fillets (or doré)
1 cup buttermilk
¼ tsp. Worcestershire sauce
2 tsp. salt
1 cup very fine dry bread OR
    cracker crumbs
1 tsp. paprika
¼ cup melted butter
    Mustard Sauce (recipe follows)

Cover fillets with mixture of buttermilk, Worcestershire sauce and salt and let stand 30 minutes.

Heat oven to 525 degrees.

Combine crumbs and paprika. Lift fish out of milk and shake to remove excess moisture. Dip each piece in crumbs to coat both sides.

Lay in a large flat baking dish in a single layer. Drizzle butter over.

Bake about 15 minutes or until fish flakes easily with a fork and is golden brown. Serve with Mustard Sauce. (Serves 6.)

Mustard Sauce

¼ cup butter
2 tbsp. flour
1 tsp. salt
⅛ tsp. pepper
    Dash cayenne
2 egg yolks
1½ cups milk
2 tbsp. prepared mustard
    Juice of half a lemon

Melt butter in saucepan. Stir in flour, salt, pepper and cayenne. Let bubble up together. Remove from heat.

Beat egg yolks, milk and mustard together with a fork. Add to flour mixture all at once and stir to blend. Return to moderate heat and cook, stirring constantly, until thick and smooth. Add lemon juice at serving time.

Serve hot over fish. (Makes 1½ cups.)

CRISPY FRIED FISH FILLETS

2 lb. pickerel fillets (or doré)
2 tsp. salt
    Buttermilk
¼ cup cooking oil (approx.)
¼ cup butter (approx.)
½ cup flour
1 tsp. paprika

Wash fillets and cut into serving-size pieces. Lay in a single layer in a large flat dish. Sprinkle with salt. Pour in enough buttermilk to cover fillets. Let stand 30 minutes. Lift out fillets and drain.

Put oil and butter in large heavy skillet and heat well (there should be about ⅛ inch of fat in pan, so add more if necessary).

Combine flour and paprika in a flat dish and dip fish in mixture to coat both sides lightly. Drop into hot fat and fry quickly until golden. Serve immediately. (Serves 4.)

CREOLE FISH FILLETS

1 lb. pickerel fillets (or doré)
3 cups chopped fresh tomatoes
¼ cup chopped onion
¼ cup chopped stuffed olives
½ medium green pepper,
    chopped

¼ cup thick chili sauce
2 tsp. salt
1 tsp. chili powder
    Dash cayenne
    Dash Tabasco

Heat oven to 350 degrees. Butter a shallow baking dish.

Wash fish fillets and cut into serving-size pieces. Put into prepared baking dish.

Combine remaining ingredients and pour over fish. Cover baking dish with foil and bake 30 minutes. Uncover and bake 15 minutes longer, or until fish is tender, basting often. (Serves 3 to 4.)

FILLETS OF SOLE IN WINE

1½ lb. sole fillets, cut in
    serving-size pieces
1 green onion (with top),
    sliced thin
½ cup thinly-sliced mushrooms
2 large tomatoes, peeled and
    chopped coarsely
1 cup dry white table wine
1 tsp. curry powder
1 cup light cream
1 tsp. salt
¼ tsp. pepper
½ cup fine dry bread crumbs
½ cup grated sharp
    Cheddar cheese
2 tbsp. butter
    Lemon wedges

Heat oven to 325 degrees.

Put pieces of fish in large flat baking dish (about 13 x 9½ x 2 inches). Sprinkle with onion, mushrooms and tomatoes.

Combine wine and curry powder and pour over.

Bake 15 to 20 minutes or until fish flakes easily with a fork. Lift fish out of baking pan and set aside.

Scald cream. Add the wine mixture from the baking dish and heat to boiling point. Then add the salt and pepper.

Return fish to baking dish. Pour cream-wine mixture over.

Mix crumbs and cheese and sprinkle over fish. Dot with butter. Put low under broiler and broil until crumbs and cheese are golden.

Serve with lemon wedges. (Serves 6.)

Fish And Chips — *recipe on page 7*

SOLE FLORENTINE

1½ lb. spinach
½ tsp. salt
¼ tsp. pepper
½ cup light cream
¼ cup butter
2 tbsp. cooking oil
2 tbsp. butter
2 tbsp. flour
½ tsp. salt
⅛ tsp. pepper
⅛ tsp. paprika
4 fillets of sole
1 cup grated Cheddar cheese
7½-oz. can tomato sauce

Heat oven to 375 degrees. Butter a shallow baking dish about 13 x 9½ x 2 inches.

Wash spinach and cook 5 minutes in water clinging to leaves. Drain and chop.

Add ½ tsp. salt, ¼ tsp. pepper, cream and ¼ cup butter and toss lightly. Spread in baking dish.

Heat oil and 2 tbsp. butter in heavy skillet. Combine flour, ½ tsp. salt, ⅛ tsp. pepper and paprika in flat dish and dip fish in mixture to coat both sides. Drop into hot oil and butter in skillet and fry quickly until golden on both sides. Lay on top of spinach and sprinkle with half of cheese.

Pour tomato sauce over and sprinkle with remaining cheese.

Bake 20 minutes or until bubbling well. (Serves 4.)

STEAMED SALMON

6 salmon steaks
¼ cup minced onion
Salt and pepper
Egg Sauce (recipe follows)
Lemon wedges

Set salmon on a piece of heavy-duty aluminum foil in a single layer. Sprinkle with onion and lightly with salt and pepper. Turn edges of foil up to catch juice, but do not wrap tightly.

Put about ½ inch of water in a pan with a large bottom surface. Bring water to a boil.

Lift salmon on foil into pan, being careful that the foil keeps the water from touching the fish. Turn heat down, cover pan and simmer about 25 minutes or until

the salmon flakes with a fork.

Lift salmon out carefully with a broad spatula and save any juice caught by the foil.

Serve with Egg Sauce and lemon wedges. (Serves 6.)

Egg Sauce

2 tbsp. butter
2 tbsp. flour
½ tsp. salt
¼ tsp. pepper
1¾ cups milk
4 hard-cooked eggs, chopped
Juice saved from cooked salmon

Melt butter in saucepan. Add flour, salt and pepper and let bubble up together. Remove from heat and add milk all at once.

Stir to blend, return to moderate heat and cook, stirring constantly, until smooth and thickened. Add chopped eggs and heat through.

Add juice saved from cooked salmon at serving time.

SALMON BROIL

¾ cup melted butter
3 tbsp. lemon juice
¼ tsp. Worcestershire sauce
½ tsp. salt
8 salmon steaks, ¾ inch thick
2 eggplants, quartered lengthwise
2 tbsp. finely-minced green onions
1 tbsp. finely-minced parsley
1 tbsp. finely-minced capers

Combine butter, lemon juice, Worcestershire sauce and salt and brush mixture on salmon steaks

and cut sides of eggplants.

Lay steaks and eggplant pieces on lightly greased broiler rack 4 inches from heat and broil 12 to 18 minutes, or until salmon flakes easily with a fork. Turn salmon once and eggplant pieces several times. (Eggplant should cook in about the same time as the salmon and will be dark brown on the outside.)

Put salmon and eggplant on large serving plate and sprinkle salmon with a mixture of the green onions, parsley and capers. Pour remaining lemon butter over salmon and serve immediately. (Serves 8.)

FISH AND CHIPS

Fat for deep frying
2 lb. haddock fillets
2 cups sifted all-purpose flour
3 tsp. salt
2 tsp. baking powder
2 eggs
1 cup milk
2 tbsp. cooking oil
French Fried Potatoes (recipe follows)

Heat fat to 375 degrees.

Cut fish into serving-size pieces.

Sift flour, salt and baking powder together and roll fish in mixture.

Beat eggs lightly and stir in milk and oil. Add flour mixture left from coating fish and stir until smooth.

Dip fish pieces in this batter and fry one or two pieces at a time in hot fat. Cook until dark golden brown and drain on paper towelling. Serve very hot with French Fried Potatoes. (Serves 6 to 8.)

French Fried Potatoes

6 to 8 medium baking potatoes
Fat for deep frying
Salt

Peel potatoes and cut into strips lengthwise (about ⅜-inch thick). Drop strips into ice water and let stand 1 hour, adding more ice cubes as needed.

Drain and dry well with paper towelling. (If you are not going to use them immediately, wrap them in a towel and store in the refrigerator.)

Heat fat to 375 degrees. Fry potatoes a handful at a time, cooking only until very lightly browned. Separate and turn potatoes with a long-handled fork. Drain well on paper towelling.

Fry potatoes a second time just before serving time. Fry until golden this time, about 5 minutes. Sprinkle with salt and serve immediately. (Serves 6 to 8.)

POACHED HALIBUT

4 slices halibut, each 1½ inch thick
Salt and pepper
2 tbsp. butter
10-oz. can cream of mushroom soup
1 small onion, finely chopped
15-oz. can evaporated milk (tall can)
¼ cup cold water
1 tbsp. flour

Put slices of halibut in heavy skillet. Sprinkle lightly with salt and pepper. Dot with butter.

Combine soup, onion and milk and pour over fish. Cover tightly and simmer about 25 minutes or until fish flakes easily with a fork.

Remove fish to a hot serving plate. Blend cold water and flour until smooth and add gradually to milk mixture, stirring constantly. Cook and stir until boiling. Serve over fish. (Serves 4.)

CREOLE SHRIMP

2 lb. shrimp, fresh or frozen
3 tbsp. olive oil
½ cup chopped onion
1 bay leaf, crushed
¼ cup diced celery
1 tbsp. minced parsley
½ cup chopped green pepper
1½ cups long-grain rice
Dash cayenne
¼ tsp. Tabasco
1 tsp. salt
28-oz. can tomatoes
7½-oz. can tomato sauce
2 cups water

Cook shrimp, shell and clean.

Heat oil and cook onion, bay leaf, celery, parsley and green pepper until tender. Add rice and cook, stirring constantly, until lightly browned.

Add remaining ingredients ex-cept shrimp. Cover and cook 30 minutes or until rice is tender. If mixture becomes too dry add a little more water.

Add shrimp and cook 10 minutes more until they are heated through.

Serve with tossed green salad and garlic French bread. (Serves 8.)

Note: To cook fresh shrimp plunge them into boiling water seasoned with salt, parsley and lemon. Bring to a boil again, turn down heat and simmer about 5 minutes, or until they turn bright pink. When cooked peel off the shell, remove the black vein and they are ready to use.

SHRIMP RISOTTO

½ cup wild rice
1 tsp. salt
3 cups boiling water
¼ cup butter
1 large green pepper, diced
½ lb. fresh mushrooms, sliced
½ cup slivered pimento
1½ lb. cooked shrimp
½ tsp. salt
⅛ tsp. pepper
Dash Tabasco
2 tbsp. lemon juice
1 tbsp. butter
Lemon wedges

Rinse wild rice in a sieve under cold running water until water is clear. Cook rice with salt in boiling water, keeping at a slow boil, until each grain is split and fluffy, about 30 minutes. Drain well but do not stir or run under water. Cover the pan with a folded towel until ready to use the rice.

Melt ¼ cup butter in large heavy skillet. Add green pepper and cook gently until it is tender. Add mushrooms and continue cooking gently for 5 minutes.

Add rice, pimento and shrimp. Season with salt, pepper, Tabasco and lemon juice and stir gently. Top with 1 tbsp. butter and let heat over lowest heat 10 minutes.

Serve at once garnished with lemon wedges. (Serves 6.)

Note: Long-grain white rice may be used instead of wild rice, if desired. Cook according to package directions.

CHINESE SHRIMP

3 lb. raw shrimp
¼ cup cooking oil
½ lb. mushrooms, sliced
4 green onions (with tops), sliced
¼ cup soy sauce
½ cup chicken stock OR water
¼ tsp. monosodium glutamate (optional)
2 tbsp. water
1 tbsp. cornstarch
Hot cooked rice

Wash and shell shrimp and remove veins.

Heat oil in heavy skillet, add mushrooms and onions and cook gently until onions are golden.

Add shrimp, soy sauce, chicken stock or water and monosodium glutamate. Cover and simmer until shrimp are tender, about 10 minutes. Stir occasionally.

Blend 2 tbsp. water and cornstarch until smooth and stir in gradually. Cook until thickened and clear.

Serve immediately with rice. (Serves 6.)

Spices and herbs deteriorate. Make sure the ones you use are fresh by dating bottles when you buy them and checking and replacing often.

Paella —
recipe on page 78

ISLAND SHRIMP

2 lb. raw shrimp
3 tbsp. cooking oil
1 small clove garlic
20-oz. can pineapple chunks
2 tbsp. slivered candied ginger
1 green pepper, slivered
$1/2$ cup celery, sliced thin on
   the diagonal
$1/2$ cup vinegar
$1/2$ cup brown sugar
$1/2$ tsp. monosodium glutamate
   (optional)
2 tbsp. soy sauce
$1/4$ cup cold water
$2^1/2$ tbsp. cornstarch
Hot cooked rice
Baked Bananas (recipe follows)

Shell, clean and wash shrimp. Heat oil in large heavy skillet. Add garlic and shrimp and cook gently and stir until shrimp are pink, about 5 minutes.

Add pineapple chunks and juice, ginger, green pepper, celery, vinegar, brown sugar, monosodium glutamate and soy sauce. Cook and stir over low heat about 2 minutes.

Measure cold water and add cornstarch. Stir until smooth and blended and add to shrimp mixture gradually, stirring constantly. Bring mixture to boiling, stirring constantly, and boil 1 minute. Serve immediately with hot rice and Baked Bananas. (Serves 6.)

Note: If raw shrimp are not available, try the recipe with canned shrimp. To do this follow the directions, *except* do not add the shrimp at the beginning. Cook the garlic in the oil 2 or 3 minutes. Proceed as directed to point where mixture has been thickened with cornstarch and boiled 1 minute. Add four cans ($4^1/4$-oz. each) of large cleaned shrimp (rinsed under cold water) at this point; continue cooking gently just until shrimp are heated through. Serve as directed.

Baked Bananas

Peel 3 bananas and cut in half lengthwise and crosswise. Put in shallow baking dish. Brush with melted butter and sprinkle lightly with brown sugar. Bake at 375 degrees about 10 minutes or until tender.

The seas around us supply a bountiful harvest

SHRIMP CURRY

3 lb. shrimp, fresh or frozen
1 slice lemon
1 small slice onion
1 clove garlic, crushed
Small piece bay leaf
6 peppercorns
2 bunches celery leaves
1 tsp. salt
Boiling water
7-oz. pkg. coconut
3 cups liquid (see below)
$1/2$ cup butter
1 cup chopped onion
1 medium apple, chopped
2 tbsp. curry powder
$2^1/2$ tsp. salt
$1/2$ tsp. ground ginger
$1/2$ cup flour
2 cups chicken stock
2 tbsp. lemon juice
Hot cooked rice
Condiments (chutney, chopped
   green onions, chopped salted
   peanuts, raisins, coconut,
   chopped hard-cooked eggs,
   etc.)

Combine washed shrimp, slice of lemon, slice of onion, garlic, bay leaf, peppercorns, celery leaves and 1 tsp. salt in large kettle. Cover with boiling water, bring back to a boil, turn down heat and simmer 7 minutes or until shrimp are a bright pink. Remove from heat and let stand 20 minutes. Drain, straining and saving liquid. Shell and clean shrimp.

Put coconut through the fine blade of the food chopper. Put in saucepan. Add 3 cups liquid (liquid drained from shrimp plus water if necessary). Bring to a boil, turn down heat and simmer 20 minutes. Strain, saving liquid and discarding coconut.

Melt butter in saucepan. Add onion and apple and cook gently until onion is yellow. Add curry powder and cook gently 2 minutes.

Stir in salt and ginger. Sprinkle in flour and stir to blend. Remove from heat and stir in chicken stock and 2 cups of the coconut water.

Return to moderate heat and cook and stir until boiling. Boil 1 minute.

Add shrimp, cover and simmer 15 minutes or until shrimp are well heated. Stir in lemon juice.

Serve immediately with rice and condiments. (Serves 6 to 8.)

Note: If desired, replace fresh shrimp with five $4^1/4$-oz. cans large shrimp (rinsed under cold water). Omit steps of cooking, shelling and cleaning shrimp. When simmering coconut use 1 cup milk and 2 cups water for 3 cups liquid called for.

SHRIMP AND MUSHROOMS

$1/4$ cup butter
$1/2$ lb. fresh mushrooms, sliced
2 tbsp. chopped green pepper
$1/4$ cup finely-chopped celery
1 tbsp. chopped green onion
$1/4$ cup flour
$1/2$ tsp. salt
$1/8$ tsp. pepper
Dash cayenne
1 chicken bouillon cube
$1/4$ cup boiling water
$1^1/4$ cups light cream
2 tbsp. chopped pimento
Three $4^1/4$-oz. cans large cleaned
   shrimp
2 tbsp. sherry
Toast OR patty shells

Heat butter in heavy saucepan. Add mushrooms, green pepper, celery and onion and cook gently 5 minutes.

Sprinkle in flour, salt, pepper and cayenne and stir to blend. Remove from heat. Dissolve bouillon cube in boiling water and add to flour mixture. Add cream. Stir to blend.

Return to moderate heat and cook and stir until thick and smooth. Stir in pimento and shrimp. Taste and adjust seasoning if necessary. Heat thoroughly, stirring gently.

Stir in sherry at serving time. Serve on toast or in patty shells. (Serves 4 to 6.)

SCALLOPS ITALIENNE

2 tbsp. butter
1½ tbsp. finely-chopped green onions
1 lb. scallops, cut in halves
1 cup sliced mushrooms
1 cup fish OR chicken stock
Juice of ½ lemon
¼ tsp. salt
⅛ tsp. pepper
1 tbsp. butter
2 tsp. flour
¼ cup heavy cream
1 tbsp. finely-chopped chives (optional)
4 oz. hot buttered noodles

Melt 2 tbsp. butter in heavy skillet. Add green onions, scallops, mushrooms, stock and lemon juice. Sprinkle with salt and pepper. Bring to a boil, turn down heat and cook gently about 5 minutes, or until scallops are tender. Do not overcook.

Remove scallops and mushrooms with slotted spoon and keep warm.

Put liquid remaining in pan over high heat and cook until nearly reduced to half.

Blend 1 tbsp. butter and flour and add little by little to hot liquid, stirring constantly until thickened and smooth.

Add cream and bring to boiling point but do not boil. Remove from heat. Return scallops and mushrooms to mixture. Stir in chives. Taste for seasoning and add more salt if desired.

Serve immediately over hot noodles. (Serves 2 to 3.)

QUICK COQUILLES ST. JACQUES

1 lb. scallops
⅔ cup dry white table wine
⅓ cup water
2 sprigs parsley
1 small onion, cut in half
3 tbsp. butter
1 cup fresh sliced mushrooms
1 tbsp. flour
½ tsp. salt
⅛ tsp. pepper
2 tbsp. lemon juice
10-oz. can frozen shrimp soup, thawed
1 egg yolk

⅓ cup heavy cream
¼ cup butter
1 cup small bread cubes (⅛ inch)
½ cup grated Parmesan cheese
Paprika

Rinse scallops. Heat wine, water, parsley and onion to boiling in saucepan. Add scallops and simmer 5 minutes. Drain, saving cooking water but discarding parsley and onion. Cut scallops in halves if large.

Heat 3 tbsp. butter in saucepan and add mushrooms. Cook gently 3 minutes. Sprinkle in flour, ½ tsp. salt, ⅛ tsp. pepper and let bubble up. Remove from heat and add lemon juice and ½ cup of scallop cooking water all at once. Return to heat and cook gently, stirring until boiling and smooth.

Add undiluted shrimp soup and blend well.

Beat egg yolk and cream together with a fork. Stir into soup mixture. Add scallops and heat.

Melt ¼ cup butter in skillet. Add bread cubes and heat, stirring until bread is golden brown. Remove from heat and mix in cheese lightly.

Pile scallop mixture into 6 scallop shells or individual serving dishes. Sprinkle with bread cubes-cheese mixture and then with paprika.

Put low under broiler (middle of the oven) and broil about 5 minutes or until heated through and browned (watch carefully so tops don't burn). Serve immediately. (Serves 6.)

LOBSTER NEWBURG

¼ cup butter
Two 5-oz. cans lobster, broken up
1½ tbsp. flour
1 cup light cream
3 egg yolks
½ cup light cream
1 tsp. salt
¼ tsp. cayenne
2 tsp. lemon juice
2 tbsp. sherry
Buttered toast

Melt butter in heavy skillet. Add lobster pieces and cook gently 5 minutes, stirring occasionally.

Sprinkle in flour and continue cooking 1 minute, stirring to blend.

Remove from heat. Add 1 cup cream all at once, stir to blend and return to moderate heat and cook and stir until bubbling.

Beat egg yolks and ½ cup cream together with a fork. Beat in salt, cayenne, lemon juice and sherry. Stir into lobster mixture gradually and cook gently until mixture thickens.

Serve immediately over toast. (Serves 4.)

CRAB IN AVOCADO HALVES

6-oz. can crab meat, drained
1 egg yolk
1 tbsp. fresh lime juice
½ tsp. salt
⅛ tsp. curry powder
Dash pepper
¼ cup ice cold butter
2 avocados
Fresh lime juice
¼ cup crushed corn flakes
1 tbsp. melted butter

Heat oven to 400 degrees.

Break up crab meat with a fork.

Stir egg yolk and 1 tbsp. lime juice together in a small saucepan. Stir in salt, curry powder and pepper. Add half of butter. Set over lowest heat and stir constantly until butter is melted. Add remaining butter and stir again over lowest heat until sauce is blended and thickened. Add to crab meat and blend lightly with a fork.

Cut avocados in halves lengthwise. (Twist halves in opposite directions to separate.) Remove seeds. Brush cut surfaces with lime juice. Put in shallow baking dish, cut side up. Fill with crab mixture.

Combine corn flakes and melted butter and sprinkle over. Bake 15 minutes. Serve at once. (Serves 4.)

To save juices when poaching fish, steam it on aluminum foil with the edges turned up so water doesn't touch fish. Use about 1/2-inch water in a tightly-covered pan.

JAMBALAYA

1/4 cup butter
1 cup finely-chopped onion
2 cloves garlic, crushed
1 cup diced cooked ham
28-oz. can tomatoes
1 1/2 cups long-grain rice
1 small bay leaf, crumbled
Pinch sweet basil
1 tsp. salt
1/4 tsp. pepper
Dash cayenne
1/2 cup chopped green pepper
1/4 cup finely-chopped parsley
1/4 cup chopped celery
Two 4 1/4-oz. cans large shrimp
6-oz. can crab meat OR 5-oz. can lobster

Heat butter in large heavy saucepan or Dutch oven. Add onion and garlic and cook gently until yellow. Add ham and cook and stir over low heat 5 minutes.

Add tomatoes and bring to a boil.

Sprinkle rice in on top of tomatoes. Add bay leaf, basil, salt, pepper and cayenne. Cover tightly and cook gently 20 minutes.

Add green pepper, parsley and celery.

Drain shrimp and rinse under cold running water. Drain and break up crab or lobster. Stir into hot mixture gently.

Cover again and cook over low heat 20 minutes more. Serve immediately. (Serves 6.)

PAELLA

3 whole chicken breasts (6 sides)
1/2 cup olive oil
2 cloves garlic, slivered
1 large green pepper, slivered
1/3 cup finely-chopped onion
2 tsp. paprika
1/2 tsp. pepper
2 cups long-grain rice
1 pkg. frozen peas
2 large tomatoes, peeled and chopped coarsely
4 cups chicken stock
1/4 tsp. saffron
1 lb. raw shrimp, shelled and cleaned
16 clams (in the shell)
Chopped parsley
Lemon wedges

Have butcher cut each side of the chicken breasts, through the bones, into 4 pieces (24 small pieces).

Heat 1/4 cup of the olive oil in each of two 10-inch heavy iron skillets (see note below). Add half of chicken pieces to each and brown well. Add half of garlic, green pepper, onion, paprika and pepper to each pan. Stir to blend and cook gently 3 minutes. Remove from heat.

Add half of rice, peas and tomatoes to each pan. Bring chicken stock to a boil. Add saffron and stir until saffron is dissolved. Add half of stock to each pan. Cook 10 minutes over moderately high heat, uncovered. Do not stir.

Add shrimp, pushing them down well into the liquid. Lower heat, cover tightly and simmer 10 to 15 minutes more or until chicken and rice are tender.

Heat oven to 350 degrees.

Uncover skillets, stir mixture lightly with fork, put in oven. Cook another 15 minutes, or until almost all liquid is absorbed.

Scrub clam shells very well with a brush. Put in steamer or sieve over boiling water and cover very tightly. Steam until shells open, about 10 minutes.

Sprinkle cooked Paella with chopped parsley and top with steamed clams and lemon wedges. (Serves 8.)

Note: If you happen to have a paella pan use only the one pan for the whole recipe.

If fresh shrimp and clams are not available use four 4 1/4-oz. cans shrimp (drained and rinsed) and a 5-oz. can clams (drained). Add them for the last 15 minutes of cooking, pushing them well down into the rice mixture.

SEAFOOD AND RICE

1 lb. raw shrimp
1 small piece celery, with leaves
1 thin slice onion
4 peppercorns
1 tsp. salt
Small piece bay leaf
3 sprigs parsley
1/2 lb. halibut
Two 5-oz. cans lobster OR 2 cups cooked lobster meat
1/4 cup olive oil
1 clove garlic, minced
2 tomatoes, chopped
1 medium green pepper, chopped
1/2 cup chopped onion
1 1/2 cups shrimp stock (directions follow)
1 1/2 tsp. salt
1/4 tsp. pepper
1 cup long-grain rice

Combine shrimp, celery, onion slice, peppercorns, 1 tsp. salt, bay leaf and parsley in saucepan. Cover with boiling water, cover and simmer until shrimp turn bright pink, about 5 minutes. Remove from heat and let stand 20 minutes.

Drain, saving stock. Shell and remove veins from shrimp. Strain stock, measure out 1 1/2 cups and set aside for use later.

Cut halibut into 1-inch cubes.

Break lobster meat into bite-size pieces.

Heat oil in large heavy skillet.

Add halibut and lobster and cook gently just until fish is lightly browned.

Add garlic, tomatoes, pepper and onion and cook gently 2 minutes, stirring carefully. Add shrimp, shrimp stock, 1½ tsp. salt and pepper.

Push fish to sides of skillet and put rice in liquid in centre. Cover and cook 5 minutes. Remove cover and gently stir rice and seafood with a fork to blend. Cover tightly and continue simmering 15 minutes longer or until liquid is absorbed but mixture is still moist. Serve immediately. (Serves 6.)

BROILED CANNED SALMON

1-lb. can red salmon
1 cup commercial sour cream
2 tsp. lemon juice
1 tbsp. finely-minced green
**   onion**
½ tsp. salt
⅛ tsp. pepper

Drain salmon and break into large pieces. Spread in single layer on shallow baking pan.

Combine remaining ingredients and spread mixture over salmon.

Put low under broiler (in middle of oven) and broil 10 minutes or until hot and lightly browned. (Serves 4.)

TUNA BURGERS

Two 7-oz. cans tuna, flaked
2 cups thinly-sliced celery
½ cup chopped peanuts
½ tsp. salt
2 tsp. grated onion
1 cup mayonnaise
2 tbsp. lemon juice
½ cup grated cheese
10 hamburger buns

Heat oven to 450 degrees.

Mix all ingredients, except buns. Split and butter buns and fill with tuna mixture.

Wrap each Tuna Burger in aluminum foil. Place in oven and heat 10 to 15 minutes. (Makes 10.)

Note: Tuna Burgers may be prepared ahead of time, wrapped in foil and put in the refrigerator until time to heat.

Eggs and Miscellaneous

SHIRRED EGGS WITH BACON

Heat oven to 350 degrees.

Circle the inside of a 3-inch shallow baking dish with partly-fried strips of bacon (not crisp) for each serving.

Break an egg into each dish. Dot with butter, and sprinkle with salt and pepper. Add 1 tbsp. cream.

Bake 15 to 20 minutes.

Serve hot in individual dishes garnished with parsley.

EGGS IN MUSHROOM SAUCE

1 lb. fresh mushrooms
¼ cup butter
1 tbsp. grated onion
¼ cup flour
½ tsp. salt
¼ tsp. pepper
2 cups light cream
2 chicken bouillon cubes
¼ cup boiling water
6 eggs
Salt and pepper
Parmesan cheese

Heat oven to 350 degrees.

Wash and slice mushrooms. Heat butter in heavy saucepan, add mushrooms and onion and cook slowly 5 minutes.

Sprinkle in flour, ½ tsp. salt and ¼ tsp. pepper and let bubble up. Remove from heat. Add cream all at once.

Dissolve bouillon cubes in boiling water and add to mushroom mixture. Stir to blend and return to moderate heat. Cook, stirring constantly, until thick and smooth.

Spoon sauce into 6 individual baking dishes. Make a hollow in the centre of the sauce with the back of a large spoon and drop an egg into each hollow. Sprinkle lightly with salt and pepper.

Bake until eggs are nearly set, about 15 minutes. Remove from oven and turn on broiler. Sprinkle the yolk of each egg generously with grated Parmesan cheese and slip under broiler for about 1 minute to brown cheese lightly. (Serves 6.)

BAKED EGGS AND CHICKEN

2 tbsp. chicken fat OR butter
½ cup sliced fresh mushrooms
2 tbsp. flour
1 tsp. salt
¼ tsp. pepper
1 cup chicken stock
1 cup milk
1½ cups cut-up cooked chicken
½ cup toasted slivered almonds
2 tbsp. chopped pimento
6 eggs
Salt and pepper
Butter
Toasted slivered almonds (optional)

Heat oven to 350 degrees. Butter 6 shallow individual baking dishes.

Melt chicken fat or butter in saucepan. Add mushrooms and cook gently until tender.

Sprinkle in flour, salt and pepper and blend well. Remove from heat. Add chicken stock and milk all at once and stir to blend. Return to moderate heat and cook and stir until smooth and slightly thickened.

Stir in chicken, ½ cup slivered almonds and pimento. Spoon mixture into prepared individual baking dishes.

Make a hollow in the centre of the sauce in each dish and drop an egg carefully into each. Sprinkle with salt and pepper and dot with butter.

Bake about 15 minutes or until eggs are done but not hard and sauce is bubbling. Sprinkle with more slivered almonds if desired and serve immediately. (Serves 6.)

BAKED TOMATOES AND EGGS

4 medium tomatoes
Salt and pepper
4 eggs
Butter
¼ cup fine dry bread crumbs
1 tbsp. melted butter
Chicken Liver Sauce (recipe follows)

Heat oven to 375 degrees.

Cut stem end off tomatoes and scoop out pulp, leaving a ¼-inch shell. Invert on paper towelling to drain.

Set tomatoes in lightly-greased large muffin cups. Sprinkle insides with salt and pepper. Break an egg into each. Dot with butter.

Combine bread crumbs and melted butter. Top each tomato with 1 tbsp. of the mixture.

Bake about 20 minutes or until eggs are set. Serve hot topped with Chicken Liver Sauce. (Serves 4.)

Chicken Liver Sauce

3 tbsp. butter
½ lb. chicken livers
1 cup sliced fresh mushrooms
1 tbsp. flour
¾ tsp. salt
1 tbsp. chopped parsley
1 tsp. minced green onion
⅛ tsp. pepper
2 tbsp. sherry
½ cup chicken stock

Heat butter in heavy skillet.

Wash chicken livers and cut in halves. Add to hot butter along with mushrooms and cook gently until livers are well browned.

Sprinkle in flour and blend gently. Add salt, parsley, onion and pepper. Remove from heat and add sherry and chicken stock. Stir to blend. Return to moderate heat and cook and stir until slightly thickened. Serve hot.

HARD-COOKED EGGS

For tender hard-cooked eggs with no dark ring around the yolk put eggs in saucepan and cover with cold water. Bring water to a boil, remove from heat, cover and let stand 20 minutes. Drain and run cold water over them until they are cool. Shell.

CURRIED EGGS

2 tbsp. butter
1 tbsp. chopped onion
1/4 cup chopped apple
2 tbsp. flour
1 tsp. curry powder
1/4 tsp. salt
1/8 tsp. pepper
1 cup milk
6 hard-cooked eggs
Hot cooked rice
Chutney

Melt butter in heavy saucepan. Add onion and apple and cook gently until tender.

Add flour, curry powder, salt and pepper, and let mixture bubble up well over low heat. Remove from heat and add milk all at once.

Return to heat, bring to boil, boil 1 minute, stirring constantly.

Cut hard-cooked eggs in half lengthwise. Reheat them in curry sauce.

Serve curried eggs over cooked rice with chutney. (Serves 4.)

Note: If you like your curry hot, double the amount of curry powder.

EGGS AND ASPARAGUS ON TOAST

1/4 cup butter
1/4 cup finely-minced green onions
3 tbsp. flour
2 tsp. curry powder
1 tsp. salt
1/4 tsp. pepper
2 cups milk
6 hard-cooked eggs, quartered
Two 10-oz. pkg. frozen asparagus
6 slices buttered whole wheat toast

Melt butter in saucepan. Add onions and cook gently until tender. Sprinkle in flour, curry powder, salt and pepper and cook gently, stirring, until blended and bubbling.

Remove from heat and add milk all at once. Stir until blended, return to moderate heat and cook, stirring constantly, until thickened and smooth.

Add eggs and heat very gently.

Cook asparagus according to package directions. Drain well. Put slices of toast on serving plates. Top with asparagus and spoon egg mixture over all. (Serves 6.)

PUFFY JELLY OMELET

(This recipe is part omelet and part soufflé and stays high and puffy even after it comes out of the oven.)

6 eggs, separated
6 tbsp. milk
1/2 tsp. salt
1/8 tsp. pepper
3 tbsp. butter
1/2 cup tart jelly

Heat oven to 350 degrees.

Beat egg whites in large bowl until stiff. In another bowl, beat egg yolks until thick and lemon-colored. Beat in milk, salt and pepper and fold into the beaten egg whites.

Melt butter in heavy skillet (about 10 inches in diameter). Pour in egg mixture. Cook over low heat until light brown underneath (about 10 minutes).

Hard-cook left-over egg yolks in sieve set in simmering water. Drain, cool and press through sieve for salad or vegetable garnish.

Place skillet in oven and bake omelet until light brown on top, and until, when touched lightly with finger, no imprint remains (10 to 15 minutes).

Make a 1/2-inch deep crease across the omelet, half-way between the skillet handle and opposite side. Make 1-inch cuts at either end of crease. Spread half of omelet with tart jelly. Using spatula, carefully fold omelet on crease line, being careful not to break. Slide on to warm platter and serve immediately. (Serves 4.)

TOMATO-CHEESE SOUFFLÉ

1/4 cup butter
1/4 cup flour
1/4 tsp. salt
1/8 tsp. pepper
1/4 tsp. dry mustard
Dash cayenne
Dash nutmeg
1 cup tomato juice
1 cup grated sharp Cheddar cheese
3 egg yolks, well beaten
3 egg whites
1/4 tsp. cream of tartar

Heat oven to 350 degrees.

Melt butter in small saucepan. Add flour, salt, pepper, mustard, cayenne and nutmeg, stir to blend and let bubble up together. Remove from heat.

Add tomato juice all at once, stirring to blend. Return to moderate heat and cook and stir until boiling. Let boil 1 minute. Stir in cheese. Remove from heat and stir in egg yolks.

Combine egg whites and cream of tartar in mixing bowl and beat until stiff peaks form. Fold in cheese mixture.

Pour into ungreased 1 1/2-qt. casserole. Run a spoon completely around mixture 1 inch from the edge to make a groove.

Set in pan of hot water (have water 1 inch deep) and bake 50 to 60 minutes until soufflé is puffed and brown. Serve immediately with asparagus and bacon if desired. (Serves 4.)

Note: This recipe can be doubled and baked in a large soufflé dish.

BROCCOLI SOUFFLÉ

4 strips bacon, finely chopped
10-oz. pkg. frozen broccoli
7 slices white bread
Melted butter
1/3 cup butter
2/3 cup flour
2 tsp. salt
1/4 tsp. pepper
1/4 tsp. dry mustard
Dash cayenne
2/3 cup milk
2/3 cup light cream
2/3 cup grated sharp Cheddar
   cheese
1 tbsp. minced green onion
5 egg yolks, well beaten
5 egg whites
2 tbsp. grated sharp
   Cheddar cheese

Heat oven to 350 degrees. Butter soufflé dish or casserole well (one that is filled right to the brim with 8 cups of water is a perfect size). Fasten a double strip of heavy aluminum foil tightly around the dish, extending 2 inches above the top of the dish.

Fry bacon until transparent but not browned. Lift out of pan with slotted spoon and drain well on paper towelling.

Cook broccoli according to package directions. Drain and cut up into quite small pieces.

Trim crusts from bread slices

and discard. Brush bread lightly with melted butter on both sides. Use 3 of the slices to line the bottom of the soufflé dish, covering it completely. (Cut up a fourth slice to fill any uncovered places.) Cut remaining 3 slices in half on the diagonal and stand them up around the outside of the soufflé dish with a point extending above the top of the dish (see black and white photo).

Melt 1/3 cup butter in saucepan. Sprinkle in flour and stir to blend. Remove from heat. Stir in salt, pepper, mustard and cayenne. Add milk and cream all at once and stir to blend. Return to moderate heat and cook, stirring constantly, until very thick and smooth (because the sauce is so thick it may appear to lump during cooking but will come smooth if stirred constantly).

Remove sauce from heat. Add 2/3 cup cheese, onion and broccoli.

Stir hot mixture gradually into beaten egg yolks. Let cool slightly.

Beat egg whites until stiff but not dry in large bowl. Add egg yolk mixture and fold together gently but quickly.

Pour immediately into prepared soufflé dish. Sprinkle with 2 tbsp. cheese and bacon bits.

Bake 1 hour or until dark golden brown and well puffed. Serve immediately. (Serves 6.)

To line soufflé dish for Broccoli Soufflé, use 3 slices of bread to line bottom (cut up a fourth slice to fill any uncovered places). Cut 3 slices of bread in half on the diagonal and stand them up around the outside of the dish with a point extending above top.

EGGS BENEDICT

4 English muffins
8 thin slices cooked ham
8 eggs
Soft butter
1 1/2 cups Hollandaise Sauce
   (recipe p. 23)
1 tbsp. chopped parsley

Split muffins. Lay muffin halves and ham slices on broiler rack. Toast muffins and broil ham under broiler element.

Poach eggs.

Butter toasted muffins, top with slice of ham then with a poached egg. Spoon Hollandaise Sauce over. Sprinkle with chopped parsley. (Serves 4.)

Note: While English muffins are traditionally used with this dish, toasted crumpets or French bread are just as good.

ONION-CHEESE TART

Pastry for 1-crust 9-inch pie
4 medium onions, sliced thin
1/2 cup chicken stock
2 tbsp. minced parsley
1 tbsp. butter
1 tbsp. flour
1/2 tsp. salt
1/8 tsp. pepper
Dash nutmeg
Dash cayenne
1/2 cup light cream
1/4 cup grated Swiss cheese
1/2 cup grated Parmesan cheese
Paprika
1 tbsp. butter

Heat oven to 450 degrees. Line a 9-inch pie pan with pastry.

Simmer sliced onions in chicken stock, covered, 10 minutes. Drain, saving stock. Spread onions on paper towelling to dry. Spread them evenly in the bottom of pastry-lined pan. Sprinkle with parsley.

Melt 1 tbsp. butter in saucepan. Sprinkle in flour, salt, pepper, nutmeg and cayenne. Let bubble up. Remove from heat and stir in stock saved from cooking onions and cream all at once. Add Swiss cheese and half of Parmesan cheese.

Return to moderate heat and cook and stir until cheese is com-

Broccoli Soufflé — *recipe on page 82*

pletely melted and sauce is smooth. Spoon over onions, spreading evenly. Sprinkle with remaining Parmesan cheese, sprinkle lightly with paprika and dot with 1 tbsp. butter.

Bake at 450 degrees 10 minutes, reduce oven temperature to 350 degrees and bake about 15 minutes more or until crust and top of pie are well browned. Serve hot. (Serves 4 to 6.)

PIZZA

4 cups biscuit mix
1 cup water
2-oz. can anchovy fillets
2 cloves garlic, crushed
1 cup grated Parmesan cheese
Pepper
Two 7½-oz. cans tomato sauce
½ lb. Mozzarella cheese OR
    pizza cheese, sliced thin
2 tbsp. chopped parsley
1 tsp. oregano
¼ cup grated onion
2 tbsp. oil

Heat oven to 425 degrees.

Mix biscuit mix and water vigorously with a fork. Dough will be very stiff. Turn out on floured board and knead 1 minute. Divide dough in two.

Roll each half of dough into a 12-inch circle and put each on a cookie sheet. Pinch edges to make a rim to hold filling in.

Drain anchovies, saving oil. Mix anchovy oil and garlic and spread on pizza shells. Sprinkle each with half of Parmesan cheese and lightly with freshly-ground pepper.

Spread each pizza with a can of tomato sauce, then top with Mozzarella or pizza cheese, parsley, oregano, onion and chopped anchovies. Drizzle 1 tbsp. oil over each pizza.

Bake at 425 degrees 20 to 25 minutes. Serve very hot. (Makes 2.)

83

QUICK MACARONI-TOMATO CASSEROLE

½ cup salad oil
2 cups uncooked elbow
   macaroni
½ cup chopped onion
½ cup chopped green pepper
1 clove garlic, crushed
28-oz. can tomatoes
½ tsp. sweet basil
1 tsp. salt
¼ tsp. pepper
2 tbsp. Worcestershire sauce

Heat oven to 350 degrees.

Heat oil in heavy skillet. Add uncooked macaroni, onion, green pepper and garlic, and cook, stirring constantly, until macaroni turns slightly yellow.

Heat tomatoes to boiling point and add remaining ingredients. Add to macaroni mixture.

Pour into 2-qt. casserole, cover and bake 30 to 40 minutes until macaroni is tender. Good served with sausages and tossed salad. (Serves 6.)

3-CHEESE MACARONI

1½ cups small bread cubes
   (¼ inch)
2 cups shell or elbow macaroni
2 tbsp. butter
2 tbsp. flour
1 tsp. salt
¼ tsp. pepper
¼ tsp. garlic salt
3 cups milk
2 tsp. grated onion
1 tsp. Worcestershire sauce
1 cup cut-up Mozzarella cheese
½ cup grated Parmesan cheese
4 medium tomatoes, sliced thin
Salt and pepper
2 tbsp. melted butter
1 cup grated sharp Cheddar
   cheese

Heat oven to 350 degrees. Butter a 2-qt. casserole.

Spread bread cubes on a large flat pan, put in oven and toast very lightly, stirring often.

Cook and drain macaroni.

Melt 2 tbsp. butter in saucepan. Add flour, salt, pepper and garlic salt and cook and stir until bubbling. Remove from heat and add milk all at once, stirring to blend.

Set over moderate heat and cook and stir until slightly thickened.

Add onion, Worcestershire sauce, Mozzarella cheese and Parmesan cheese. Cook gently, stirring, until cheese is melted. Remove from heat and stir in cooked macaroni.

Put half of mixture in prepared casserole. Top with a layer of tomato slices. Sprinkle tomatoes lightly with salt and pepper. Pour in remaining macaroni mixture and top with remaining tomato slices, sprinkling again with salt and pepper.

Toss toasted bread cubes and 2 tbsp. butter together and sprinkle cubes on top of casserole. Bake 25 minutes. Remove from oven and sprinkle Cheddar cheese over bread cubes. Bake 10 minutes longer or until Cheddar cheese has melted. Serve hot. (Serves 6.)

BAKED BEANS

2 lb. dried navy beans
1 small bay leaf
1 small onion
2 whole cloves
1 cup molasses
2 tbsp. dry mustard
2 tsp. salt
½ lb. salt pork, sliced thin
2 medium onions, sliced thin
¼ lb. thinly-sliced salami
   (optional)

Wash and look over beans. Cover them with cold water and let stand overnight. Drain.

Cover with fresh cold water, bring to a boil, turn down heat, cover and simmer 30 minutes. Add bay leaf and onion stuck with cloves and continue simmering until tender, about 30 minutes longer.

Drain, saving cooking water. Discard bay leaf, onion and cloves.

Heat oven to 275 degrees.

Combine molasses, mustard, salt and 1 cup of bean cooking water.

Lay 2 or 3 slices of salt pork in the bottom of a large bean pot. Top with a thick layer of beans, a few slices of salt pork, some of the onion slices, some of the salami slices (cut in halves) and pour

some of molasses mixture over. Repeat layers, starting with bean layer, until all ingredients are used, ending with a layer of beans and one of salt pork.

Cover pot with aluminum foil and bake at least 8 hours, adding more bean cooking water if necessary to keep moist. Bake for last hour uncovered to brown beans. (Serves 12.)

PEPPY BAKED BEANS

Four 15-oz. cans pork and beans
1 large onion, sliced thin
¾ cup molasses
1 tsp. dry mustard
3 tbsp. vinegar
¼ cup ketchup
6 strips bacon, cut in halves
Baked Back Bacon
   (recipe p. 42)

Heat oven to 350 degrees.

Combine beans, onion, molasses, mustard, vinegar and ketchup in 3-qt. casserole. Lay bacon strips on top.

Bake 1 hour and 15 minutes then increase temperature to 400 degrees and bake 15 minutes more.

Serve very hot with Baked Back Bacon. (Serves 12.)

WIENER TREATS

2 tbsp. butter
4 large onions, thinly sliced
1 clove garlic
½ tsp. salt
⅛ tsp. pepper
2 tbsp. Worcestershire sauce
1 tbsp. prepared mustard
1 lb. wieners
10 to 12 slices bacon

Heat butter in skillet. Add onions, garlic, salt and pepper. Cover and simmer until onions are tender, about 10 minutes. Add Worcestershire sauce and mustard.

Split wieners almost through, open out and fill with onion mixture. Close around onion filling and wrap each wiener with a slice of bacon. Fasten bacon at each end with a toothpick or small metal skewer.

Broil, turning several times, until bacon is crisp. (Makes 10 to 12.)

Add new Weekend Magazine Tested Recipes here

Add new Weekend Magazine Tested Recipes here

Add new Weekend Magazine Tested Recipes here

Add new Weekend Magazine Tested Recipes here

Add new Weekend Magazine Tested Recipes here

SECTION III

Happy Endings

Who wants a meal without a happy ending?

I often hear people say they never eat desserts — but I don't really believe them. I've even seen them refuse dessert in a restaurant. But somehow (have you noticed?) a home-made dessert, chosen with care to compliment the rest of the meal, never seems to be refused.

And I'm glad. I'd hate to be the only one to crave a touch of sweet as a perfect ending to a good meal.

My only trouble with this large selection of recipes was to keep it from being any larger. As usual I had to include many of my own favorites plus as many as possible of the favorites readers request over and over again.

There are cakes of many colors and shapes, including some planned for special occasions. And there are cookies and more cookies.

Pastries of any kind make the meal ending especially happy for the male members of the family. What man ever refuses a piece of hot apple pie? So there are recipes for plently of pies, tarts and special pastries here too.

And not to be forgotten are puddings — hot, cold and frozen — and some extra-special fresh fruit desserts.

You'll be all set for a really happy ending with any of these happiest of desserts.

Butterscotch Sundae Cake — *recipe on page 94*

Cakes

Cakes

PICNIC CHOCOLATE CAKE

2 cups sifted all-purpose flour
1 tsp. soda
3/4 tsp. salt
2 cups brown sugar, packed
1/2 cup shortening
1 cup buttermilk OR sour milk
1 tsp. vanilla
3 eggs
2 squares (2 oz.) unsweetened chocolate, melted
Choco-O-Nut Frosting (recipe follows)

Heat oven to 350 degrees. Grease and flour a 13 x 9 1/2 x 2-inch oblong pan.

Sift dry ingredients into bowl. Add sugar and shortening, then milk and vanilla.

Beat 2 minutes at medium speed on mixer, or 300 strokes by hand.

Add eggs and chocolate and beat 2 minutes more.

Pour into prepared pan and bake 40 to 45 minutes. Cool in pan.

Frost with Choc-O-Nut Frosting.

Choc-O-Nut Frosting

1/3 cup soft butter
3 cups sifted icing sugar
4 to 5 tbsp. cream
1 1/2 tsp. vanilla
2 squares (2 oz.) unsweetened chocolate, melted
1/2 cup seedless raisins
1/2 cup chopped walnuts

Blend butter and sugar. Stir in cream, vanilla and chocolate, stirring until smooth.

Add raisins and nuts.

CHOCOLATE-NUT LOAF

1 cup soft butter
2 cups sugar
5 eggs, well beaten
1 cup pecans, coarsely broken
3 squares (3 oz.) unsweetened chocolate, melted and cooled
1 tsp. vanilla
2 1/2 cups sifted all-purpose flour
1/2 tsp. salt
1 tsp. soda
1 cup buttermilk OR sour milk

Creamy Mocha Icing (recipe follows)
Whole pecans

Heat oven to 350 degrees. Grease and flour two 9 x 5 x 3-inch loaf pans.

Cream butter until fluffy. Add sugar gradually, beating constantly. Beat in eggs.

Stir in nuts, chocolate and vanilla.

Sift flour, salt and soda together and add alternately with milk, beating well after each addition.

Spoon batter into prepared pans and bake 50 to 60 minutes, or until a toothpick stuck in the centre comes out clean.

Turn out on racks and cool. Ice with Creamy Mocha Icing and decorate with whole pecans.

Creamy Mocha Icing

2 2/3 cups sifted icing sugar
3 tbsp. cocoa
1/3 cup soft butter
1/4 tsp. vanilla
1 tbsp. instant coffee
3 tbsp. hot water

Sift sugar and cocoa into bowl. Add butter and vanilla and blend. Dissolve coffee in hot water and add enough to sugar mixture to make icing the right consistency to spread.

BEST CHOCOLATE CAKE

1/2 cup soft shortening
2 cups sugar
4 egg yolks
4 squares (4 oz.) unsweetened chocolate, melted
2 1/4 cups sifted cake flour
2 tsp. baking powder
1/2 tsp. salt
1 cup milk
1 tsp. vanilla
4 egg whites
Creamy Chocolate Icing (recipe follows)

Heat oven to 350 degrees. Grease and flour two 9-inch layer cake pans at least 1 1/2 inches deep.

Cream shortening. Add sugar and beat to blend well. Add egg yolks one at a time, beating well after each addition. Stir in chocolate.

Sift flour, baking powder and salt together and add to chocolate mixture alternately with milk and vanilla, beating well after each addition.

Beat egg whites until stiff but not dry and fold in quickly.

Pour batter into prepared pans and bake about 35 minutes or until tops spring back when touched lightly in the centre. Cool on cake racks and fill and ice with Creamy Chocolate Icing.

Creamy Chocolate Icing

1/4 cup butter
2 squares (2 oz.) unsweetened chocolate, cut up
3 tbsp. flour
1/4 tsp. salt
2/3 cup milk
4 cups sifted icing sugar (approx.)
1 tsp. vanilla

Melt butter and chocolate in saucepan over low heat. Remove from heat and blend in flour and salt. Stir in milk slowly and return to low heat. Cook, stirring constantly, until very thick and smooth.

Remove from heat and stir in sugar and vanilla. Set in ice water and continue stirring until of spreading consistency. Add a little more sugar if necessary.

CHOCOLATE CREAM CAKE

2 squares (2 oz.) unsweetened chocolate
Hot strong coffee
1 egg
1 cup sugar
1/3 cup cooking (salad) oil
1 tsp. vanilla
1 1/3 cups sifted all-purpose flour
1 tsp. baking powder
1 tsp. soda
1/2 tsp. salt
Cream Filling (recipe follows)
1 large ripe banana
Chocolate Glaze (recipe follows)
Walnut halves

Heat oven to 350 degrees. Grease generously and flour one 9-inch round layer cake pan at least 1 1/2 inches deep.

Put chocolate in measuring cup

92

and add hot coffee to make 1 cup liquid. Let stand until chocolate is soft, stir and cool to lukewarm.

Beat egg in small mixing bowl until light. Add sugar, oil and vanilla and beat well.

Sift flour, baking powder, soda and salt together and add to egg mixture alternately with chocolate mixture, beginning and ending with dry ingredients. Pour into prepared pan and bake about 30 minutes or until top springs back when touched lightly in the centre.

Turn out on cake rack and cool. Split crosswise into 2 layers shortly before serving time. Put bottom of cake on serving plate and spread with cooled Cream Filling. Put thin slices of banana on top of filling, saving a few slices to garnish top. Put top on cake and pour Chocolate Glaze over. Garnish with banana slices and walnut halves. Chill a few minutes. Cut in wedges to serve. (Serves 6 to 8.)

Cream Filling

½ cup sugar
3 tbsp. flour
⅛ tsp. salt
1 cup milk
1 egg
1 tsp. vanilla

Combine sugar, flour and salt in small saucepan. Stir in milk gradually, blending until smooth. Set over low heat and cook and stir until bubbling and thick.

Beat egg lightly and add at least half of hot mixture gradually, stirring constantly. Stir back into saucepan and bring back to boil. Remove from heat, cover and cool. Stir in vanilla.

Chocolate Glaze

1 square (1 oz.) unsweetened
   chocolate
1 tsp. butter
1 cup sifted icing sugar
2 tbsp. boiling water
¼ tsp. vanilla

Put chocolate and butter in top of double boiler and set over simmering water until melted. Remove from heat. Blend in icing sugar, boiling water and vanilla and stir until smooth (not thick). Pour over cake letting it drip down sides.

CHOCOLATE JELLY ROLL

1 cup sifted cake flour
1 tsp. baking powder
¼ tsp. salt
¼ cup cocoa
3 large eggs
1 cup sugar
⅓ cup water
1 tsp. vanilla
Powdered instant chocolate
   drink
Orange Filling (recipe follows)
Chocolate Glaze (recipe p. 93)

Heat oven to 375 degrees. Grease and line the bottom of a 15 x 10 x 1-inch jelly roll pan with greased brown paper or aluminum foil.

Sift flour, baking powder, salt and cocoa together.

Beat eggs in a small bowl until thick and lemon-colored (about 5 minutes, high speed on mixer).

Pour beaten eggs into a large bowl. Gradually beat in sugar. Blend in water and vanilla.

Mix in dry ingredients slowly just until the batter is smooth. Pour into prepared pan.

Bake 12 to 15 minutes, until top springs back when lightly touched in centre.

Sprinkle top of cake with sifted instant chocolate drink.

Loosen edges and turn out on clean towel. Peel off paper and trim off crisp edges if necessary. Roll up in towel from narrow end while hot. Cool on wire rack.

Unroll when cool and fill with Orange Filling. Roll up again. Pour Chocolate Glaze over top of roll.

Cut in 1-inch slices to serve.

Orange Filling

1 cup sugar
¼ cup cornstarch
½ tsp. salt
1 cup orange juice
2 tbsp. butter
2 tbsp. grated orange rind
2 tbsp. lemon juice

Mix sugar, cornstarch and salt in saucepan. Stir orange juice in gradually. Bring to a boil over moderate heat, stirring constantly. Boil 1 minute.

Remove from heat. Stir in remaining ingredients. Cool.

THE ICING ON YOUR CAKE

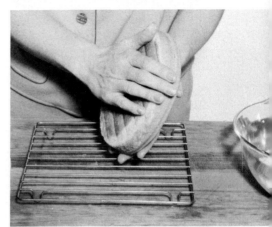

To ice cake, brush loose crumbs from layer with fingers. Anchor cake to plate with dab of icing. Put top side down and spread layer with filling.

Set second layer on filling, top side up, and put thin coat of icing on outside of cake. Let it set. Spread frosting thickly on sides, bringing icing up to form rim around top. Put remaining frosting on top of cake, spreading to meet built-up rim.

CRUMB CAKE

2 cups brown sugar, packed
2 1/2 cups sifted all-purpose flour
1/2 cup soft butter
1 tsp. cinnamon
1/2 tsp. cloves
1/2 tsp. nutmeg
1 cup buttermilk OR sour milk
1 tsp. soda
1 egg
1 cup raisins

Heat oven to 350 degrees. Grease and flour 13 x 9 1/2 x 2-inch oblong pan.

Mix sugar, flour, butter, cinnamon, cloves and nutmeg together with fingers or on low speed of mixer. Take out 1/2 cup of dry mixture and save for topping.

Add remaining ingredients and beat all together thoroughly.

Spread batter in prepared pan. Sprinkle with 1/2 cup dry mixture saved for topping.

Bake about 45 minutes or until top springs back when touched lightly.

Note: To sour milk put 1 tbsp. white vinegar in bottom of cup, then fill cup to 1 cup line with milk. Stir together.

ROASTED SPICE CAKE

1 3/4 cups sifted all-purpose flour
3 tsp. baking powder
1 tsp. salt
1 tsp. cloves
1 tsp. cinnamon
1 1/3 cups brown sugar, packed
1/3 cup soft shortening
1 cup milk
1 tsp. vanilla
2 egg yolks
1 whole egg
2 egg whites
1 cup brown sugar, packed
1/2 cup chopped nuts

Heat oven to 350 degrees. Grease and flour 13 x 9 1/2 x 2-inch pan.

Sift flour, baking powder, salt, cloves and cinnamon together into a bowl. Add 1 1/3 cups brown sugar, shortening, milk and vanilla.

Beat 2 minutes (medium speed on the mixer or 300 strokes by hand). Add egg yolks and whole egg and beat another 2 minutes.

Pour into prepared pan.

Beat egg whites until frothy. Gradually beat in 1 cup brown sugar, beating well after each addition, and continue beating until stiff and glossy. Spread meringue on uncooked cake batter. Sprinkle with nuts. Bake 35 to 40 minutes.

Cool in pan.

KENTUCKY GINGERBREAD

3 eggs
1 cup sugar
1 cup molasses
1 cup shortening, melted
1 tsp. cloves
1 tsp. ginger
1 tsp. cinnamon
2 tsp. soda
2 tbsp. hot water
2 cups sifted all-purpose flour
1 cup boiling water
Granulated sugar
Sweetened whipped cream

Heat oven to 350 degrees. Grease a 13 x 9 1/2 x 2-inch oblong pan.

Blend eggs, sugar, molasses, shortening and spices in large bowl. Beat very well until batter is smooth.

Dissolve soda in 2 tbsp. hot water and stir in. Sift flour into mixture and beat very well again.

Add boiling water and beat a few seconds to blend well. Batter will be very thin.

Pour into prepared pan and bake about 45 minutes or until top springs back when touched lightly in centre. Remove from oven and sprinkle generously with granulated sugar. Serve warm, cut in squares and topped with whipped cream.

BANANA CAKE

1 1/2 cups sifted cake flour
3/4 cup brown sugar, packed
3/4 tsp. baking powder
3/4 tsp. soda
3/4 tsp. salt
1/4 cup cooking (salad) oil
3/4 cup mashed ripe bananas
1/4 cup buttermilk OR sour milk
1 tsp. vanilla
1/4 cup buttermilk OR sour milk
2 egg yolks
2 egg whites
1/4 cup brown sugar, packed
1/2 cup finely-chopped nuts

Heat oven to 350 degrees. Grease and flour a 9-inch square cake pan.

Sift flour, 3/4 cup brown sugar, baking powder, soda and salt into a bowl. Add oil, bananas, 1/4 cup buttermilk or sour milk and vanilla and beat hard 1 minute.

Add remaining 1/4 cup buttermilk or sour milk and egg yolks and beat another 1 minute.

Beat egg whites until frothy. Add 1/4 cup brown sugar and continue beating until soft peaks form. Fold into flour mixture along with nuts.

Pour into prepared pan and bake about 40 minutes or until top springs back when touched lightly in the centre. Set on cake rack and cool in pan. Ice with your favorite butter or fudge icing.

BUTTERSCOTCH SUNDAE CAKE

1 cup soft butter
2 cups brown sugar, packed
4 egg yolks
2 2/3 cups sifted cake flour
3 tsp. baking powder
1 tsp. salt
1 cup milk
1 1/2 tsp. vanilla
4 egg whites
Butterscotch Filling (recipe follows)
2 medium bananas
Boiled Icing (recipe follows)
Butterscotch Glaze (recipe follows)

Heat oven to 350 degrees. Grease generously and flour three

8- or 9-inch round layer pans, at least 1½ inches deep.

Cream butter until light and fluffy. Add sugar gradually, creaming well after each addition. Continue beating until fluffy.

Add egg yolks one at a time, beating well after each addition.

Sift flour, baking powder and salt together. Combine milk and vanilla. Add sifted dry ingredients to creamed mixture alternately with milk mixture, stirring until blended after each addition and beginning and ending with dry ingredients.

Beat egg whites until stiff but not dry and fold into first mixture. Pour into prepared pans.

Bake 25 to 30 minutes or until tops spring back when touched lightly in the centre. Cool in pans about 5 minutes then turn out on cake racks. Cool.

Put Butterscotch Filling between layers, topping each layer of filling with a layer of sliced bananas.

Ice sides and top of assembled cake with Boiled Icing and drizzle Butterscotch Glaze around edge of top allowing it to run down sides.

Butterscotch Filling

1 cup brown sugar, packed
3 tbsp. flour
Pinch salt
1 cup milk
2 egg yolks, lightly beaten
2 tbsp. butter
1 tsp. vanilla
½ cup chopped walnuts

Combine sugar, flour and salt in saucepan, stirring to blend well. Add milk gradually, stirring until smooth. Set over moderate heat and bring to a boil, stirring constantly. Boil 1 minute.

Stir at least half of the hot mixture gradually into egg yolks. Pour back into pan and return to heat. Bring back to a boil, stirring constantly. Boil 1 minute. Remove from heat. Stir in butter, vanilla and nuts and cool.

Boiled Icing

½ cup sugar
2 tbsp. water
¼ cup corn syrup
2 egg whites
1 tsp. vanilla

Combine sugar, water and corn syrup in small saucepan. Bring to boil and boil hard, without stirring, to 242 degrees (syrup spins 6- to 8-inch thread when dropped from the tines of a fork).

Beat egg whites until stiff. Pour hot syrup in a thin stream into egg whites, beating constantly. Continue beating until stiff peaks form. Blend in vanilla.

Butterscotch Glaze

¼ cup brown sugar, packed
3 tbsp. butter
2 tbsp. water

Combine all ingredients in small saucepan. Bring to a boil and boil hard 1½ minutes without stirring. Cool slightly.

CHERRY-NUT LOAF

2 cups sifted all-purpose flour
1 cup sugar
3 tsp. baking powder
½ tsp. salt
2 eggs
¼ cup maraschino cherry juice
¾ cup milk
3 tbsp. cooking (salad) oil
¼ tsp. almond extract
1 cup maraschino cherries, drained and cut in halves
½ cup chopped walnuts

Heat oven to 350 degrees. Grease a 9 x 5 x 3-inch loaf pan.

Sift flour, sugar, baking powder and salt together into mixing bowl.

Beat eggs, cherry juice, milk, oil and almond extract together with a fork. Stir into dry ingredients and beat hard until smooth, about 30 seconds. Stir in cherries and nuts.

Spoon into prepared pan. Bake about 1 hour or until a toothpick inserted in centre comes out clean.

CURRANT CAKE

1 cup soft butter
1 cup sugar
3 eggs
1 tbsp. water
1 tsp. lemon extract
2 cups sifted all-purpose flour
½ tsp. baking powder
½ tsp. salt
1½ cups currants
½ cup coarsely-broken pecans
2 tbsp. corn syrup

Heat oven to 275 degrees. Grease and line with greased heavy brown paper a 9 x 5 x 3-inch loaf pan.

Cream butter. Add sugar gradually, creaming well after each addition. Add eggs, one at a time, beating well after each addition. Beat in water and lemon extract.

Sift flour, baking powder and salt together into mixture and stir to blend. Stir in currants and pecans.

Spoon into prepared pan and bake about 1¾ hours or until a toothpick stuck in the centre comes out clean. Remove from oven. Drizzle corn syrup over top and spread evenly. Return to oven for 5 minutes to glaze. Turn out on rack to cool.

A clever way to quick-frost cupcakes is to dip each one in fluffy icing, then twist and lift out.

JELLY ROLL

3 large eggs
1 cup sugar
5 tbsp. water
1 tsp. vanilla
1 cup sifted all-purpose flour
1 tsp. baking powder
¼ tsp. salt
Icing sugar
1 cup thick jam OR jelly

Heat oven to 375 degrees. Grease sides of 15 x 10 x 1-inch jelly roll pan and line bottom with waxed paper or greased heavy brown paper.

Beat eggs in small mixer bowl until very thick and fluffy. Add sugar gradually and beat well after each addition. Beat in water and vanilla.

Sift flour, baking powder and salt together into egg mixture and beat until smooth. Pour into prepared pan and spread evenly.

Bake 12 to 15 minutes or until top springs back when touched lightly in centre. Sift icing sugar over top of cake and turn out on towel. Roll cake and towel up together loosely from narrow end and let stand on cake rack until cool (see black and white photos).

Unroll and spread cake with jam or jelly and roll up again. Sprinkle top with more icing sugar if desired. Cut in thick slices to serve.

DATE SPONGE ROLL

Jelly Roll (recipe p. 96)
Date-Almond Filling (recipe follows)
Butter Cream Icing (recipe follows)
Finely-chopped toasted almonds

TO ROLL JELLY ROLL

Sift icing sugar generously over top of cake. Loosen edges from pan.

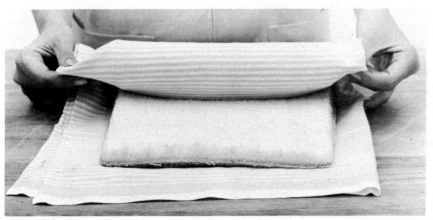

Turn cake out on clean towel. Roll cake and towel up together loosely from narrow end and let stand on cake rack until cool. Fill and roll again as directed in recipe.

Bake and cool Jelly Roll as directed in recipe but unroll and spread with lukewarm Date-Almond Filling. Roll up again. Ice outside of roll with Butter Cream Icing and sprinkle with almonds. (Serves 8 to 10.)

Date-Almond Filling

⅔ cup light cream
⅔ cup sugar
2 egg yolks
1 cup chopped dates
½ tsp. vanilla
½ tsp. almond extract
½ cup chopped toasted almonds

Mix cream, sugar, egg yolks and dates in saucepan and set over low heat. Cook, stirring constantly, just until it comes to a boil and thickens slightly.

Remove from heat and stir in vanilla, almond extract and almonds. Cool to lukewarm and use to fill cake as directed in recipe.

Butter Cream Icing

2 cups sifted icing sugar
1 egg yolk
1 tbsp. soft butter
½ tsp. almond extract
¼ tsp. vanilla
1½ tbsp. light cream (approx.)

Combine sugar, egg yolk, butter and flavorings in small bowl. Add enough of the cream to make icing a good spreading consistency. Ice outside of roll as directed in recipe.

STRAWBERRY ROLL

1 cup sifted all-purpose flour
1 tsp. baking powder
¼ tsp. salt
3 large eggs
1 cup sugar
⅓ cup orange juice
Grated rind of 1 orange
Icing sugar
1½ cups whipping cream
6 tbsp. sifted icing sugar
2 cups sliced strawberries

Heat oven to 375 degrees. Grease sides of 15 x 10 x 1-inch jelly roll pan. Line bottom of pan with waxed paper or greased heavy brown paper.

Sift flour, baking powder and salt together.

Beat eggs in small mixing bowl with rotary beater or electric mixer until thick and light-colored. Gradually beat in sugar.

Blend in orange juice. Add sifted dry ingredients and orange rind and blend only until smooth.

Pour into prepared pan, spreading evenly. Bake 12 to 15 minutes or until top springs back when touched lightly in centre.

Loosen edges of cake and sprinkle top generously with sifted icing sugar. Turn out on towel. Peel off paper. Roll cake and towel up together loosely from narrow end and let stand on cake rack until cake is cool.

Whip cream and 6 tbsp. icing sugar until stiff, 30 minutes before serving time.

Unroll cooled cake. Spread with whipped cream and sprinkle with strawberries. Roll up again loosely. Refrigerate until serving time. Cut in 1-inch slices to serve.

LAZY-DAISY CAKE

2 eggs
1 cup sugar
1 tsp. vanilla
1 cup sifted all-purpose flour
1 tsp. baking powder
$1/4$ tsp. salt
$1/2$ cup milk
1 tbsp. butter
3 tbsp. butter
3 tbsp. brown sugar
2 tbsp. cream
$1/2$ cup coconut

Heat oven to 350 degrees. Grease and flour an 8 x 8 x 2-inch pan.

Beat eggs well. Beat in sugar and vanilla.

Sift flour, baking powder and salt together and stir in.

Heat milk and 1 tbsp. butter together just to the boiling point. Pour into batter and beat well.

Pour into prepared pan and bake about 35 minutes or until top springs back when touched lightly in the centre.

Blend 3 tbsp. butter, brown sugar and cream in small saucepan. Put over moderate heat and let bubble up together. Stir in coconut and spread on top of baked cake. Put low under broiler for 2 or 3 minutes to brown.

LEMON LOAF

$1/4$ cup sugar
Juice of 1 lemon
$1/2$ cup soft butter
1 cup sugar
2 eggs
$1 1/2$ cups sifted all-purpose flour
1 tsp. baking powder
$1/2$ tsp. salt
$1/2$ cup milk
2 tsp. grated lemon rind

Heat oven to 350 degrees. Grease a loaf pan approximately $10 1/4$ x $3 1/2$ x $2 1/2$ inches.

Combine $1/4$ cup sugar and lemon juice and set in warm place, stirring occasionally, until needed.

Cream butter. Add 1 cup sugar and beat until fluffy. Add eggs one at a time, beating well after each addition.

Sift flour, baking powder and salt together and add to creamed mixture alternately with milk, beginning and ending with dry ingredients. Stir in grated lemon rind.

Spoon into prepared pan and bake about 1 hour or until a toothpick stuck in centre comes out clean. Leave in pan and set on cake rack. Pour lemon juice mixture slowly over the baked loaf while it is hot. Cool in pan.

Turn out of pan when cool and wrap in aluminum foil and store for a day or so to mellow. Slice thick and serve as cake or cut thin and butter to serve as bread with fruit salad.

PINEAPPLE CAKE

$3/4$ cup soft shortening
2 cups sugar
5 egg yolks
$2 2/3$ cups sifted all-purpose flour
$1/2$ tsp. salt
3 tsp. baking powder
1 cup pineapple juice
1 tbsp. lemon juice
3 egg whites
$3/4$ cup well-drained crushed pineapple
Pineapple Filling (recipe follows)
Seven Minute Icing (recipe follows)

Heat oven to 350 degrees. Grease and flour three 8- or 9-inch round layer pans, $1 1/2$ inches deep.

Cream shortening. Add sugar gradually and cream well after each addition. Add egg yolks one at a time, beating well after each addition. Continue beating until light and fluffy.

Sift dry ingredients together and stir into creamed mixture alternately with pineapple juice and lemon juice, beginning and ending with dry ingredients.

Beat egg whites until stiff and fold in. Quickly fold in crushed pineapple.

Divide batter evenly between the 3 prepared pans, and bake about 30 minutes or until tops spring back when touched lightly in centre. (If you only have room to bake 2 layers keep the batter for the third layer in the refrigerator until baking time.)

Cool on cake racks. Put layers together with Pineapple Filling and ice with Seven Minute Icing. If desired, ice only about $1 1/2$ inches in from sides on top of cake and fill centre with some of pineapple filling.

Pineapple Filling
20-oz. can crushed pineapple
2 tbsp. cornstarch
$1/4$ cup sugar
$1/4$ tsp. salt
1 tsp. lemon juice
1 tbsp. butter

Drain pineapple very well. Measure juice and add water if necessary to make 1 cup.

Combine cornstarch, sugar and

Recipe continued on next page

salt in saucepan. Add the 1 cup pineapple juice gradually, stirring and blending until smooth.

Set over moderate heat and cook, stirring constantly, until mixture boils and is thick and clear.

Remove from heat and stir in pineapple, lemon juice and butter. Cool thoroughly before filling cake.

Seven Minute Icing

2 egg whites
1½ cups sugar
¼ tsp. cream of tartar
⅓ cup water
1 tsp. vanilla

Combine egg whites, sugar, cream of tartar and water in top of double boiler.

Set over boiling water and beat with rotary beater until stiff peaks form (about 7 minutes). Remove from over hot water, add vanilla and continue beating until cooled and a good consistency to spread.

RUM CAKE

1 tsp. soda
1 cup boiling water
1 cup soft butter
1½ cups brown sugar, packed
3 eggs, well beaten
2½ cups sifted all-purpose flour
¼ tsp. salt
1 lb. dates, put through fine blade of food chopper
1 cup walnuts, finely chopped
3 tbsp. dark rum
Rum Icing (recipe follows)

Heat oven to 350 degrees. Line a 9-inch spring-form pan (with tube centre) or angel food pan with greased heavy brown paper.

Add soda to boiling water and set aside.

Cream butter and sugar until fluffy. Add eggs and beat well. Sift flour and salt together and add alternately with water-soda mixture, blending well after each addition.

Stir in dates and nuts.

Spoon into prepared pan and bake 60 to 70 minutes or until a toothpick inserted in centre comes out clean.

Remove from oven and spoon

rum over slowly, allowing it to soak into cake. Cool in pan.

Remove from pan when cool, wrap in aluminum foil and let mellow a few days. Ice with Rum Icing when ready to use.

Rum Icing

¼ cup butter
2 cups sifted icing sugar
2 tbsp. rum

Blend butter and icing sugar and add enough rum to make mixture of right consistency to spread.

AS-YOU-LIKE-IT CAKE
(Nice for afternoon teas)

2 cups sifted cake flour
1⅓ cups sugar
3 tsp. baking powder
1 tsp. salt
⅓ cup soft shortening
⅔ cup milk
½ tsp. lemon extract
½ tsp. vanilla
⅓ cup milk
2 egg yolks
1 whole egg
Brown Sugar Meringue OR
 As-You-Like-It Frosting
 (recipes follow)

Heat oven to 350 degrees. Grease and flour 15 x 10 x 1-inch jelly roll pan.

Sift together into mixing bowl flour, sugar, baking powder and salt.

Add shortening, ⅔ cup milk, lemon extract and vanilla. Beat 2 minutes at medium speed on mixer or 300 strokes by hand.

Add remaining milk and unbeaten egg yolks and whole egg. Beat 2 minutes more.

Pour into prepared pan.

Bake about 25 minutes or until top springs back when touched lightly in the centre. While hot, top with Brown Sugar Meringue, or cool and ice with As-You-Like-It Frosting.

Cut each third of the cake into different shapes such as fingers, squares and diamonds.

Ginger-Pear Upside-Down Cake —
recipe on page 101

CURRANT CUPCAKES

³/₄ cup soft shortening (part butter)
³/₄ cup sugar
¹/₄ cup corn syrup
3 eggs
2 tsp. grated orange rind
¹/₂ tsp. grated lemon rind
1³/₄ cups sifted all-purpose flour
¹/₂ tsp. baking powder
¹/₂ tsp. salt
1 cup currants

Heat oven to 375 degrees. Line 20 large muffin cups with paper baking cups.

Cream shortening, sugar and corn syrup together until fluffy. Add eggs one at a time and beat well after each addition. Stir in orange and lemon rind.

Sift flour, baking powder and salt together into creamed mixture and blend. Stir in currants.

Spoon batter into paper baking cups filling ¹/₂ to ²/₃ full. Bake 20 to 25 minutes or until tops spring back when touched lightly in centre. (Makes 20 large.)

ORANGE BLOSSOMS

1 cup sifted cake flour
1 tsp. baking powder
¹/₄ tsp. salt
3 large eggs
1 cup sugar
¹/₃ cup orange juice
1 tbsp. grated orange rind
¹/₂ cup whipping cream
1 tbsp. grated orange rind
3 tbsp. honey

Heat oven to 375 degrees.

Sift flour, baking powder and salt together and set aside.

Beat eggs in small mixer bowl until thick and lemon-colored, about 5 minutes at high speed.

Pour eggs into large mixer bowl and beat in sugar gradually, beating well after each addition.

Blend in orange juice at low speed and stir in sifted dry ingredients and 1 tbsp. orange rind.

Fill smallest-size greased and floured muffin pans (1¹/₂ inches in diameter) half full, and bake 8 to 10 minutes or until tops spring back when touched lightly in the centre. Cool.

Whip cream and fold in 1 tbsp. orange rind and honey. Cut a small cone from the top of each cake. Fill with whipped cream mixture, replace top and sift icing sugar over. (Makes 48.)

PINEAPPLE PUFFS

¹/₂ cup soft butter
1 cup sugar
1 egg
2 cups sifted all-purpose flour
1 tsp. baking powder
¹/₂ tsp. soda
¹/₂ tsp. salt
¹/₂ tsp. cinnamon
¹/₄ tsp. cloves
1 cup crushed pineapple with juice (see note below)

Heat oven to 350 degrees. Line 20 medium muffin cups with paper baking cups.

Combine butter, sugar and egg and beat together until light. Sift flour, baking powder, soda, salt, cinnamon and cloves together and add to creamed mixture alternately with pineapple, beginning and ending with dry ingredients.

Spoon into paper cups, filling about ²/₃ full. Bake 20 to 25 minutes or until tops spring back when touched lightly. (Makes 20 medium cupcakes.)

Note: Stir crushed pineapple before measuring.

DUTCH APPLE CAKE

4 cups sifted all-purpose flour
6 tsp. baking powder
1 tsp. salt
¹/₄ cup sugar
¹/₂ cup butter
2 tsp. grated lemon rind
2 eggs
1¹/₃ cups milk
4 cups sliced unpeeled apples (¹/₄ inch thick)
¹/₄ cup soft butter
¹/₂ cup sugar
2 tsp. cinnamon
Pouring cream OR whipped cream

Heat oven to 400 degrees. Grease 13 x 9¹/₂ x 2-inch baking pan.

Sift flour, baking powder, salt and ¹/₄ cup sugar into mixing bowl. Add ¹/₂ cup butter and cut in with pastry blender or 2 knives. Stir in lemon rind with fork.

Add eggs to milk and beat together with a fork. Add to flour mixture and stir gently with fork until blended.

Spread in prepared pan. Top with rows of apple slices. Put the slices close together and press into the dough. Spread with ¹/₄ cup soft butter.

Combine ¹/₂ cup sugar and cinnamon and sprinkle over.

Bake 30 to 35 minutes or until a toothpick stuck in centre comes out clean.

Serve warm topped with pouring cream or whipped cream. (Serves 12.)

GINGER-PEAR UPSIDE-DOWN CAKE

20-oz. can pear halves
¹/₃ cup butter
¹/₄ cup molasses
¹/₄ cup brown sugar, packed
³/₄ tsp. ginger
Maraschino cherries
1¹/₃ cups sifted all-purpose flour
1 cup sugar
2 tsp. baking powder
¹/₂ tsp. salt
¹/₃ cup soft butter
²/₃ cup milk
1 tsp. vanilla
1 egg
Pear Sauce (recipe follows)

Heat oven to 350 degrees.

Drain pears, saving juice for sauce. Dry pear halves well on paper towelling.

Put ¹/₃ cup butter in 9-inch square pan or 10-inch skillet and set in oven to melt. Remove from oven and add molasses, brown sugar and ginger. Stir to blend. Lay pear halves, cut side down, in a design in butter mixture. Add a few cherries for color.

Sift flour, sugar, baking powder and salt into mixing bowl. Add ¹/₃ cup butter, milk and vanilla. Beat 2 minutes, medium speed on the mixer or 300 strokes by hand. Add egg and beat 2 minutes more. Pour over pears.

Bake 40 to 50 minutes or until cake springs back when touched lightly in the centre. Serve warm with warm Pear Sauce. (Serves 9.)

Pear Sauce

1½ tbsp. cornstarch
2 cups liquid (pear juice plus water)
1 tbsp. lemon juice
1 tbsp. butter

Combine cornstarch and ¼ cup of the cold liquid, stirring until smooth.

Combine remaining liquid and lemon juice in saucepan and heat to boiling. Turn heat to low and stir in cornstarch mixture gradually, stirring constantly. Bring back to boiling and boil 1 minute, stirring constantly. Stir in butter. Serve warm.

HONEY UPSIDE-DOWN CAKE

20 dried prunes
20 dried apricots
½ cup liquid honey
¼ cup brown sugar, packed
¼ cup butter
Nut halves
½ cup soft butter
½ cup sugar
¼ cup liquid honey
1 egg
1½ cups sifted all-purpose flour
1 tsp. baking powder
¼ tsp. soda
½ tsp. nutmeg
½ cup milk
Honey Sauce (recipe follows)

Cook fruit separately as directed on packages or cover with water, cover and simmer until tender. Drain well. Remove stones from prunes.

Heat oven to 350 degrees.

Put ½ cup honey, brown sugar and ¼ cup butter in a 10-inch heavy iron skillet, and let melt slowly on top of stove. Blend.

Remove from heat and arrange cooked prunes and apricots alternately in pan, working in circles from the outside to the centre. Put nut halves in any spaces between fruit. Set aside and make batter.

Cream ½ cup butter, sugar, ¼ cup honey and egg until light and fluffy.

Sift dry ingredients together and add to creamed mixture alternately with milk, beginning and ending with dry ingredients. Stir just to blend.

Spoon batter over fruit in skillet. Bake 30 to 35 minutes, or until top springs back when touched lightly in centre.

Turn out on large plate and leave pan inverted over cake for a minute to allow all fruit and syrup to drop out of pan.

Serve warm or cold with Honey Sauce.

Note: A 9-inch square pan may be used instead of skillet.

Honey Sauce

½ cup liquid honey
½ cup butter

Place ingredients in small saucepan and heat until butter melts. Serve warm.

FROZEN CHOCOLATE ROLL

4 eggs
¾ cup sugar
½ cup sifted cake flour
½ tsp. baking powder
½ tsp. salt
1 tsp. peppermint extract
2 tbsp. sugar
¼ tsp. soda
3 tbsp. cold water
2 squares (2 oz.) unsweetened chocolate, melted
Granulated sugar
1½ pts. vanilla ice cream
Chocolate Sauce (recipe follows)

Heat oven to 375 degrees. Grease a jelly roll pan, 15 x 10 x 1 inches, and line bottom with greased heavy brown paper.

Put eggs in small mixer bowl and beat at high speed until they begin to get light. Add ¾ cup sugar gradually, beating well after each addition. Transfer to large mixer bowl and continue beating at high speed until very thick and light.

Sift flour, baking powder and salt together into egg mixture, add peppermint extract and blend well.

Add 2 tbsp. sugar, soda and water to melted chocolate and stir well until completely blended. Add to batter and fold in quickly.

Spread batter evenly in prepared pan and bake 15 to 20 minutes or until top springs back when touched lightly in centre.

Sprinkle top of cake generously with granulated sugar, loosen sides and invert on towel. Lift off pan and strip off paper carefully. Roll up from one narrow side with the towel inside to keep cake from sticking to itself. Set on cake rack and cool.

Chill a large mixer bowl and beaters well. Put ice cream in bowl and soften it by beating it with mixer (work quickly so ice cream softens but doesn't melt). Unroll cake and spread softened ice cream thickly across one narrow end. Roll up again and immediately wrap in heavy aluminum foil and put in freezer.

Remove from freezer at least 10 minutes before serving so ice cream will soften a little. Cut in thick slices to serve and top with Chocolate Sauce. (Serves 8.)

Chocolate Sauce

6-oz. pkg. semi-sweet chocolate chips
½ cup corn syrup
¼ cup milk
1 tbsp. butter
½ tsp. vanilla

Combine all ingredients in top of double boiler. Set over hot (not boiling) water. Stir until chocolate is melted and sauce is blended and smooth. Serve warm or cold. (Makes 1½ cups.)

There comes a time when you must count the blessings and ignore the calories

SWISS CHOCOLATE CAKE

³/₄ cup sifted cake flour
¹/₂ tsp. baking powder
¹/₂ tsp. salt
2 squares (2 oz.) unsweetened chocolate
5 eggs
¹/₂ tsp. vanilla
³/₄ cup sugar
¹/₄ cup cold water
¹/₄ tsp. soda
2 tbsp. sugar
1 cup whipping cream
2 tbsp. icing sugar
¹/₂ cup whipping cream
1 tbsp. icing sugar
1 tbsp. cocoa
Chocolate cake decorations

Grease 15 x 10 x 1-inch jelly roll pan and line bottom with waxed paper.

Heat oven to 375 degrees. Sift flour, baking powder and salt together.

Melt chocolate over hot water.

Beat eggs in large mixing bowl until thick and lemon-colored (about 10 minutes at high speed with electric mixer).

Add vanilla, then ³/₄ cup sugar, 1 tbsp. at a time, beating well after each addition. Fold in flour mixture.

Add cold water, soda and 2 tbsp. sugar to melted chocolate and stir until smooth. Fold quickly into batter and pour into prepared pan.

Bake 12 to 15 minutes, or until top springs back when touched lightly.

Turn out on to towel which has been dusted with icing sugar. Remove waxed paper and cool.

Divide cake into 4 equal parts crosswise, then split each of these pieces into 2 layers, making 8 very thin layers in all.

Beat 1 cup whipping cream and 2 tbsp. icing sugar together until stiff. Spread between layers.

Beat ¹/₂ cup whipping cream, 1 tbsp. icing sugar and cocoa together until stiff. Spread on top and sides of cake. Sprinkle with chocolate cake decorations and chill.

Note: This cake freezes well, so can be made the day before and frozen unwrapped until shortly before serving time.

CHOCOLATE COOKIE TORTE

1 cup soft shortening
2 cups sugar
2 eggs
3 squares (3 oz.) unsweetened chocolate, melted
1 tsp. vanilla
2³/₄ cups sifted all-purpose flour
1 tsp. salt
1 cup finely-ground walnuts
Cocoa Fluff (recipe follows)
Walnut halves (optional)

Draw a 9-inch circle on each of 2 sheets of heavy-duty aluminum foil which have been cut the size of cookie sheets (I trace around 9-inch layer cake pans). Lay foil on cookie sheets.

Heat oven to 375 degrees.

Cream shortening and sugar until fluffy. Add eggs, melted chocolate and vanilla and beat very well.

Sift in flour and salt and add walnuts. Mix first with spoon and then with hand until completely blended.

Take ¹/₂ cup of dough and shape it into a round with hands. Lay it in centre of one of circles on aluminum foil. Spread the dough with a rubber scraper or spatula as thin as possible inside circle. Round up with hands, then spread further by pressing with heel of hand until it is even and fills the circle to within ¹/₄ inch of guide line.

Repeat with a second ¹/₂ cup of dough on second sheet of aluminum foil. Put both sheets in oven

at once (move bottom rack up a little from the bottom of oven and have top rack just above middle of oven). Bake 8 minutes or until set.

Put a cake rack over each and invert carefully. Peel off foil and let cool. Using the same sheets of foil, repeat the shaping and baking until all the dough is used. There should be 10 crisp chocolate layers.

Store in a dry place until needed.

Put layers together with Cocoa Fluff 1 hour before serving. Top with Cocoa Fluff and garnish with walnut halves if desired. Chill until served. (Serves 12.)

Cocoa Fluff

3 cups chilled whipping cream
1¹/₂ cups sifted icing sugar
³/₄ cup sifted cocoa
Dash salt
1 tsp. vanilla

Combine cream, icing sugar, cocoa and salt in chilled mixing bowl. Beat until stiff. Stir in vanilla.

BLITZ TORTE

¹/₂ cup soft shortening
³/₄ cup sifted icing sugar
4 egg yolks, well beaten
1 cup sifted all-purpose flour
1 tsp. baking powder
¹/₄ tsp. salt
3 tbsp. milk
4 egg whites
¹/₂ cup sugar
¹/₂ cup icing sugar
¹/₂ cup slivered blanched almonds
2 tbsp. sugar
¹/₂ tsp. cinnamon
Rich Custard Filling (recipe follows)

Heat oven to 325 degrees.

Cream shortening and ³/₄ cup icing sugar well. Beat in egg yolks.

Sift flour, baking powder and salt together. Stir into creamed mixture. Stir in milk and spread in 2 greased and floured 8-inch layer pans.

Beat egg whites until frothy. Beat in ¹/₂ cup sugar and ¹/₂ cup icing sugar gradually, beating well after each addition. Beat until stiff and glossy. Spread half on batter in each pan.

Recipe continued on next page

103

HOW TO PREPARE ANGEL FOOD FOR FILLING

Turn the angel food cake upside down on waxed paper or plate. Cut top from the cake one inch down.

Cut into cake one inch from hole and one inch from edge leaving one inch base. Scoop out "trench" with fork. Put cake on serving plate and fill cavity with prepared filling. Replace top, press down gently.

Sprinkle meringue with almonds. Mix sugar and cinnamon and sprinkle over almonds.

Bake 35 to 40 minutes or until cake tests done and meringue is lightly browned. Cool. Remove from pans.

Place 1 layer on serving plate, meringue side up. Spread with Rich Custard Filling. Set other layer on top, meringue side up. (Serves 12.)

Rich Custard Filling

½ cup sugar
½ tsp. salt
⅓ cup flour
2 cups milk
4 egg yolks, well beaten
2 tsp. vanilla OR almond extract

Mix sugar, salt and flour in saucepan. Stir in milk.

Set over medium heat and cook, stirring constantly, until mixture boils. Boil 1 minute.

Remove from heat. Stir a little over half of mixture gradually into egg yolks. Pour back into saucepan, and continue cooking just until mixture reaches the boiling point. Cool. Add flavoring.

AMBROSIA ANGEL FOOD

4¼-oz. pkg. lemon pie filling
½ cup orange juice
1 tbsp. grated orange rind
2 tsp. grated lemon rind
1 tsp. unflavored gelatin
1 tbsp. water
½ pt. whipping cream
½ cup toasted flaked OR cut-up shredded coconut
10-inch angel food cake
1 cup whipping cream
¼ cup sifted icing sugar
½ tsp. vanilla
¼ tsp. almond extract
½ cup toasted flaked or cut-up shredded coconut

Prepare lemon pie filling as directed on package *except* reduce total liquid by ½ cup and substitute orange juice for ½ cup of remaining liquid. Cool. Stir in orange and lemon rind. Take out and set aside ½ cup of this mixture to use on top of cake. (Do not chill lemon filling or it will be too stiff.)

Measure gelatin into small dish, add water and let stand a few minutes. Set in pan of boiling water and heat until gelatin is dissolved. Cool slightly.

Whip ½ pt. cream until it begins to stiffen. Add gelatin in a thin stream, beating constantly. Continue beating until cream holds stiff peaks. Add the large amount of lemon pie filling and continue beating just until mixture is smooth and blended. Fold in ½ cup toasted coconut.

Hollow out angel food for filling. (See black and white photos for directions.) Fill with lemon-cream mixture. Replace top. Chill 4 to 8 hours.

Whip 1 cup cream until it begins to thicken at serving time. Add icing sugar, vanilla and almond extract and continue beating until cream is stiff.

Thin remaining ½ cup lemon filling to spreading consistency by adding a few drops boiling water. Spread on top of cake.

Spread sides of cake with whipped cream. Sprinkle with ½ cup toasted coconut. Serve immediately. (Serves 12.)

Note: To toast coconut, spread in flat pan. Heat in oven (350 degrees) until golden, stirring often.

CHIFFON PARFAIT CAKE

15-oz. pkg. frozen raspberries
2 tbsp. port
1 cup liquid (raspberry juice plus water if necessary)
3-oz. pkg. raspberry gelatin
1 pt. vanilla ice cream
1 cup miniature marshmallows
1 Orange-Chiffon Cake (recipe follows OR use a mix)
½ pt. whipping cream
2 tbsp. sugar

Put frozen berries into bowl. Pour port over and let stand several hours, stirring occasionally. When berries are completely thawed drain well. Measure juice and add water to make 1 cup if necessary.

Heat raspberry juice to boiling point. Remove from heat and stir in gelatin, stirring until dissolved.

Add ice cream a spoonful at a time, stirring until melted. Stir in marshmallows and drained raspberries.

Chill in ice water until mixture is thick and jelly-like but not set.

Remove chiffon cake from tube pan and wash pan. Cut cake into three layers. Put bottom layer of cake back into tube pan. Spoon half of gelatin mixture on to layer, spreading it evenly. Don't worry if a little of the red mixture runs down the sides. Set middle layer of cake on top, add remaining gelatin mixture and top with remaining layer of cake.

Chill until gelatin layers are set, about 1 hour.

Whip cream and sugar until stiff at serving time. Unmould cake and spread cream over outside. Cut in wedges to serve.

Orange Chiffon Cake

2¼ cups sifted cake flour
1½ cups sugar
3 tsp. baking powder
1 tsp. salt
½ cup cooking (salad) oil
5 egg yolks
¾ cup cold water
3 tbsp. grated orange rind
1 cup egg whites (7 or 8)
½ tsp. cream of tartar

Heat oven to 325 degrees.

Sift flour, sugar, baking powder and salt together into a bowl. Make a well in the centre of the dry ingredients and add the oil, egg yolks, water and orange rind in order. Beat with a spoon until smooth.

Put egg whites and cream of tartar in a large mixing bowl. Beat until whites form very stiff peaks.

Pour egg yolk mixture gradually over beaten whites, folding gently all the time with a rubber scraper. Fold just until blended.

Pour into 10-inch ungreased tube pan. Bake at 325 degrees 55 minutes. Increase oven temperature to 350 degrees and bake 10 to 15 minutes longer or until top springs back when touched lightly in centre.

Invert on funnel or neck of a small bottle to cool.

Cookies

Would you like to own the most popular cookie jar in town?

NORWEGIAN OATMEAL COOKIES

1 cup soft butter
1 cup brown sugar, packed
3 cups rolled oats
1 cup sifted all-purpose flour
1/2 tsp. salt
1 tsp. soda
1/4 cup boiling water

Cream butter and sugar thoroughly. Add rolled oats. Sift flour and salt together into creamed mixture.

Add soda to boiling water. Add to first mixture, blending well. Shape into a roll and freeze.

Heat oven to 375 degrees.

Slice dough very thin (1/16 inch) with a sharp knife. Place on lightly-greased cookie sheet and bake 5 to 7 minutes until lightly browned. Cookies will be soft when baked, but crisp when cool. (Makes 4 dozen.)

NORA'S MOLASSES CRISPS

1 cup molasses
1 cup shortening
1 tsp. cinnamon
1 tsp. ginger
1 tsp. salt
1 tsp. soda
2 1/2 cups sifted all-purpose flour
Sugar

Put molasses in saucepan and boil 2 minutes. Remove from heat. Add shortening, spices and salt, stir until shortening is melted, then cool.

Add soda and beat well. Beat in flour.

Shape into 2 rolls about 1 1/2 inches in diameter. Wrap in waxed paper and chill several hours or overnight.

Heat oven to 375 degrees.

Slice as thin as possible and put on lightly-greased cookie sheets. Sprinkle with sugar. Bake 5 to 7 minutes. Cool slightly before removing from pan. (Makes 8 dozen.)

ORANGE ICEBOX COOKIES

3/4 cup soft butter
1 cup sugar
1 egg
1 tbsp. grated orange rind
3 cups sifted all-purpose flour
1/2 tsp. soda
1/2 tsp. salt
1/4 cup milk
2 tsp. orange extract
Sesame seeds (optional)

Cream butter until fluffy. Add sugar and beat together thoroughly. Beat in egg. Stir in orange rind.

Sift flour, soda and salt together. Combine milk and orange extract. Add sifted dry ingredients to creamed mixture alternately with milk mixture, blending well after each addition.

Shape into 2 rolls about 2 inches in diameter, wrap in waxed paper and chill several hours or overnight.

Heat oven to 375 degrees.

Slice very thin (1/8 inch) and put on greased cookie sheets. Sprinkle with sesame seeds.

Bake 8 to 10 minutes or until golden. (Makes about 10 dozen.)

DELICIOUS COOKIES

1 cup soft shortening
1 cup brown sugar, packed
1 cup sugar
2 eggs
1 tsp. vanilla
1 tsp. almond extract
1 3/4 cups sifted all-purpose flour
1 tsp. baking powder
1 tsp. soda
1/2 tsp. salt
1/2 tsp. nutmeg
1/4 tsp. cloves
2 cups shredded coconut
1 cup chopped walnuts
2 cups rolled oats

Heat oven to 375 degrees.

Combine shortening, brown sugar, sugar and eggs in large mixing bowl and beat well until light and fluffy. Stir in vanilla and almond extract.

Sift flour, baking powder, soda, salt, nutmeg and cloves together and blend into creamed mixture. Stir in coconut, nuts and rolled oats.

Form dough into small balls and put on greased cookie sheet. Flatten with the tines of a fork dipped in cold water.

Bake about 12 minutes or until nicely browned. They should be soft when they come from the oven but will crisp as they cool. (Makes 6 dozen.)

GINGERSNAPS

1/2 cup melted shortening
1 cup sugar
1 egg
1/2 cup molasses
2 cups sifted all-purpose flour
1 tsp. soda
1 tsp. ginger
1 tsp. cinnamon
1/2 tsp. salt

Beat shortening and sugar together until well blended. Add egg and beat again. Stir in molasses.

Sift flour, soda, ginger, cinnamon and salt together into first mixture and blend well. Chill a few minutes.

Heat oven to 375 degrees.

Shape dough into small balls, 1 inch in diameter, and put on ungreased cookie sheets. Bake about 12 minutes or until set and cracked on top. (Makes 4 dozen.)

HERMITS

1 cup soft shortening
2 cups brown sugar, packed
2 eggs
1/2 cup water
3 1/2 cups sifted all-purpose flour
1 tsp. soda
1 tsp. salt
1 tsp. nutmeg
1 tsp. cinnamon
1 tsp. instant coffee
1 cup raisins
1 cup broken nuts

Cream shortening, sugar and eggs thoroughly. Add water.

Sift together flour, soda, salt, spices and instant coffee, and add to creamed mixture.

Stir in raisins and nuts. Chill about 1 hour.

Heat oven to 400 degrees.

Drop dough by rounded teaspoonfuls on lightly-greased cookie sheet. Bake 8 to 10 minutes. (Makes 6 dozen.)

HONEY DROPS

1 cup soft shortening (part butter)
1 cup brown sugar, packed
2 eggs
1/3 cup liquid honey
1 tsp. vanilla
3 1/2 cups sifted all-purpose flour
2 tsp. soda
Apricot jam

Mix shortening, sugar and eggs together thoroughly.

Stir in honey and vanilla. Add flour and soda sifted together.

Chill dough until firm, several hours or overnight.

Heat oven to 350 degrees.

Roll dough into balls the size of walnuts and place on ungreased cookie sheet.

Bake 10 to 12 minutes or until, when lightly touched with finger, almost no imprint remains. When slightly cooled, put together in pairs with apricot or other jam between. (Makes about 3 1/2 dozen double cookies.)

SAUCEPAN KISSES

2 cups brown sugar, packed
1/2 cup milk
1/2 cup butter
1/2 tsp. salt
1 tsp. vanilla
3 cups rolled oats
1/2 cup cocoa
1 cup shredded coconut

Combine brown sugar, milk, butter and salt in saucepan. Bring to a boil, stirring constantly. Boil gently, stirring, 5 minutes.

Remove from heat and stir in vanilla, rolled oats, cocoa and coconut. Drop by rounded teaspoonfuls on waxed paper. Cool. (Makes 3 to 4 dozen.)

SWEDISH PASTRIES

½ cup soft butter
¼ cup brown sugar, packed
1 egg yolk
1 cup flour
1 egg white
1 cup finely-chopped nuts
Jelly

Heat oven to 375 degrees.

Cream butter, brown sugar and egg yolk together well. Add flour and blend thoroughly.

Roll dough in balls the size of small walnuts. Dip each ball in egg white and roll in nuts. Place on ungreased cookie sheet.

Press a dent in the top of each cookie with finger.

Bake 10 to 12 minutes. Fill each cookie with a dab of red jelly at serving time. (Makes 3 dozen.)

ICED BROWNIES

½ cup soft butter
1 cup sugar
2 eggs
1 tsp. vanilla
2 squares (2 oz.) unsweetened chocolate, melted
1 cup sifted cake flour
¾ tsp. baking powder
½ tsp. salt
1 cup chopped walnuts
Fudge Icing (recipe follows)

Heat oven to 350 degrees. Grease a 13 x 9½ x 2-inch oblong pan.

Beat butter, sugar, eggs and vanilla together well. Add melted chocolate.

Sift dry ingredients together and add to first mixture. Beat well and stir in nuts.

Pour into prepared pan and bake 25 minutes. While slightly warm, ice with Fudge Icing.

Fudge Icing

2 cups brown sugar, packed
6 tbsp. butter
6 tbsp. light cream
1 tsp. corn syrup
1 square (1 oz.) unsweetened chocolate, cut up
2 tsp. vanilla

Combine sugar, butter, cream, corn syrup and chocolate in sauce-

pan. Bring to boil, stirring constantly.

Boil hard 2 minutes without stirring. Remove from heat and add vanilla. Beat until right consistency to spread.

BEST BROWNIES

4 squares (4 oz.) unsweetened chocolate
⅔ cup cooking (salad) oil
4 eggs
2 cups sugar
2 tsp. vanilla
1½ cups sifted all-purpose flour
1 tsp. baking powder
1 tsp. salt
1 cup chopped nuts
Icing sugar

Heat oven to 350 degrees. Grease a 13 x 9½ x 2-inch oblong pan.

Combine chocolate and oil in small saucepan. Heat over low heat until chocolate is melted. Remove from heat and cool.

Beat eggs thoroughly. Beat in sugar and vanilla. Add chocolate mixture and blend well.

Sift flour, baking powder and salt together into mixture and blend well. Stir in nuts.

Spoon into prepared pan and bake about 30 minutes or until sides test done but centre is still a little soft. Cool in pan. Sift icing sugar over top and cut in squares or bars to serve.

BROWNIE TEA SQUARES

½ cup butter
2 squares (2 oz.) unsweetened chocolate
2 eggs, lightly beaten
1 cup sugar
½ tsp. vanilla
½ cup plus 1 tbsp. sifted all-purpose flour
1 cup finely-chopped walnuts
Orange Butter Icing (recipe follows)

Heat oven to 350 degrees. Grease and flour two 8-inch square cake pans.

Put butter and chocolate in small saucepan and set over moderate heat to melt. Cool slightly.

Combine eggs, sugar and vanilla in mixing bowl. Blend in butter-chocolate mixture. Stir in flour.

Divide batter between the two prepared pans and spread in thin layers. Sprinkle each with half of nuts.

Bake about 12 minutes or until the centres spring back when touched lightly. Cool in pans.

Cut into small squares at serving time and put squares together in pairs with Orange Butter Icing.

Note: The recipe is correct with no leavening.

Orange Butter Icing

⅓ cup soft butter
3 cups sifted icing sugar
1 egg yolk
1½ tbsp. grated orange rind
2 to 3 tbsp. orange juice

Blend butter, sugar and egg yolk. Stir in orange rind and enough juice to make a thick icing.

CHERRY CHEWS

1 cup sifted all-purpose flour
1 cup rolled oats
1 cup brown sugar, packed
1 tsp. soda
¼ tsp. salt
½ cup butter
2 eggs
1 cup brown sugar, packed
½ tsp. almond extract
2 tbsp. flour
1 tsp. baking powder
½ tsp. salt
1 cup coconut
1 cup well-drained maraschino cherries, halved
½ cup pecan halves
Cherry-Almond Icing (recipe follows)

Heat oven to 350 degrees. Grease 13 x 9½ x 2-inch oblong pan.

Mix flour, rolled oats, 1 cup brown sugar, soda and ¼ tsp. salt. Add butter and mix until crumbly, first with a fork, then with fingers.

Press mixture into bottom of prepared pan. Bake 10 minutes.

Beat eggs, stir in 1 cup brown sugar and almond extract. Mix flour, baking powder and ½ tsp. salt and stir in. Add coconut and cherries and stir to blend.

Pour over first mixture and spread evenly. Sprinkle with pecans. Return to oven and bake 25 minutes until lightly browned.

Cool and ice with Cherry-Almond Icing. Cut in squares or bars to serve.

Cherry-Almond Icing

3 tbsp. soft butter
2 cups sifted icing sugar
2 tbsp. maraschino cherry juice
¼ tsp. almond extract

Blend butter and sugar. Add cherry juice and almond extract, using enough juice to make the icing easy to spread. Stir until smooth.

UNBAKED DREAM SQUARES

18 graham wafers (approx.)
1 cup brown sugar, packed
½ cup butter
½ cup milk
1 cup fine graham wafer crumbs
1 cup chopped walnuts
1 cup flaked coconut
¼ cup chopped candied cherries
1½ cups sifted icing sugar
2 tbsp. butter
½ tsp. almond extract
¼ tsp. vanilla
1 tbsp. cream (approx.)
Finely-chopped walnuts

Lightly butter an 8-inch square cake pan. Line the bottom with half of the graham wafers, cutting an extra wafer to fill in spaces if necessary.

Combine brown sugar, ½ cup butter and milk in saucepan. Bring to a full boil. Remove from heat and add graham wafer crumbs, nuts, coconut and cherries immediately. Spoon over graham wafers in pan while hot. Top with remaining graham wafers, cutting an extra wafer to fill spaces if necessary. Press them down firmly.

Combine icing sugar, 2 tbsp. butter, almond extract, vanilla and enough cream to make a thick icing that is easy to spread. Ice top of squares and sprinkle with finely-chopped walnuts. Let cool. Cut in squares to serve.

TROPICAL BARS

1 cup sifted all-purpose flour
¼ tsp. salt
¼ cup brown sugar, packed
¼ cup butter
1 egg
1 cup brown sugar, packed
1 tsp. rum extract
½ cup sifted all-purpose flour
½ tsp. baking powder
¼ tsp. salt
1 cup flaked coconut
¼ cup cut-up maraschino cherries
½ cup well-drained crushed pineapple

Heat oven to 350 degrees. Lightly grease a 9-inch square cake pan.

Sift 1 cup flour and ¼ tsp. salt into bowl. Add ¼ cup brown sugar and blend lightly. Add butter and work into dry ingredients first with a fork and then with fingers until mixture is crumbly. Press firmly into bottom of prepared pan. Bake 15 minutes. Remove from oven.

Beat egg thoroughly. Add 1 cup brown sugar gradually, beating well after each addition. Beat in rum extract.

Sift ½ cup flour, baking powder and ¼ tsp. salt together into mixture and stir to blend. Stir in coconut, cherries and pineapple. Spread over hot pastry layer and return to oven. Bake about 35 minutes or until well browned. Cool in pan and cut in bars.

CHINESE CHEWS

2 eggs
1 cup brown sugar, packed
1 cup chopped walnuts
1 cup cut-up dates
1 tsp. vanilla
¾ cup sifted all-purpose flour
1 tsp. baking powder
Granulated sugar

Heat oven to 350 degrees. Grease a 13 x 9½ x 2-inch oblong pan.

Beat eggs and sugar well. Add walnuts, dates and vanilla.

Blend in flour and baking powder, sifted together. Spread in prepared pan.

Bake about 20 minutes or until top springs back when lightly touched in centre.

Cut, while hot, in small oblongs and shape with hands into tiny rolls. Roll in granulated sugar. (Makes about 42.)

To make an interesting pattern on cookies use a greased and sugared potato masher instead of a fork to flatten dough after moulding it in balls.

SKILLET CHEWS

2 eggs
1 cup brown sugar, packed
1/3 cup butter
1 1/2 cups chopped dates
1 tsp. vanilla
1/4 tsp. salt
2 1/2 cups crispy rice cereal
1 cup chopped nuts
1/2 cup sugar
1 tsp. pumpkin pie spice

Beat eggs and brown sugar together thoroughly.

Melt butter in heavy skillet over low heat. Remove from heat and stir in egg mixture and dates. Set back over low heat and cook, stirring constantly, 10 minutes. Remove from heat and stir in vanilla and salt.

Combine rice cereal and nuts in bowl. Pour date mixture over and blend well. Cool to lukewarm.

Combine sugar and pumpkin pie spice in shallow dish. Butter hands lightly and shape cereal mixture into small rolls. Coat outside with sugar mixture. Cool.

FIG BARS

1 lb. dried figs
1 1/2 cups water
1/2 cup sugar
Pinch of salt
1 cup soft shortening
1 cup brown sugar, packed
2 eggs
3 cups sifted all-purpose flour
3/4 tsp. salt
1 tsp. cream of tartar
1 tsp. vanilla
1/2 tsp. soda
1 tbsp. hot water

Put figs through coarse blade of the food chopper. Combine with water, sugar and pinch of salt in saucepan. Bring to a boil, then turn down heat and simmer until mixture is very thick, about 15 minutes. Stir often. Remove from heat and cool.

Cream shortening, add brown sugar and continue creaming until light and fluffy. Add eggs and beat well.

Sift flour, salt and cream of tar-

tar together. Add half to creamed mixture. Add vanilla and soda which has been dissolved in hot water. Beat well.

Stir in remaining dry ingredients and mix until well blended. Chill several hours or overnight.

Heat oven to 375 degrees.

Roll dough 1/8 inch thick on floured board and cut into long strips 3 inches wide. Spoon some of fig filling down centre of each strip and fold sides of dough over filling so they overlap. (Because it is hard to give an exact amount of filling for each strip you might like to try a few test cookies so you can judge the amount to use.)

Cut strips into 1 1/2-inch lengths. Put on lightly-floured cookie sheet, folded side down. Bake 12 to 15 minutes or until golden brown. (Makes about 7 dozen.)

MATRIMONIAL CAKE
(Date Squares)

1 1/2 cups rolled oats
1 1/2 cups sifted all-purpose flour
1 tsp. soda
1 cup brown sugar, packed
1 tsp. salt
3/4 cup shortening
Nut-Date Filling (recipe follows)

Heat oven to 400 degrees.

Blend dry ingredients. Add shortening and rub together with fork and then with fingers to make a crumbly mixture.

Press half of mixture firmly into a greased 13 x 9 1/2 x 2-inch oblong pan.

Spread with cooled Nut-Date Filling. Sprinkle remaining crumbly mixture on top and pat lightly.

Bake 25 to 30 minutes, or until golden brown.

Nut-Date Filling

3 cups dates
1/2 cup brown sugar, packed
1 cup water
1/2 cup chopped nuts

Cook dates, sugar and water together slowly until thick, 5 to 10 minutes. Stir frequently. Add nuts and cool.

BUTTERSCOTCH OAT THINS

2 cups rolled oats
1 tsp. baking powder
1/2 tsp. salt
1 cup brown sugar, packed
1/2 cup butter, melted
1/2 tsp. vanilla
Sugar

Heat oven to 300 degrees.

Combine rolled oats, baking powder, salt and brown sugar, blending well with a fork. Stir in melted butter and vanilla.

Spread in a thin layer in ungreased 13 x 9 1/2 x 2-inch baking pan. Press down firmly with the back of a spoon. Sprinkle generously with sugar.

Bake until golden, about 20 minutes. Let stand 5 minutes, then cut into squares or bars. Cool before removing from pan.

PECAN FINGERS

1 cup dark brown sugar, packed
1 cup soft butter
1 egg
1/2 tsp. vanilla
2 cups sifted all-purpose flour
1 egg, well beaten
1/2 cup dark brown sugar, packed
1 cup coarsely-chopped pecans
1/2 cup dark brown sugar, packed

Heat oven to 350 degrees. Lightly grease a jelly roll pan, 15 x 10 x 1 inches.

Combine 1 cup sugar and butter and cream together until fluffy. Add 1 egg and vanilla and beat until well blended.

Add flour and work into creamed mixture until well blended. Spread in prepared pan. Brush with beaten egg. Sprinkle with 1/2 cup sugar, then with nuts and then with remaining sugar, spreading evenly over top.

Bake 20 to 25 minutes or until nicely browned. Cool in pan and cut in fingers to serve.

Note: Dark brown sugar gives the best flavor in this recipe but any brown sugar will be satisfactory.

SPICY SESAME SQUARES

¹/₄ cup sesame seeds
1 egg
³/₄ cup brown sugar, packed
3 tbsp. melted butter
¹/₂ cup sifted all-purpose flour
¹/₄ tsp. salt
¹/₄ tsp. soda
¹/₄ tsp. allspice
¹/₄ tsp. ground cardamom
¹/₄ tsp. nutmeg

Heat oven to 350 degrees. Spread sesame seeds on a large flat pan and toast in oven until golden, about 10 minutes.

Grease an 8-inch square cake pan. Sprinkle half of the toasted sesame seeds evenly over the bottom of the prepared pan.

Beat egg lightly. Add sugar gradually, beating after each addition. Stir in melted butter.

Sift flour, salt, soda, allspice, cardamom and nutmeg together into mixture and blend well. Spoon batter into prepared pan and spread carefully and evenly. Sprinkle remaining sesame seeds over top.

Bake about 25 minutes or until top springs back when touched lightly but centre is still chewy. Cool in pan and cut in bars to serve.

Note: If you are familiar with the flavor of cardamom and like it you may increase the amount to ¹/₂ tsp. for a delicious but rather strong flavor.

ALMOND CRISPS

2 cups soft butter
1¹/₂ cups sifted icing sugar
2¹/₂ cups sifted all-purpose flour
1 cup grated unblanched almonds
¹/₂ tsp. vanilla
¹/₈ tsp. salt
Red currant jelly
1¹/₂ cups sifted icing sugar
2 tbsp. warm water
¹/₄ tsp. almond extract
Blanched almonds

Cream butter and 1¹/₂ cups sugar until light and fluffy. Mix in flour and blend very well.

Add grated almonds (use finest

grater — do not grind), vanilla and salt and blend.

Wrap dough in waxed paper and chill several hours or overnight.

Heat oven to 350 degrees.

Roll dough very thin (1/16 inch) and cut into 2-inch rounds. Put on ungreased cookie sheets and bake 8 to 10 minutes or until very lightly browned.

Put a small spoonful of currant jelly on half the cookies and cover with another cookie while they are still hot.

Mix 1¹/₂ cups sugar, water and almond extract to a thick paste and spread thinly on cooled cookies. Top with blanched almonds. (Makes about 5 dozen double cookies.)

SOFT GINGER COOKIES

³/₄ cup soft shortening
¹/₂ cup brown sugar, packed
1 cup molasses
4¹/₂ cups sifted all-purpose flour
3 tsp. soda
2 tsp. ginger
¹/₂ tsp. cloves
¹/₂ tsp. cinnamon
¹/₂ tsp. salt
²/₃ cup cold water
Sugar

Cream shortening. Add brown sugar and cream well. Beat in molasses.

Sift together flour, soda, ginger, cloves, cinnamon and salt and add to creamed mixture alternately with water. Blend well and chill several hours or overnight.

Heat oven to 350 degrees.

Roll dough into a square ¹/₈ inch thick. Sprinkle generously with

sugar and cut into 2-inch squares with a knife. Put on ungreased cookie sheet and bake about 10 minutes or until a light touch in the centre leaves almost no mark.

Cool on racks and store in a tin box with a tight lid. (Makes 5 to 6 dozen.)

LEMON-GINGER COOKIES

1 cup soft butter OR shortening
¹/₂ cup sugar
1 egg
2 tbsp. lemon juice
2 tsp. grated lemon rind
¹/₂ cup finely-chopped preserved ginger
3 cups sifted all-purpose flour
1 tsp. baking powder
¹/₂ tsp. salt
1 tsp. ground ginger

Heat oven to 425 degrees.

Cream butter or shortening, sugar and egg together until light and fluffy.

Stir in lemon juice, rind and chopped ginger. Sift flour, baking powder, salt and ground ginger together and blend in.

Roll dough thin (1/16 inch), cut in rounds and bake on ungreased cookie sheet 6 minutes or until lightly browned. (Makes 6 dozen medium.)

THIN OATMEAL COOKIES

1 cup soft shortening
1 cup brown sugar, packed
3 cups rolled oats
2 cups sifted all-purpose flour
1 tsp. soda
1 tsp. salt
¹/₂ cup water
Sugar
Date Filling (recipe follows)

Cream shortening and brown sugar thoroughly.

Add rolled oats, sifted dry ingredients and water. Chill dough.

Heat oven to 375 degrees.

Roll dough very thin (1/16 inch). Cut with cookie cutter and sprinkle with sugar.

Bake on lightly-greased cookie sheet until lightly browned (about 5 minutes). If desired, put cookies together with Date Filling at serving time. (Makes 12 dozen single cookies.)

Date Filling

3 cups cut-up dates
¼ cup brown sugar
1½ cups water

Mix all ingredients in saucepan. Cook over low heat, stirring constantly, until thick (about 10 minutes). Cool. (Makes 2½ cups.)

VANILLA CREAMS

1 cup soft butter
⅓ cup whipping cream
2 cups sifted all-purpose flour
¼ tsp. salt
Sugar
¼ cup soft butter
¾ cup sifted icing sugar
1 egg yolk
1 tsp. vanilla

Mix 1 cup butter, cream, flour and salt thoroughly. Chill several hours or overnight.

Heat oven to 375 degrees. Roll dough ⅛ inch thick and cut into 1½-inch rounds.

Dip each round in sugar, coating on both sides. Use a spatula to lift cookies so they don't break.

Put on ungreased cookie sheet, prick several times with the tines of a fork and bake until puffy but not brown, 7 to 9 minutes. Cool.

Blend ¼ cup butter, icing sugar, egg yolk and vanilla. Put cookies together in pairs with this mixture. (Makes about 5 dozen double cookies.)

To make vanilla sugar for special flavor in baking, split a vanilla bean lengthwise, put in a canister of sugar and leave it for two weeks.

Pastries

113

STANDARD PASTRY
(For 2-crust 9-inch pie)

2 cups sifted all-purpose flour
1 tsp. salt
2/3 cup lard OR 3/4 cup shortening
1/4 cup ice water

Measure flour into bowl. Mix in salt with a fork. Add lard or shortening and cut in coarsely with a pastry blender or 2 knives. Sprinkle in water, a tablespoonful at a time, mixing lightly with a fork just until all flour is dampened.

Gather into a ball with fingers and press firmly.

Divide in two and shape each half into a round. Flatten slightly with hand. Roll one half thin (slightly less than 1/8 inch) on floured board or pastry cloth, using as little extra flour as possible on board and rolling pin. Roll gently from centre rather than back and forth. Keep rounding up edges with hands. Roll to 1 inch larger than inverted pie pan.

Lift on rolling pin to pan and ease pastry loosely into pan. Do not stretch. Add filling then trim off pastry even with edge of pie pan.

Roll remaining dough 1 inch larger than top of pie pan. Fold in quarters and cut several slits to let steam escape.

Dampen edge of bottom pastry with water and put folded top crust in place. Unfold, press to bottom crust to seal, trim evenly to 1/2 inch. Roll edge of top crust under edge of bottom crust. Flute.

Cover edge of pie with a narrow strip of aluminum foil to keep it from browning too much during baking. Bake as directed in recipe.

(For 1-crust 9-inch pie)

Use half of preceding ingredients. Roll out and put in pan as for lower crust of 2-crust pie. Trim to 1/2 inch, roll edge under and flute. Hook points of flutes under edge of pie pan (see black and white photo).

Do not prick if filling goes in unbaked crust. Fill and bake as directed in recipes.

Prick all over with tines of a fork if baked pie shell is called for. Bake 475 degrees 8 to 10 minutes or until browned. Cool and fill.

APPLE PIE WITH CHEESE CRUST

Cheese Pastry (recipe follows)
1/2 cup brown sugar, packed
1/2 cup sugar
1 tsp. cinnamon
6 cups sliced apples
1 1/2 tbsp. butter
Milk
Sugar

Heat oven to 425 degrees.
Line a 9-inch pie pan with half of Cheese Pastry.
Combine brown sugar, sugar and cinnamon. Sprinkle over apples and mix through slices lightly.
Pile apples into pastry-lined pan. Dot with butter.
Roll out remaining pastry and top pie, fluting edge. Cut slits in top crust.
Brush pastry lightly with milk and sprinkle generously with sugar.
Bake 50 to 60 minutes or until apples are tender. Serve slightly warm or cold.

Cheese Pastry

2 cups sifted all-purpose flour
1 tsp. salt
2/3 cup lard
1/2 cup grated sharp Cheddar cheese
1/4 cup ice water

Sift flour and salt together into mixing bowl. Add lard and cut in coarsely. Stir in grated cheese with a fork.

Sprinkle with water, a tablespoonful at a time, mixing lightly with a fork until flour is completely moistened.

Gather into a ball with fingers and roll out as directed in recipe above.

DUTCH APPLE PIE

Pastry for 2-crust 9-inch pie
5 to 6 cups peeled sliced tart apples
1 cup brown sugar, packed
1 tsp. cinnamon
1 tbsp. butter
1/2 cup heavy cream

Heat oven to 425 degrees.
Line pie pan with half of pastry. Combine apples, sugar, cinnamon. Heap into pan. Dot with butter.
Roll out remaining pastry and cover pie, sealing edges well and making extra-large slits in the top.
Bake 50 to 60 minutes, or until apples are tender. Five minutes before baking time is up pour cream into slits in top of pie. Serve warm.

TO SECURE EDGE OF PASTRY FOR BAKED PIE SHELL

Roll edge of pastry under and flute. Hook the point of each flute under the edge of the pie pan. The little hooks will break off when pie is cut but will keep edge from slipping during baking.

HONEY-APPLE PIE

Pastry for 2-crust 9-inch pie
³/₄ cup sugar
1 tsp. nutmeg
6 cups sliced peeled apples
1¹/₂ tbsp. butter
¹/₂ cup liquid honey
1 tbsp. grated orange rind
Icing sugar

Heat oven to 425 degrees. Line 9-inch pie pan with half of pastry, leaving 1 inch of pastry hanging over the edge of the pan.

Combine sugar and nutmeg and add to apple slices, mixing lightly. Put apples into prepared pan. Dot with butter.

Roll remaining pastry and cut into ¹/₂ inch strips. Moisten edge of bottom pastry with water and make lattice top with strips, sealing them to bottom crust.

Turn bottom crust and strips under and flute to make a high edge. Cover edge with 1¹/₂-inch wide strip of aluminum foil to keep it from getting too brown.

Bake 50 to 60 minutes or until apples are tender and pastry is well browned.

Combine honey and orange rind and pour mixture through the openings in the lattice when the pie is baked. Return to the oven for 5 minutes.

Cool to lukewarm and sift icing sugar over top. Serve warm or cold.

APPLESAUCE CHIFFON PIE

²/₃ cup sugar
1 envelope (1 tbsp.) unflavored gelatin
1 cup thick unsweetened applesauce
3 egg whites
¹/₄ tsp. cream of tartar
¹/₄ tsp. salt
¹/₃ cup sugar
¹/₂ cup whipping cream
2 tbsp. finely-chopped candied ginger
Ginger Crumb Crust (recipe follows)

Combine ²/₃ cup sugar and gelatin in saucepan. Stir in applesauce. Bring to a full boil over moderate heat, stirring constantly. Set pan in ice water and chill until mixture begins to mound when dropped from a spoon.

Beat egg whites, cream of tartar and salt together until frothy. Add ¹/₃ cup sugar gradually, beating constantly and continue beating until stiff and glossy. Fold into applesauce mixture.

Whip cream until stiff. Fold into applesauce mixture along with ginger. Spoon into prepared shell, sprinkle with ginger wafer crumbs (see following recipe) and chill several hours or until set.

Ginger Crumb Crust

1¹/₂ cups ginger wafer crumbs
3 tbsp. butter

Heat oven to 350 degrees. Mix crumbs and butter thoroughly. Take out ¹/₄ cup of mixture for top of pie and press remainder firmly and evenly against the bottom and sides of 9-inch pie pan. Bake 10 minutes. Cool.

GLAZED BLUEBERRY PIE

1¹/₂ cups fine graham wafer crumbs
3 tbsp. sugar
¹/₃ cup butter, melted
4-oz. pkg. cream cheese (room temperature)
1 tbsp. lemon juice
1 tsp. grated lemon rind
11-oz. pkg. frozen blueberries
¹/₃ cup water
¹/₂ cup sugar
1¹/₂ tbsp. cornstarch
3 tbsp. water
Sweetened whipped cream

Heat oven to 350 degrees.

Blend graham wafer crumbs, 3 tbsp. sugar and melted butter thoroughly. Put in 9-inch pie pan and press firmly in an even layer against the bottom and sides of the pan. Bake 10 minutes. Cool.

Blend cream cheese and lemon juice together with rotary beater or electric mixer until fluffy. Stir in lemon rind. Spread on crust.

Empty about ¹/₄ of the package of frozen berries into a saucepan. Add the ¹/₃ cup water. Simmer, breaking up berries with a fork, for 3 minutes.

Blend ¹/₂ cup sugar and corn-starch in a small bowl. Add 3 tbsp. water and blend until smooth. Add to simmering berries gradually and cook gently, stirring constantly, until thick and clear. Cool slightly.

Top cream cheese mixture with remaining blueberries. Then cover with cooked blueberry mixture, spreading it to cover the raw berries. Chill until firm, about 2 hours.

Serve topped with sweetened whipped cream.

MOCK CHERRY PIE

1¹/₂ cups sugar
2 tbsp. flour
3 cups seeded raisins
3 cups raw cranberries
1 tsp. vanilla
1 tsp. almond extract
1 tbsp. corn syrup
1 tbsp. butter
Pastry for 2-crust 9-inch pie

Heat oven to 425 degrees.

Blend sugar and flour. Combine raisins and cranberries in large bowl and add sugar-flour mixture. Add vanilla, almond extract and corn syrup and toss all together lightly until blended.

Roll half of pastry and line a 9-inch pie pan. Fill with fruit mixture. Dot with butter.

Roll remaining pastry and use to cover pie, fluting edge and cutting vents in top to let steam escape. Cover edge of pie with a strip of aluminum foil to keep it from getting too brown.

Bake 40 to 50 minutes or until pastry is well browned and cranberries are cooked. Serve slightly warm or cold with ice cream or whipped cream if desired.

LATTICE PEACH PIE

8 cups sliced fresh peaches
1 cup sugar
¹/₂ cup water
¹/₂ tsp. mace
Pastry for 2-crust 9-inch pie
1 tbsp. lemon juice
2 tbsp. butter

Peel and cut peaches into thin slices. Put them in heavy saucepan and add sugar, water and mace. Cover and simmer until peaches are tender. Drain well, saving juice. Cool.

Recipe continued on next page

Heat oven to 425 degrees.

Line 9-inch pie pan with pastry, leaving a 1 inch overhanging edge. Pile peaches in pastry-lined pan. Sprinkle with lemon juice. Dot with butter.

Make a lattice top with remaining pastry. Roll edge of bottom crust and strips of lattice together, turning them under. Crimp, making a high edge.

Bake until pastry is well browned, about 30 minutes.

Boil juice saved from simmering peaches very hard until reduced in half. Pour over whole top of pie as soon as it comes from the oven. Serve slightly warm or cold.

RHUBARB-STRAWBERRY DEEP-DISH PIE

15-oz. pkg. frozen strawberries
4 cups cut-up rhubarb
2 tsp. grated lemon rind
1 tbsp. lemon juice
1 cup sugar
3 tbsp. quick-cooking tapioca
2 tbsp. butter
Pastry for 1-crust 9-inch pie
Milk
Sugar
Vanilla ice cream

Thaw strawberries enough to break apart.

Heat oven to 400 degrees. Butter an 8-inch square glass baking dish.

Combine rhubarb, strawberries and lemon rind lightly in a large bowl. Sprinkle in lemon juice.

Combine sugar and tapioca and toss lightly through the fruit. Put in prepared baking dish. Dot with butter.

Roll pastry in a square larger than the baking dish. Lay it over the fruit, turn the edges of the pastry under and crimp and seal them well to the sides of the dish. Cut vents in top to let steam escape.

Brush the pastry with milk and then sprinkle it generously with sugar.

Bake about 45 minutes or until pastry is well browned and filling is bubbling well.

Serve slightly warm with ice cream. (Serves 6.)

BANANA CREAM PIE

1½ cups fine chocolate wafer crumbs
¼ cup sugar
⅓ cup melted butter
3¼-oz. pkg. vanilla pudding mix (cooked type)
1 tbsp. butter
½ cup whipping cream
¼ tsp. vanilla
2 medium bananas

Heat oven to 350 degrees.

Mix crumbs, sugar and melted butter. Measure out ¼ cup of mixture and set aside. Press remaining crumbs evenly and firmly on bottom and up sides of a buttered 8-inch pie pan. Bake 5 minutes. Cool.

Make pudding according to package directions, using ½ cup less milk than called for. When cooked stir in butter. Cool.

Beat whipping cream until stiff peaks form. Add vanilla and spoon in cooled pudding. Beat with rotary beater until smooth.

Slice bananas into cooled pie shell. Spoon in cream mixture. Sprinkle with ¼ cup crumbs saved from crust. Chill until filling is firm, at least 30 minutes. Serve same day as made.

CHOCOLATE VELVET PIE

½ cup soft butter
¾ cup sugar
1 square (1 oz.) unsweetened chocolate, melted
1 tsp. vanilla
2 eggs
9-inch baked pie shell

Cream butter and add sugar gradually, creaming well after each addition. Blend in chocolate and vanilla.

Add eggs, one at a time, beating 5 minutes, medium speed on the mixer (or with a rotary beater) after each addition.

Turn into cooled pie shell and chill several hours.

Serve garnished with whipped cream, if desired.

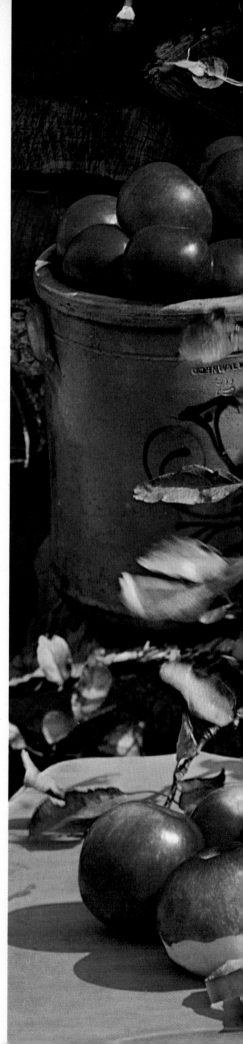

Honey-Apple Pie — *recipe on page 115*

LEMON MERINGUE PIE

1½ cups sugar
⅓ cup cornstarch
1½ cups water
3 egg yolks, slightly beaten
3 tbsp. butter
¼ cup lemon juice
1 tbsp. grated lemon rind
9-inch baked pie shell
3 egg whites
¼ tsp. cream of tartar
6 tbsp. sugar

Heat oven to 400 degrees.

Mix 1½ cups sugar and cornstarch in saucepan. Gradually stir in water. Cook over medium heat, stirring constantly, until mixture thickens and boils. Boil 1 minute.

Stir about half of the mixture slowly into egg yolks. Pour egg yolk mixture back into saucepan, blending thoroughly. Boil 1 minute, stirring constantly. Remove from heat and stir until smooth.

Blend in butter, lemon juice and lemon rind. Pour into baked pie shell.

Beat egg whites and cream of tartar until frothy. Beat in 6 tbsp. sugar, a little at a time, beating well after each addition. Beat until stiff and glossy.

Pile on to hot pie filling. Seal carefully to edge of crust. Bake 8 to 10 minutes until delicately browned. Cool before serving.

CREAMY PUMPKIN PIE

Pastry for 1-crust 9-inch pie
1¾ cups canned pumpkin
15-oz. can sweetened condensed milk
1 large egg
½ tsp. salt
½ tsp. cinnamon
¼ tsp. nutmeg
¼ tsp. cloves
¼ tsp. ginger
1 cup hot water

Heat oven to 375 degrees. Line pie pan with pastry, building up a high fluted edge. Do not prick.

Beat remaining ingredients together with rotary beater. Pour into pastry-lined pan. Bake 50 to 55 minutes, until knife inserted in side of filling comes out clean. Serve cold.

PUMPKIN PIE

Pastry for 1-crust 9-inch pie
Melted butter
½ cup coarsely-chopped pecans
2 tbsp. red currant jelly
1¾ cups canned pumpkin
1 cup brown sugar, packed
1 tbsp. molasses
½ tsp. salt
1¼ tsp. cinnamon
½ tsp. ginger
½ tsp. nutmeg
16-oz. can evaporated milk (tall can)
3 eggs
Sweetened whipped cream
Pecan halves

Heat oven to 425 degrees.

Roll pastry thin and line 9-inch pie pan, leaving 1 inch hanging over edge. Fold this extra pastry under and crimp, building up sides as much as possible.

Brush bottom of crust with melted butter. Sprinkle with chopped pecans and dot with red currant jelly.

Combine pumpkin, sugar, molasses, salt, cinnamon, ginger, nutmeg, evaporated milk and eggs in a large bowl. Beat with rotary beater until smooth. Pour into prepared shell.

Put a narrow strip of aluminum foil around the pie to keep the crimped edge from getting too brown.

Bake 45 to 55 minutes or until a knife inserted near the edge of the filling comes out clean. The centre should still be a little soft. Cool. Serve garnished with whipped cream and pecan halves.

SHOOFLY PIE

9-inch unbaked pie shell
1 tsp. soda
⅔ cup boiling water
⅔ cup molasses
⅓ cup butter
½ cup brown sugar, packed
1½ cups sifted all-purpose flour
½ cup raisins
Sweetened whipped cream

Heat oven to 350 degrees.

Prepare pie shell from your favorite recipe or pie crust mix. Do not prick.

Dissolve soda in boiling water. Stir in molasses.

Mix butter, sugar and flour to make a crumbly mixture. Sprinkle some of crumbly mixture in pie shell.

Pour over part of molasses mixture and sprinkle with some of raisins. Repeat layers until all is used, ending with crumbly mixture.

Bake 30 minutes until filling is browned and firm.

Serve slightly warm with whipped cream.

SOUR CREAM PIE

Pastry for 1-crust 9-inch pie
3 eggs
1½ tbsp. flour
¾ cup brown sugar, packed
½ tsp. salt
3 tsp. cinnamon
¾ tsp. cloves
1½ cups commercial sour cream
1½ cups seeded raisins, cut in halves

Heat oven to 350 degrees.

Line 9-inch pie pan with pastry and flute edge.

Beat eggs until very fluffy and light-colored (if using electric mixer, use small bowl).

Mix flour, sugar, salt, cinnamon and cloves together and blend them into eggs.

Fold in cream and raisins. Pour into pastry-lined pan and bake 50 to 60 minutes or until a silver knife inserted 1 inch from the side of the filling comes out clean.

Serve slightly warm or cold.

When the main course is over it's time for deserving desserts

PECAN PIE

3 eggs
²/₃ cup sugar
¹/₂ tsp. salt
¹/₃ cup butter, melted
³/₄ cup corn syrup
¹/₄ cup maple syrup
1 cup pecan halves
9-inch unbaked pie shell

Heat oven to 350 degrees.

Beat eggs, sugar, salt, butter, corn syrup and maple syrup together.

Place pecans in bottom of unbaked pie shell and pour in sugar mixture.

Bake about 50 minutes or until filling is set and pastry is browned. Cool.

STRAWBERRY-LEMON TARTS

Pastry for 2-crust pie
8-oz. pkg. cream cheese
2 tbsp. cream
2 tsp. grated lemon rind
Toasted slivered almonds
Strawberry Sauce (recipe follows)

Heat oven to 475 degrees.

Roll out pastry very thin and cut eighteen 3-inch rounds. Place on cookie sheet and prick. Bake 5 to 8 minutes until golden brown. Cool.

Beat softened cream cheese and cream together until light and fluffy. Stir in lemon rind.

Put pastry rounds together in threes with cream cheese mixture between and a dab on top. Sprinkle with toasted slivered almonds.

Place on cookie sheet and return to oven for 3 minutes to warm cheese.

Serve warm with Strawberry Sauce. (Makes 6.)

Strawberry Sauce

15-oz. pkg. frozen strawberries, thawed
¹/₄ tsp. almond extract
1 tsp. grated lemon rind

Stir all ingredients together.

APRICOT TARTS

2 cups sifted all-purpose flour
¹/₂ tsp. salt
¹/₂ cup sifted icing sugar
1 tsp. baking powder
³/₄ cup shortening (part butter)
1 egg
1 tbsp. milk
Apricot Filling (recipe follows)
Marshmallow Topping (recipe follows)
Candied cherries

Heat oven to 425 degrees.

Sift flour, salt, icing sugar and baking powder together into bowl. Add shortening and cut in coarsely.

Beat egg and milk together with a fork. Add to flour mixture and blend lightly with fork until dough sticks together and leaves sides of bowl.

Form dough into small balls, about 1 inch in diameter, and press into 36 small (2-inch) tart tins, pressing to sides to form shells. Prick bottoms of shells.

Bake about 10 minutes, or until nicely browned. Cool on cake rack.

Fill with Apricot Filling and top with a spoonful of Marshmallow Topping. Decorate with a small piece of candied cherry. (Makes 36 small tarts.)

Apricot Filling

¹/₂ lb. dried apricots (about 2 cups, packed)
1¹/₂ cups water
³/₄ cup sugar
Juice of ¹/₂ lemon
Pinch of salt

Cut apricots into small pieces. Combine with water in a saucepan, bring to a boil, turn down heat and simmer until mushy. Press through coarse sieve (or use a blender if you have one) to form a purée.

Return to saucepan, add sugar, lemon juice and salt and heat, stirring, until sugar is dissolved and mixture is thick.

Marshmallow Topping

¹/₄ cup lemon gelatin
¹/₄ cup boiling water
1 egg white
³/₄ cup sugar
2¹/₂ tbsp. water
1 tsp. corn syrup
Pinch of salt

Dissolve gelatin in boiling water and set aside.

Combine egg white, sugar, water, corn syrup and salt in the top of a double boiler. Set over boiling water and cook, beating constantly with a rotary beater, about 5 minutes or until mixture holds firm peaks. Beat in gelatin mixture.

Remove from heat and continue beating until mixture cools and forms peaks.

QUICK AMBROSIA TARTS

4¹/₄-oz. pkg. orange pie filling
2 egg whites
¹/₄ cup sugar
1 tbsp. grated orange rind
1 cup shredded coconut
Thirty-two 3-inch baked tart shells
Sweetened whipped cream (optional)

Prepare orange pie filling as directed on package. Cool.

Beat egg whites until frothy. Add sugar gradually and continue beating until mixture is glossy and holds firm peaks. Fold in prepared pie filling, orange rind and coconut.

Spoon 2 tbsp. of mixture into each tart shell and chill until about 20 minutes from serving time. (Both pastry and filling will taste better if allowed to warm up slightly before eating.)

Top with sweetened whipped cream at serving time. (Makes 32 tarts.)

Note: If desired, make half of orange mixture into tarts and serve remainder as pudding.

119

STRAWBERRY CREAM TARTS

Pastry for 2-crust 9-inch pie
3¼-oz. pkg. vanilla pudding mix
   (cooked type)
1½ cups milk
   ½ cup whipping cream
   2 tbsp. cornstarch
   ½ cup sugar
   1 cup strawberries, cut up
   1 tbsp. grated orange rind
   2 tbsp. orange juice
   1 cup whole strawberries

Heat oven to 475 degrees.

Roll pastry very thin and cut 60 rounds with a 2¼-inch cookie cutter. Put 1 round in bottom of each of ten 2¾-inch muffin cups. Overlap 5 more rounds around the sides of each cup, moistening where they overlap and pressing together. Prick well with the tines of a fork.

Bake 8 to 10 minutes until lightly browned. Cool.

Make vanilla pudding as directed on package, using 1½ cups milk. Chill. Whip cream stiff and fold into pudding. Spoon into baked tart shells. Chill.

Combine cornstarch and sugar in saucepan. Add cut-up berries, orange rind and orange juice. Cook over low heat, mashing berries and stirring until thick and clear. Cool slightly.

Put whole berries on top of vanilla pudding in tart shells. Spoon cornstarch mixture over. Chill. (Makes 10 large.)

Note: If desired, food coloring may be added to the pastry along with the liquid to make pink or pale green petal tart shells.

APPLE STRUDEL

2½ cups sifted all-purpose flour
   ½ tsp. salt
   2 eggs, slightly beaten
   3 tbsp. cooking (salad) oil
   ½ cup lukewarm water
   Flour
   ¼ cup melted butter
   ¼ cup butter
1½ cups fine dry bread crumbs
1½ cups ground walnuts
   5 cups coarsely-grated
      peeled apples

Grated rind of 2 lemons
   1 cup seedless raisins
   ½ cup sugar
   1 tsp. cinnamon
   Melted butter
   Icing sugar

Sift flour and salt into a large bowl. Make a well in the centre and pour in eggs and oil. Add water gradually, stirring constantly with a fork. Dough will be fairly soft and sticky. Continue mixing with fork until dough becomes firmer and leaves the sides of the bowl.

Knead the dough in the bowl for 10 to 15 minutes or until it is very smooth and elastic. Pick it up and slap it down into the bowl or on a board often. (Dough won't stick to hands or bowl when it is kneaded enough.)

Shape into a ball, put back into bowl and cover with a towel which has been wrung out in hot water. Set in a warm place and let it rest 1 hour.

Cover a table at least 36 x 30 inches (if you don't have a kitchen table a card table will do) with a clean smooth cloth. (I use an old sheet.) The table must be away from the wall so you can move all around it.

Sprinkle the cloth lightly with flour and rub it in very well. Brush off all excess.

Warm rolling pin in warming oven or oven turned to lowest temperature.

Put dough in centre of cloth and start rolling, turning and lifting often so it doesn't stick. Roll it as thin as possible, about ⅛ inch.

Flour backs of hands lightly. Slip hands under dough (palms down and fingers turned under). Lift and stretch dough with backs of hands, working from centre and stretching toward the outside. Work carefully keeping knuckles down so they do not puncture the dough.

Move around the table as the dough stretches so each part is stretched as thin as possible but no part is strained too much. (Don't worry if, by accident, you make a few small holes — they can be patched.) Continue stretching the dough this way until it is tissue-paper thin and transparent. (The dough is surprisingly elastic and this is not as difficult as it sounds.)

Stretch until dough is hanging over the edges of the table and is a rectangle about 40 inches long and 30 to 36 inches wide. Trim off thick edges. (There will still be 2 inches or so hanging down from table.) Patch main part of dough with bits of these trimmings if necessary.

Brush entire surface of dough with melted butter.

Melt remaining butter in heavy skillet. Add crumbs and heat gently, stirring, until crumbs are golden.

Standing at long side of rectangle of dough, sprinkle middle third of dough with crumbs, spreading them evenly with hand. (Ignore edges of dough hanging down over table; these will be folded in later.) Sprinkle ground nuts on top of crumbs and spread evenly again.

Combine grated apples, lemon rind and raisins and sprinkle evenly over nuts. Mix sugar and cinnamon and sprinkle over all.

Fold in edges of dough hanging down over table on long sides of rectangle. Standing at one long side of rectangle, fold right-hand third of dough over filling. Fold left-hand third of dough over preceding fold. You should now have a rectangle the width of the table one way and the width of the filling the other.

Roll up like a jelly roll from one of the wide sides. Lift on to well-greased cookie sheet and turn to shape into a "U". Brush with melted butter.

Heat oven to 375 degrees. Bake strudel until golden brown, about 40 minutes. Sift icing sugar over top while hot and serve warm cut into 1½-inch slices.

Gâteau Saint-Honoré — *recipe on page 123*

Surprisingly simple but somewhat on the sensational side

CREAM PUFFS

1 cup water
1/2 cup butter
1 cup sifted all-purpose flour
4 eggs
Sweetened whipped cream
Icing sugar

Heat oven to 400 degrees.

Put water and butter in medium-size saucepan. Set over high heat and bring to a full rolling boil. Turn heat to low.

Add flour all at once and stir vigorously until mixture leaves sides of pan and forms into a ball (about 1 minute). Remove from heat.

Add eggs, one at a time, beating well after each addition. Continue beating until mixture is smooth and velvety in appearance.

Drop mixture by large spoonfuls on ungreased cookie sheet, making 8 to 12 mounds. Leave 3 inches between mounds.

Bake 45 to 50 minutes or until puffed, golden brown and dry and firm to touch. Cool on cake rack.

Cut tops from puffs at serving time. Pull any moist filaments from inside. Fill with sweetened whipped cream. Replace tops and sift icing sugar over. (Makes 8 to 12.)

PRALINE PUFFS

Cream Puffs (recipe p. 122)
Praline Filling (recipe follows)
Chocolate Glaze (recipe p. 93)

Prepare Cream Puffs as directed in recipe except drop the dough by heaping tablespoonfuls on ungreased cookie sheet, making 16 mounds of dough. Leave 2 inches around each mound to give dough room to puff. Bake about 45 minutes or until golden and firm to touch. Cool.

Cut a slit in the side of each puff shortly before serving time and fill with Praline Filling. Spread tops with Chocolate Glaze and sprinkle with almond mixture left over from making Praline Filling. Serve as soon as possible after filling. (Makes 16 small.)

Praline Filling

1/2 cup coarsely-chopped
    blanched almonds
1/2 cup sugar
2 tbsp. water
3 1/4-oz. pkg. vanilla pudding mix
    (cooked type)
1/4 tsp. almond extract
1/2 cup whipping cream

Heat oven to 350 degrees.

Spread almonds in a single layer on a baking sheet. Toast about 10 minutes or until golden, stirring often.

Boil sugar and water together in a small saucepan over moderate heat, shaking the pan often, until the sugar caramelizes and is golden brown. Add almonds, stir and bring back to a boil. Pour out on cookie sheet immediately, spreading thin.

Cool. Mixture should be brittle. Break up and put through the fine blade of the food chopper.

Prepare vanilla pudding mix according to package directions. Cool. Stir in almond extract. Just before filling puffs, whip cream until stiff and fold into pudding along with 1 cup of almond mixture. (Save remaining almond mixture to sprinkle on top of puffs.)

ORANGE CREAM PUFFS

Cream Puffs (recipe p. 122)
Grated rind of 1 orange
Orange Cream (recipe follows)
Orange Glaze (recipe follows)
Grated orange rind (optional)

Prepare Cream Puffs as directed in recipe *except* add grated rind of 1 orange with last egg.

Drop and bake dough as directed for Cream Puffs making 12 mounds.

Cut tops from puffs at serving time. Pull out any moist filaments and fill with Orange Cream. Replace tops and spoon a little Orange Glaze on top of each. (Glaze should be thin enough to run a little.) Sprinkle with grated orange rind if desired. (Makes 12.)

Orange Cream

7 1/2-oz. pkg. lemon pie filling
2 eggs, lightly beaten
1/2 cup orange juice
2 tsp. grated orange rind
1/2 pt. whipping cream

Prepare lemon pie filling as directed on the package, *except* use the 2 whole eggs instead of egg yolks and replace 1/2 cup of liquid called for with the 1/2 cup orange juice. Cool.

Stir in grated orange rind.

Whip cream until stiff and fold into lemon-orange mixture. Fill Cream Puffs as directed.

Orange Glaze

1 1/2 cups sifted icing sugar
1 egg yolk
2 tsp. grated orange rind
1 1/2 tbsp. orange juice (approx.)

Combine sugar, egg yolk, orange rind and enough orange juice to make a rather thin icing.

STRAWBERRY DESSERT PANCAKES

8-oz. pkg. cream cheese
2 tbsp. light cream
2 tbsp. sugar
2 tsp. grated orange rind
1/4 cup butter
1/2 cup sifted icing sugar
1/2 cup orange juice
2 cups sliced strawberries
Thin Pancakes (recipe follows)

Put cheese and cream in the top of a double boiler and set over simmering water, heating just until well blended and of spreading consistency. Add 2 tbsp. sugar and grated orange rind.

Combine butter, 1/2 cup icing sugar and orange juice in a small saucepan and heat gently until hot and well blended. Keep warm. Stir strawberries into this mixture at serving time.

Spread a large spoonful of cheese mixture on each pancake at serving time. Roll up and spoon some of strawberry mixture over. (Serves 4 — 2 per serving.)

Thin Pancakes

1 cup flour
¼ cup icing sugar
½ tsp. salt
2 eggs
1 cup milk

Sift flour, icing sugar and salt together. Beat eggs and milk well and stir in dry ingredients. Cover and let stand 30 minutes.

Grease a heavy skillet or griddle lightly and heat.

Pour on ¼ cup batter and spread it to 5 to 6 inches in diameter. Cook one side and turn carefully to brown second side. Keep warm between the folds of a towel in a warm oven until all are baked. (Makes 8.)

GÂTEAU SAINT-HONORÉ

¼ cup soft butter
¼ cup sugar
 Dash salt
1 egg yolk
½ tsp. almond extract
1 cup sifted all-purpose flour
¾ cup water
6 tbsp. butter
¾ cup sifted all-purpose flour
3 eggs
1 egg yolk
1 tbsp. cold water
 Vanilla Cream Filling (recipe follows)
½ cup whipping cream
1 tbsp. icing sugar
¼ tsp. vanilla
 Caramel Syrup (recipe follows)

Beat ¼ cup butter, sugar, salt and egg yolk together until light and fluffy. Beat in almond extract.

Add 1 cup flour and mix with a wooden spoon until well blended. (If very dry add a few drops cold water.)

Gather dough into a ball, wrap in waxed paper and chill at least 1 hour.

Heat oven to 375 degrees.

Work dough with hands until pliable again then roll into a 9-inch circle on floured pastry cloth. Slip on to ungreased cookie sheet, prick in several places and bake about 15 minutes or until light golden brown.

Cool on sheet a few minutes, then slip off on to cake rack and cool.

Heat oven to 400 degrees.

Combine water and 6 tbsp. butter in saucepan. Bring to a full rolling boil. Add ¾ cup flour all at once and stir vigorously over low heat until mixture leaves the sides of the pan and forms into a ball, about 1 minute.

Remove from heat. Add eggs one at a time, beating well after each addition and continuing to beat until smooth and velvety. Spoon paste into pastry tube or bag. Pipe a ring of the paste about 1 inch wide in a 9-inch circle on ungreased cookie sheet or inside 9-inch layer cake pan (see black and white photos). Force remaining paste through tube in little mounds about the size of small walnuts on small cookie sheet or bottom of cake pan (see black and white photos). You should have 10 to 14 small mounds.

Beat egg yolk and cold water together with fork and brush over ring.

Bake little puffs about 25 minutes or until well browned and firm to the touch. Take them out of the oven and continue baking the ring for about 20 minutes more or until dark golden brown and firm to the touch. Cool little puffs and ring on cake racks.

Make Vanilla Cream Filling about 2 hours before serving time. Cool but do not chill.

Whip cream, icing sugar and vanilla until stiff and make Caramel Syrup about 1½ hours before serving time.

Assemble cake in the following manner about 1 hour before serving time. Lay sweet pastry round on serving plate. Spoon a little of the Caramel Syrup on to the pastry near the outside edge. Set cream-puff ring on top.

Make a small hole in the side of each small puff and pipe sweetened whipped cream into each. Dip the bottom of puffs in Caramel Syrup and set them close together on top of the ring. Drizzle a little of the Caramel Syrup over the top of each puff. Pour thickened (but not set) Vanilla Cream Filling into centre of cake. Chill about 1 hour. Cut in wedges to serve. (Serves 8.)

QUICK TRICKS FOR GÂTEAU SAINT-HONORÉ

For cream puff ring, pipe paste one inch wide in a nine-inch circle on ungreased cookie sheet, or for a more exact size, inside a layer cake pan.

For little puffs, pipe paste in little mounds on small cookie sheet or on bottom of cake pan. Bake both ring and puffs at the same time.

Vanilla Cream Filling

½ cup sugar
2 tbsp. cornstarch
¼ tsp. salt
2 cups milk
3 egg yolks, lightly beaten
1 envelope (1 tbsp.) unflavored
  gelatin
2 tbsp. cold water
2 tsp. vanilla
3 egg whites
3 tbsp. icing sugar

Combine sugar, cornstarch and salt in saucepan. Add milk gradually, stirring until smooth. Set over moderate heat and cook and stir until mixture thickens and boils. Boil 1 minute.

Add half of hot mixture gradually to egg yolks, stirring constantly. Return to pan and boil 1 minute. Remove from heat.

Soak gelatin in cold water 5 minutes. Add to hot mixture and stir until dissolved. Cool. Do not chill. Stir in vanilla.

Beat egg whites until frothy. Add icing sugar gradually and continue beating until stiff and glossy. Fold into cooled cream. Pour into centre of assembled cake as directed above.

Caramel Syrup

¾ cup sugar
½ cup boiling water

Put sugar in large heavy skillet and set over moderate heat. Cook, stirring often, until syrupy and golden. Remove from heat and add boiling water (be careful of the steam). Return to moderate heat and cook and stir until sugar melts again, then continue to boil until syrupy.

APPLE TART

1 cup sifted all-purpose flour
¼ tsp. salt
2 tbsp. sugar
½ cup butter
1 tbsp. white vinegar
1 cup sugar
2 tbsp. flour
½ tsp. cinnamon
3 cups coarsely-grated apples
Icing sugar
Sweetened whipped cream
  (optional)

Heat oven to 400 degrees. Have ready 9-inch spring-form pan.

Combine 1 cup flour, salt and 2 tbsp. sugar lightly with a fork. Cut in butter and then blend with a fork until mixture looks like a shortbread dough. Stir in vinegar with fork.

Spread dough thickly on the bottom of spring-form pan and thinly about 1 inch up the sides. (I use a rubber scraper to spread the dough and then pat it evenly with my hand.)

Combine 1 cup sugar, 2 tbsp. flour, cinnamon and apples and spread evenly over the dough.

Bake 1 hour. Remove from oven, cool and remove from pan. Sift icing sugar over top. Pipe whipped cream on top at serving time, if desired.

BRANDY BASKETS

1 cup sifted all-purpose flour
1 cup finely-chopped walnuts
½ cup corn syrup
½ cup shortening
⅔ cup brown sugar, packed
Vanilla ice cream
Honey-Orange Sauce (recipe
  follows)

Heat oven to 375 degrees. Grease the outside of four 5-oz. custard cups.

Blend flour and nuts together.

Combine syrup, shortening and sugar in saucepan, set over moderate heat and bring to a boil, stirring constantly.

Remove from heat and gradually blend in flour-nuts mixture.

Drop by level tablespoonfuls 3 inches apart on lightly-greased cookie sheet (see note below).

TO SHAPE BRANDY BASKETS

Let baked mixture stand on cookie sheet till each can be lifted (about 3 minutes). Try them every few seconds after the first 2 minutes of cooling.

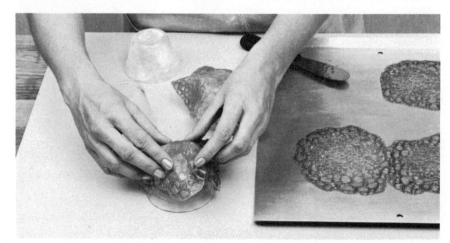

Shape mixture into baskets by moulding it around the outside of some greased 5-oz. custard cups.

Bake 6 minutes or until outside edges are browned but centre still seems soft.

Let stand on sheet about 3 minutes or just until they can be lifted off the sheet (check them every few seconds after the first 2 minutes so they don't get too hard). Shape each into a basket by moulding around the greased custard cups (see black and white photos). Lift off and set on racks as they cool so cups will be ready for next batch.

Set each basket on a plate at serving time and fill with a scoop of ice cream. Top with warm Honey-Orange Sauce. (Makes 24.)

Note: It is very important to shape the baskets at just the right moment since they will get too hard quickly, but will tear apart if too hot. I suggest trying them one at a time at first — just until you are sure you can handle them. Then bake no more than 4 at a time. If they do get too hard they can be softened by returning them to the oven for a minute.

Variation: If you would like to make some baskets and some cookies, make the baskets first so you will be sure you have the number you need for dessert. The remaining mixture can then be dropped on aluminum foil and baked slightly longer than for the baskets, about 8 minutes. Cool on the foil until it can be peeled off easily, about 4 minutes.

Honey-Orange Sauce

1 cup orange juice
1 cup liquid honey
1 cup brown sugar
1 cup chopped nuts
¼ cup butter
1 tsp. grated orange rind
¼ tsp. salt
½ tsp. almond extract
¼ tsp. vanilla

Combine orange juice, honey and brown sugar in saucepan. Bring to a boil and boil until mixture forms a soft ball in cold water, about 15 minutes. Remove from heat and stir in remaining ingredients. Serve warm over vanilla ice cream in Brandy Baskets.

Puddings

BAKED PRUNE WHIP

1 cup finely cut-up cooked
   prunes
3 egg whites
1/3 cup sugar
1/4 tsp. salt
1 tbsp. lemon juice
1/4 cup chopped pecans
  Soft Custard (recipe p. 130)

Heat oven to 350 degrees.

Beat prunes, egg whites, sugar and salt together until stiff enough to hold shape. Fold in lemon juice and pecans.

Pour into 6 custard cups and set in a pan of hot water (1 inch deep).

Bake until puffed and lightly browned, about 20 minutes.

Serve topped with Soft Custard. (Serves 6.)

EASY SUNSHINE SOUFFLÉ

3 egg whites
Pinch salt
3 tbsp. sugar
2 tbsp. orange marmalade (chop
   fruit before measuring)
1 tbsp. grated orange rind
1 tsp. grated lemon rind
2 egg yolks
1/4 cup sifted icing sugar
1 tsp. vanilla
1/2 cup whipping cream, whipped
  Toasted slivered almonds
   (optional)

Butter inside of top pan and lid of 2-qt. double boiler thoroughly.

Beat egg whites and salt in a small bowl until frothy. Beat in 3 tbsp. sugar gradually and beat until stiff.

Fold in orange marmalade, orange rind and lemon rind.

Spoon into prepared top of double boiler, cover and set over boiling water. Cook 1 hour without lifting lid. Turn off heat and let stand over water until serving time (not more than 30 minutes).

Beat egg yolks lightly. Beat in sugar and vanilla. Whip cream and fold into egg yolk mixture at serving time.

Turn hot soufflé out on hot serving dish or spoon into individual dishes at serving time. Serve immediately with whipped cream mixture spooned over and sprinkled with almonds. (Serves 4.)

BAKED CRANBERRY PUDDING

1 cup fresh cranberries
1 cup seedless raisins
1/2 cup sugar
1/4 cup soft butter
2/3 cup sugar
1 egg
1 1/4 cups sifted all-purpose flour
1/2 tsp. salt
2 tsp. baking powder
1/3 cup milk
1/2 cup chopped almonds
  Vivian's Pudding Sauce
   (recipe follows)

Wash and drain cranberries. Put raisins and cranberries through food chopper, using medium blade. Add 1/2 cup sugar, stir well and let stand at room temperature 1 hour.

Heat oven to 350 degrees. Grease an 8-inch square cake pan.

Cream butter and 2/3 cup sugar. Add egg and beat thoroughly.

Sift flour, salt and baking powder together and add to creamed mixture alternately with milk. Stir in fruit and almonds, blending well.

Spoon into prepared pan and bake 40 to 45 minutes or until top springs back when touched lightly in the centre. Cut in squares to serve. Serve warm with Vivian's Pudding Sauce. (Serves 6 to 9.)

Vivian's Pudding Sauce

1/2 cup butter
1/2 cup sugar
1/2 cup brown sugar, packed
2 egg whites
1 tsp. vanilla
1/2 cup whipping cream

Combine butter, sugar and brown sugar in top of double boiler. Set over boiling water and stir until blended.

Beat egg whites until stiff peaks form and fold into sugar mixture. Continue cooking over boiling water until sugar is all melted (graininess disappears and mixture appears syrupy), stirring occasionally. Cool. Stir in vanilla. Chill.

Stir to blend at serving time. Whip cream until stiff and fold in. Serve over Baked Cranberry Pudding. (Makes 2 cups.)

CRUMB PUDDING

1 cup very fine dry bread crumbs
1 cup buttermilk OR sour milk
1/4 cup soft shortening
1 cup brown sugar, packed
1/4 cup molasses
1 egg
1/2 cup sifted all-purpose flour
1 tsp. soda
1 tsp. nutmeg
1/2 tsp. cloves
1/2 tsp. cinnamon
1/2 tsp. salt
1 cup finely-chopped dates
1/2 cup finely-chopped nuts
  Fluffy Sauce (recipe follows)

Put crumbs in small bowl (be sure they are fine). Add milk, stir to blend and let stand 1 hour.

Heat oven to 300 degrees. Grease a 9-inch square cake pan at least 2 inches deep. Put a pan with some hot water in it in the bottom of the oven.

Beat shortening, sugar, molasses and egg together until well blended.

Sift dry ingredients together into mixture and stir to blend. Add crumbs-milk mixture and beat until smooth. Stir in dates and nuts.

Pour into prepared pan and bake about 45 minutes or until set. Serve hot topped with Fluffy Sauce. (Serves 9.)

Fluffy Sauce

2 egg yolks
1/3 cup melted butter
1 1/2 cups sifted icing sugar
1 tsp. vanilla
2-oz. pkg. dessert topping mix

Beat egg yolks in small bowl until foamy. Blend in butter, icing sugar and vanilla.

Prepare dessert topping mix according to package directions at serving time. Fold into first mixture. Spoon over servings of hot pudding.

JIFFY PUDDING

1 cup sifted all-purpose flour
2 tsp. baking powder
1/4 tsp. salt
1/2 tsp. nutmeg
1/2 cup brown sugar, packed
1/2 cup milk
1 cup raisins
2 tsp. soft butter
1 cup brown sugar, packed
1 3/4 cups boiling water

Heat oven to 350 degrees. Butter a 1 1/2-qt. casserole.

Sift flour, baking powder, salt and nutmeg into bowl. Add 1/2 cup brown sugar and stir in milk and raisins. Spoon into casserole. Dot with butter.

Sprinkle with 1 cup brown sugar.

Pour boiling water over all. Do not stir. Put in oven at once. (During baking batter will rise to top and sauce will be on bottom.)

Bake about 45 minutes or until well browned and set. (Serves 6.)

CARROT PUDDING

1 cup grated raw carrots
1 cup grated raw potatoes
1 cup chopped suet
1 cup raisins
1 cup currants
1/4 cup mixed peel
1 1/2 cups sifted all-purpose flour
1 tsp. salt
1 tsp. soda
1/2 tsp. cinnamon
1/2 tsp. nutmeg
1/2 tsp. cloves
1 cup brown sugar, packed
Grated rind and juice of 1 lemon
1 egg, beaten
2 tbsp. milk
Lemon Sauce (recipe follows)

Combine carrots, potatoes, suet and fruit in a large bowl.

Measure flour, salt, soda and spices into sifter and sift together over fruit. Add brown sugar and blend well.

Add lemon rind and juice, egg and milk. Blend well.

Spoon into well-greased 1 1/2-qt. pudding pan or mould. Cover with foil.

Steam 4 hours. (Serves 10.)

To make grinding easy and juiceless, try freezing fresh cranberries before putting them through the chopper.

Lemon Sauce

1 cup sugar
2 eggs
1/2 cup butter
Grated rind and juice of 1 lemon
1/2 cup boiling water

Measure sugar into saucepan. Add eggs and beat thoroughly with a wooden spoon. Add butter and lemon rind and juice. Stir in boiling water gradually. Set over moderate heat and cook and stir until thick and smooth. Serve hot.

STEAMED CRANBERRY PUDDING

1/2 cup molasses
1/2 cup boiling water
2 tsp. soda
1 1/2 cups sifted all-purpose flour
1 tsp. baking powder
1/2 tsp. salt
1 cup whole fresh cranberries
Butter Sauce (recipe follows)

Combine molasses, boiling water and soda. Stir to blend and let cool to lukewarm.

Sift flour, baking powder and salt together into cooled mixture. Stir to blend. Stir in cranberries.

Put in 1-qt. greased mould. Cover loosely with foil. Steam 1 1/2 hours. Serve hot with Butter Sauce. (Serves 6 to 8.)

Butter Sauce

1/2 cup sugar
1/2 cup light cream
1/4 cup butter

Combine all ingredients in small saucepan. Simmer 15 minutes. Serve hot over Steamed Cranberry Pudding.

ST. JAMES PUDDING

1 cup molasses
1 cup buttermilk OR sour milk
1 cup suet
2 cups sifted all-purpose flour
1 tsp. soda
1 tsp. cinnamon
1 tsp. ginger
1/2 tsp. salt
Brown Sugar Sauce (recipe follows)

Blend molasses, milk and suet.

Add sifted dry ingredients and pour into shallow 1 1/2-qt. baking dish or pudding pan.

Steam 1 hour. (If you use a deep dish, use one with a tube in the centre, or steam for an extra half-hour to be sure pudding is done.)

Serve with Brown Sugar Sauce.

Brown Sugar Sauce

1 cup brown sugar, packed
2 tbsp. soft butter
2 egg yolks
1 tsp. vanilla
2 egg whites

Beat sugar, butter, egg yolks and vanilla well.

Beat egg whites stiff and fold into sugar mixture.

CHEESECAKE

1/2 cup fine Zwieback or graham wafer crumbs
1 tbsp. sugar
1/4 tsp. cinnamon
1/4 tsp. nutmeg
5 eggs
1 cup sugar
8-oz. carton cottage cheese
Two 8-oz. pkg. cream cheese (room temperature)
Grated rind and juice of 1 lemon
1 cup commercial sour cream
1/2 cup toasted slivered almonds
Raspberry Sauce (recipe follows)

Heat oven to 350 degrees. Butter generously an 8- or 9-inch spring-form pan (or use a 9-inch layer pan with sides built up with aluminum foil).

Mix crumbs, 1 tbsp. sugar and spices.

Dust the bottom and sides of pan with the crumb mixture.

Beat eggs until thick and lemon-colored and beat in sugar gradually. *Recipe continued on next page*

Press cottage cheese through a sieve and add along with cream cheese. Beat until thick and smooth. Stir in lemon rind and juice.

Pour into crumb-lined pan and bake 1 hour or until set.

Remove from oven and increase oven temperature to 450 degrees.

Spread sour cream over top and sprinkle with almonds. Bake 5 minutes more. Cool. Serve with Raspberry Sauce. Best served the day it's made. (Serves 12 to 16.)

Raspberry Sauce

15-oz. pkg. frozen raspberries, thawed
4 tsp. cornstarch
¼ cup sugar
1 tbsp. butter
2 tbsp. lemon juice
¼ cup port

Force raspberries through a sieve to remove seeds. Mix cornstarch and sugar in saucepan.

Stir in raspberry purée and cook, stirring constantly until mixture boils.

Remove from heat, add butter and stir until melted. Add lemon juice and port. Chill. Makes 2 cups.)

UNBAKED CHEESECAKE

⅔ cup graham wafer crumbs
2 tbsp. butter, melted
1 tbsp. sugar
¼ tsp. cinnamon
¼ tsp. nutmeg
20-oz. can crushed pineapple
2 envelopes (2 tbsp.) unflavored gelatin
½ cup sugar
Pinch of salt
2 egg yolks, well beaten
2 tbsp. lemon juice
1 tsp. grated lemon rind
Two 8-oz. cartons cream-style cottage cheese
2 egg whites
¼ cup sugar
1 cup whipping cream

Mix graham wafer crumbs, melted butter, 1 tbsp. sugar and spices. Press into bottom of spring-form pan.

Drain pineapple thoroughly. Measure out ¾ cup juice and 1 cup pineapple.

Blend the ¾ cup pineapple juice, gelatin, ½ cup sugar and salt in top of double boiler. Stir until sugar is dissolved. Stir in egg yolks.

Place over simmering water and cook, stirring constantly, until gelatin dissolves and mixture thickens slightly (about 5 minutes).

Remove from heat and stir in lemon juice and rind and the 1 cup drained pineapple. Cool.

Press cottage cheese through a sieve into a large bowl. Stir in cooled gelatin mixture. Set bowl in ice water and cool until mixture begins to set.

Beat egg whites until frothy, then add ¼ cup sugar a little at a time, beating well after each addition and continuing to beat until stiff. Fold into cheese mixture. Whip cream stiff and fold into cheese mixture.

Pour into spring-form pan on top of crumb mixture. Chill until firm, 4 to 6 hours. (Serves 12 to 16.)

PUMPKIN CHEESECAKE

1½ cups ginger wafer crumbs
⅓ cup melted butter
6 egg yolks
Two 8-oz. pkg. cream cheese (room temperature)
1¾ cups canned pumpkin
15-oz. can sweetened condensed milk
1¼ tsp. cinnamon
½ tsp. ginger
½ tsp. nutmeg
½ tsp. salt
6 egg whites
1 cup commercial sour cream
¼ cup brown sugar, packed
¼ cup chopped pecans

Heat oven to 350 degrees. Butter a 9-inch spring-form pan.

Mix ginger wafer crumbs and melted butter thoroughly. Pack firmly into bottom of spring-form pan and bake 15 minutes. Set aside while preparing filling.

Beat egg yolks at high speed until thick and lemon-colored in small mixer bowl (about 5 minutes). Add cheese and beat until smooth. Transfer mixture to large mixer bowl.

Add pumpkin, condensed milk, spices and salt and beat again until well blended.

Beat egg whites until stiff but not dry. Fold into pumpkin mixture.

Pour into spring-form pan on top of ginger crust. Bake 1 hour or until set.

Remove from oven and increase oven temperature to 450 degrees.

Combine sour cream and brown sugar and spread evenly on top of cheesecake. Sprinkle with pecans. Return to oven as soon as temperature reaches 450 degrees. Bake 5 minutes. Cool. Refrigerate until serving time. (Serves 12 to 16.)

DELUXE CHEESECAKE

1 cup sifted all-purpose flour
¼ cup sugar
½ cup butter
6 apples
½ cup sugar
½ tsp. cinnamon
Two 8-oz. pkg. cream cheese (room temperature)
3 egg yolks
½ cup sugar
1 tsp. vanilla
3 egg whites
Two 15-oz. cans prune plums
2 tbsp. cornstarch
⅓ cup sugar
Blue food coloring
Red food coloring

Heat oven to 350 degrees.

Sift flour and ¼ cup sugar together into a small bowl. Add butter and cut in with pastry blender or two knives until butter is very fine, then work with hands until thoroughly blended (looks like shortbread).

Pack dough into 9-inch spring-form pan, pressing into an even layer. Bake 20 minutes or until golden brown and set.

Peel, core and slice apples and place in saucepan with ½ cup sugar and cinnamon. Cover and cook without water until apples are very tender, stirring occasionally. Press through sieve.

Recipe continued on page 130

Orange-Lime Pudding — *recipe on page 130*

Spread on top of shortbread and return to oven for 10 minutes.

Cream cheese, egg yolks, 1/2 cup sugar and vanilla, and beat to blend.

Beat egg whites stiff and fold in. Spread over applesauce layer and return to oven until cheese mixture is set, about 30 minutes. Cool.

Drain plums thoroughly, saving juice. Cut plums in half carefully and remove stones. Set cut side down on paper towelling to dry.

Mix cornstarch and 1/3 cup sugar, and add enough of cold plum juice to make a smooth paste.

Bring 1 1/2 cups of the plum juice to a boil and add cornstarch mixture gradually, stirring constantly. Boil 1 minute. Add blue and red food coloring to make glaze a rich plum color. Cool.

Trim plum halves if necessary and arrange on top of cake, cut side down, in a design, using only halves which are firm and well shaped. Pour cooled glaze over, spreading to cover top of cake.

Chill until a few minutes before serving. (Serves 12 to 16.)

STRAWBERRY-CHEESE PIE

1 1/2 cups graham wafer crumbs
3 tbsp. sugar
1/3 cup butter, melted
Three 4-oz. pkg. cream cheese
   (room temperature)
1/2 cup sugar
3 egg yolks
1 tsp. vanilla
1/4 tsp. almond extract
3 egg whites
1 cup commercial sour cream
1 tbsp. sugar
1/2 tsp. vanilla
Sugared strawberries

Heat oven to 325 degrees.

Combine graham wafer crumbs, 3 tbsp. sugar and melted butter, mixing first with fork then with fingers until well blended. Press into 9-inch pie pan, building up sides well to hold filling.

Cream cheese, add 1/2 cup sugar and blend thoroughly. Add egg yolks one at a time beating well after each addition. Stir in 1 tsp. vanilla and almond extract.

Beat egg whites stiff and fold into cheese mixture, blending well. Pour into prepared graham wafer shell.

Bake about 50 minutes or until set and lightly browned. Increase oven temperature to 450 degrees.

Combine sour cream, sugar and 1/2 tsp. vanilla and spread over top of pie. Bake another 5 minutes.

Serve cold with sugared strawberries spooned over. (Serves 8.)

SOFT CUSTARD

1 1/2 cups milk
4 egg yolks
1/4 cup sugar
1/4 tsp. salt
1 1/2 tsp. vanilla

Scald milk in top of double boiler over direct heat.

Beat egg yolks in small bowl. Blend in sugar and salt. Gradually stir in scalded milk.

Return to top of double boiler and set over simmering water. Cook, stirring constantly, until mixture coats a silver spoon. Remove from heat and cool quickly. Blend in vanilla. Use as dessert or as sauce with fruit or cold puddings.

ORANGE-LIME PUDDING

2 1/2 cups graham wafer crumbs
1/4 cup sugar
1/2 cup butter, melted
1/2 cup coarsely-broken walnuts
1 1/2 cups sugar
Dash salt
1/3 cup cornstarch
1 3/4 cups orange juice
2 tbsp. fresh lime juice
4 egg yolks, lightly beaten
1 tbsp. grated orange rind
1/4 tsp. grated lime rind
4 egg whites
1/4 cup sugar
Orange sections (optional)

Heat oven to 350 degrees.

Combine graham wafer crumbs, 1/4 cup sugar and butter, blending well. Stir in walnuts. Spread on large shallow pan and toast lightly in oven, stirring often, about 10 minutes.

Mix 1 1/2 cups sugar, salt and cornstarch in saucepan. Add or-

ange juice (use all or part reconstituted frozen orange juice, if desired) and lime juice gradually, stirring until smooth and blended.

Set over moderate heat and cook, stirring constantly, until boiling. Boil 1 minute, stirring.

Add at least half of hot mixture gradually to egg yolks, stirring constantly. Return mixture to saucepan, set over moderate heat and boil 1 minute more, stirring constantly.

Remove from heat and stir in orange and lime rind. Cool to lukewarm, stirring occasionally.

Combine egg whites and 1/4 cup sugar and beat until stiff peaks form. Fold into orange mixture.

Sprinkle 1/3 of graham wafer crumb mixture into serving bowl. Spoon in half of pudding mixture. Sprinkle with 1/3 of crumb mixture and spoon in remaining pudding mixture. Sprinkle top with remaining crumbs. (Or layer in sherbet or parfait glasses for individual servings.) Chill until serving time. Garnish with orange sections. (Serves 6 to 8.)

FRENCH PUDDING

1/2 cup soft butter
1 1/2 cups sifted icing sugar
2 eggs
2 cups graham wafer crumbs
Two 4 3/4-oz. cans strained
   apricots (baby food)
1/2 cup toasted slivered almonds
1 cup whipping cream,
   whipped

Beat butter and sugar together until light and fluffy. Add eggs and beat thoroughly.

Put a layer of about half the crumbs in the bottom of a buttered 8-inch square pan. Add the butter mixture and spread evenly. Spread this with the contents of one can of strained apricots.

Fold remaining can of strained apricots and almonds into whipped cream. Spread this over layers in pan and top with remaining crumbs, pressing them down gently.

Chill 24 hours before serving, then cut into squares or spoon out of pan. (Serves 9.)

STRAWBERRY-CHEESE PUDDING

16-oz. carton cream-style cottage cheese
1/4 cup sugar
1 tsp. vanilla
2 cups fresh strawberries, sliced
1/2 cup graham wafer crumbs
1 tbsp. melted butter
1/8 tsp. nutmeg

Press cottage cheese through a sieve. Blend in sugar and vanilla. Fold in berries. Spoon into serving dishes. Chill well.

Combine graham wafer crumbs, melted butter and nutmeg at serving time and sprinkle over desserts. (Serves 6.)

CHILLED CHOCOLATE SOUFFLÉ

4 squares (4 oz.) semi-sweet baking chocolate
2 cups milk
1/3 cup water
2 envelopes (2 tbsp.) unflavored gelatin
1/2 cup cold water
4 egg yolks
1/2 cup sifted icing sugar
3 tsp. vanilla
4 egg whites
2 cups whipping cream
Icing sugar
1 cup whipping cream
2 tbsp. icing sugar
1/4 tsp. cinnamon

Put chocolate in top of double boiler. Add milk and water and set over simmering water. Heat, stirring occasionally until chocolate is melted and milk scalded.

Soak gelatin in cold water 5 minutes.

Beat egg yolks in a small bowl until thick, about 5 minutes at high speed on the mixer. Beat in icing sugar. Add hot chocolate mixture gradually, stirring to blend. Pour back into top of double boiler and cook over simmering water until mixture coats a silver spoon, about 5 minutes. Stir constantly.

Add gelatin and stir to dissolve.

Remove mixture from heat and set in ice water to chill until it begins to mound when dropped from a spoon. Stir in vanilla.

Beat egg whites until stiff but not dry.

Beat 2 cups whipping cream until stiff. Fold cream into chilled chocolate mixture. Fold egg whites into chocolate mixture.

Pour into 2-qt. soufflé dish or casserole. Chill until firm, at least 2 hours.

Sift icing sugar thickly over top of soufflé at serving time.

Whip remaining 1 cup cream with 2 tbsp. icing sugar and cinnamon just until it begins to thicken. Serve separately to pour over soufflé. (Serves 8.)

Note: To make soufflé appear to have risen above dish, use a 1 1/2-qt. soufflé dish or straight-sided casserole. Extend sides as shown in black and white photo.

ORANGE FLUFF

3 cups corn flakes
1/4 cup sugar
1/4 tsp. salt
1/4 cup butter
1 envelope (1 tbsp.) unflavored gelatin
1/4 cup cold water
1 cup orange juice
1/3 cup sugar
2 tsp. grated orange rind
1/4 tsp. grated lemon rind
1 tsp. lemon juice
2 egg whites
1/3 cup sugar
1 cup whipping cream
1/2 cup whipping cream (optional)
Orange sections (optional)

Measure corn flakes and crush into fine crumbs. Blend in 1/4 cup sugar and salt. Melt butter, add to corn flake mixture and stir with fork until well blended. Take out 1/4 cup of mixture and set aside.

Press remaining corn flake mixture firmly and evenly into the bottom of a well buttered 8 x 8 x 2-inch pan. Chill well.

Put gelatin in a mixing bowl. Add water and let stand 5 minutes.

Combine orange juice and 1/3 cup sugar in a small saucepan. Heat and stir until mixture reaches the boiling point. Add to gelatin and stir until gelatin is dissolved. Stir in orange and lemon rind and lemon juice.

Set in ice water and chill until mixture mounds slightly when dropped from a spoon.

Beat egg whites until foamy. Add remaining 1/3 cup sugar gradually and beat well after each addition. Continue beating until stiff peaks form. Fold into gelatin mixture.

Beat 1 cup whipping cream until stiff. Fold into gelatin mixture.

Pour over chilled corn flake crust. Sprinkle remaining 1/4 cup of corn flake crumbs over top. Chill thoroughly until set.

Cut in oblongs 4 x 2 inches to serve. Whip remaining 1/2 cup cream and top pieces with a spoonful and 2 or 3 orange sections if desired. (Serves 8.)

EXTENDING SIDES OF SOUFFLÉ DISH

Extend sides of dish with a double piece of waxed paper to make chilled soufflés look as if they had risen above the dish. Tape the paper firmly to the dish. Pour the mixture, chill and peel off paper.

PINK SNOW

1 envelope (1 tbsp.) unflavored
 gelatin
1/4 cup cold water
2 cups sliced strawberries
1/4 cup water
3/4 cup sugar
1/4 cup orange juice
2 egg whites
Whole strawberries
Soft Custard (recipe p. 130)

Add gelatin to 1/4 cup cold water and let stand 5 minutes.

Combine sliced strawberries and 1/4 cup water in saucepan, cover and bring to a boil. Cook about 2 1/2 minutes or just until berries are breaking up. Strain through sieve, pressing through as much of berry pulp as possible. Pour strawberry juice back into saucepan.

Add gelatin mixture and sugar to strawberry juice and heat, stirring constantly, until gelatin and sugar are dissolved. Remove from heat. Stir in orange juice.

Set in ice water and chill until mixture begins to hold shape when dropped from the tip of a spoon.

Beat egg whites stiff. Slowly add gelatin mixture to egg whites, continuing to beat with a rotary beater. Set mixture back in ice water and chill, stirring gently, until mixture begins to hold shape.

Spoon into serving dishes and chill. Serve with whole berries and Soft Custard. (Serves 6.)

ALMOND FLUFF WITH STRAWBERRIES

1/2 cup sugar
1/3 cup toasted chopped almonds
1 envelope (1 tbsp.) unflavored
 gelatin
3 tbsp. cold water
3 eggs
1/2 cup sugar
1 tsp. almond extract
1 cup whipping cream
1 pt. strawberries
Sugar

Heat 1/2 cup sugar in heavy skillet until melted and golden. Stir in toasted almonds and turn out on buttered cookie sheet immediately, pulling with the tines of two forks to spread as thinly as possible. Cool. Crush to crumbs with a rolling pin.

Add gelatin to cold water in small dish and let stand 5 minutes. Melt gelatin by setting dish in simmering water. Cool slightly.

Beat eggs until frothy in small deep bowl. Beat in 1/2 cup sugar and almond extract and continue beating until thick (5 minutes at high speed on the mixer).

Whip cream until just beginning to get thick. Beat in melted gelatin and continue beating until cream is stiff. Fold into egg mixture along with crushed almond mixture.

Spoon into serving dishes and chill well. Slice and lightly sweeten strawberries and spoon over almond mixture at serving time. (Serves 8.)

GRAHAM WAFER TORTE

1 tsp. unflavored gelatin
1 tbsp. cold water
1/2 pt. whipping cream
2 tbsp. sugar
4 3/4-oz. can strained apricots
 (baby food)
1/2 cup chopped toasted almonds
16 double graham wafers
4 3/4-oz. can strained apricots
1/2 cup slivered toasted almonds

Soak gelatin in cold water, then set in hot water to dissolve. Cool slightly.

Whip cream until foamy, add sugar and whip until beginning to thicken. Add gelatin drop by drop, beating constantly until stiff. Fold in 1 can strained apricots and chopped toasted almonds.

Spread half of this mixture thickly between graham wafers, standing them on end, side by side, to form a cake. Chill about 1 hour. Keep remaining whipped cream mixture cold.

Spread outside of graham wafer cake with remaining can of strained apricots and spread remaining whipped cream mixture over all. Sprinkle thickly with slivered toasted almonds. Chill again until serving time.

Cut on diagonal. (Serves 6.)

POT DE CRÈME AU CHOCOLAT

1/4 cup blanched almonds
4 squares (4 oz.) sweet baking
 chocolate
1 tbsp. sugar
Dash salt
1/2 cup light cream
3 egg yolks
1/2 tsp. vanilla
Whipping cream

Heat oven to 350 degrees.

Chop almonds quite fine, spread on baking sheet and put in oven. Toast, stirring often, until golden, about 10 minutes. Set aside to cool.

Melt chocolate in top of double boiler over simmering water. Gradually stir in sugar, salt and cream and continue heating until smooth and glossy. Lift off heat.

Beat egg yolks until frothy and slowly blend in the hot mixture. Stir in vanilla.

Pour into 4 small dessert dishes, custard cups or demi-tasse cups. Sprinkle with toasted almonds. Cool and chill.

Whip cream at serving time and top each dessert with a spoonful of whipped cream. (Serves 4.)

STRAWBERRY MOUSSE

1 qt. strawberries
3 egg whites
1 cup sugar
1 pt. whipping cream
2 tbsp. lemon juice
2 tsp. almond extract
1/8 tsp. salt
Whole strawberries

Wash, hull and mash strawberries with fork until there are no large pieces. Add egg whites and sugar and beat until thick and fluffy (about 5 minutes at high speed on the mixer).

Whip cream until it begins to thicken. Add lemon juice, almond extract and salt and continue beating until stiff. Fold into berry mixture.

Pour into two 9-inch ring moulds or one large mould. Freeze until firm.

Serve with sugared whole berries. (Serves 16.)

Chilled Chocolate Soufflé — *recipe on page 131*

MELON MOUSSE

½ cup sugar
½ cup water
2 cups diced cantaloup
  (1 small)
1 envelope (1 tbsp.)
  unflavored gelatin
¼ cup water
Yellow food coloring (optional)
2 cups whipping cream

Combine sugar and ½ cup water in saucepan. Bring to a boil, turn down heat and simmer 5 minutes. Add cantaloup and simmer about 5 minutes or until melon is very tender.

Soak gelatin in ¼ cup water 5 minutes.

Strain melon and press the pulp through the sieve. Add the gelatin to the hot melon mixture and stir until dissolved.

Chill melon-gelatin mixture in ice water until beginning to set. Beat with rotary beater until foamy. Beat in a few drops of yellow food coloring.

Whip cream until very stiff. Fold in chilled melon mixture. Pour into ice cube trays or mould and freeze until firm. (Serves 6 to 8.)

DELICIOUS BANANA ICE CREAM

3 large fully-ripe bananas
1 tbsp. lemon juice
½ cup sugar
1 pt. whipping cream
3⅝-oz. pkg. vanilla
  instant pudding

Break bananas up into large bowl and beat with rotary beater or electric mixer until puréed. Add lemon juice and sugar and beat until smooth.

Add whipping cream and pudding mix and beat with rotary beater or mixer at medium speed until smooth and thickened, about 2 minutes.

Pour into ice cube trays or mould and freeze until quite firm around the outside but still soft in the middle. Put into chilled bowl and beat again until smooth. Pour back into trays or mould and freeze until firm. (Serves 6 to 9.)

BLUEBERRY RIPPLE ICE CREAM

¼ cup soft butter
¾ cup sugar
2 eggs
½ cup ice water
½ cup instant powdered skim milk
1½ tsp. vanilla
2 tbsp. lemon juice
1 cup fresh or thawed frozen blueberries
1 tsp. grated lemon rind
Blueberries

Beat butter and sugar together with electric mixer until very light and fluffy. Add eggs, one at a time, beating well after each addition. Continue beating at high speed 5 minutes.

Mix ice water, powdered skim milk and vanilla in another bowl. Beat at high speed on mixer until soft peaks form (3 to 4 minutes). Add lemon juice and continue beating until stiff peaks form (3 to 4 minutes longer). Fold into butter mixture. Spoon into ice cube tray or mould. Freeze until holding shape but still soft.

Whirl 1 cup blueberries in blender to make a purée. Stir lemon rind into purée and spoon over first mixture. Run a wooden spoon or rubber scraper through the ice cream in each direction so the blueberry mixture is rippled through but not blended completely.

Freeze until firm. Spoon into serving dishes and top with more blueberries. (Serves 4 to 6.)

PEACH ICE CREAM

2 to 3 medium peaches (very ripe)
¼ cup soft butter
¾ cup sugar
2 eggs
1 small peach
½ cup instant powdered skim milk
1½ tsp. vanilla
2 tbsp. lemon juice
Red food coloring (optional)

Peel and cut up medium peaches. Press the pulp through a sieve (or use a blender if you have one). Use enough to give you ½ cup thick purée. Chill thoroughly.

Cream butter and sugar together very well, using medium speed on electric mixer. Add eggs, one at a time, beating well after each addition. Turn mixer speed to high and beat 5 minutes.

Mash small peach with a fork (you should have about ¼ cup peach pulp). Stir into creamed mixture.

Combine the ½ cup chilled peach purée, instant powdered skim milk and vanilla in small mixer bowl. Beat at high speed until soft peaks form (3 to 4 minutes). Add lemon juice and red food coloring to tint a delicate pink and continue beating until firm peaks form (another 3 to 4 minutes).

Fold whipped mixture into creamed mixture. Pour into ice cube tray or mould. Freeze until firm. (Serves 6.)

CHERRY TORTONI

2 egg whites
2 tbsp. sugar
½ cup coarse vanilla wafer crumbs
½ cup coarsely-chopped toasted almonds
½ cup maraschino cherries, cut up
1 tbsp. sherry
1 cup whipping cream
¼ cup sifted icing sugar
½ cup coarse vanilla wafer crumbs

Beat egg whites until foamy. Add sugar and beat until stiff. Fold in ½ cup crumbs, almonds, cherries and sherry.

Whip cream with icing sugar and fold into egg white mixture.

Sprinkle bottom of 9 large paper baking cups (cupcake cups) with some of remaining crumbs. Spoon in cherry mixture. Sprinkle tops with remaining crumbs. Freeze. (Makes 9.)

FROZEN NEAPOLITAN TORTE

4-oz. pkg. chocolate pudding and pie filling
1½ cups milk
2 egg yolks
1 square (1 oz.) unsweetened chocolate
½ tsp. vanilla
15-oz. pkg. frozen strawberries
Milk
3¼-oz. pkg. vanilla pudding and pie filling
2 egg yolks
Red food coloring
4-oz. pkg. butterscotch pudding and pie filling
1 tbsp. instant coffee
1½ cups milk
2 egg yolks
1 pt. whipping cream
½ cup sugar
Sweetened whipped cream
½ cup coarsely-chopped walnuts or walnut halves

Prepare chocolate pudding according to package directions except use only 1½ cups milk. Beat 2 egg yolks lightly and stir at least half of hot mixture into them gradually. Return to pan and bring

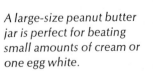

A large-size peanut butter jar is perfect for beating small amounts of cream or one egg white.

back to a full rolling boil. Remove from heat, cover with waxed paper and cool. Grate chocolate on coarse grater and stir into cooled pudding along with vanilla.

Heat frozen strawberries to boiling and cook gently until berries are broken up. Force through sieve and measure strawberry purée. Add enough milk to make 1¾ cups liquid. Prepare vanilla pudding mix according to package directions, using this strawberry-milk mixture as the liquid. Beat 2 egg yolks lightly and stir at least half of hot mixture into them gradually. Return to pan and bring back to a full rolling boil. Remove from heat, add a few drops of red food coloring to tint a good strawberry color. Cover with waxed paper and cool.

Prepare butterscotch pudding mix according to package directions, *except* stir instant coffee into dry mix and use only 1½ cups milk. Beat 2 egg yolks lightly and stir at least half of hot mixture into them gradually. Return to pan and bring back to a full rolling boil. Remove from heat, cover with waxed paper and cool.

Whip 1 pt. cream with ½ cup sugar when all puddings are cool. Fold ⅓ of the whipped cream into each of the cooled puddings.

Spoon butterscotch mixture into 10-inch angel food pan, levelling it as much as possible. Spoon strawberry mixture on top of butterscotch and level it off. Spoon chocolate mixture on top.

Cover pan with aluminum foil and freeze several hours or overnight. Unmold about 20 minutes before serving and ice outside edge with sweetened whipped cream, sprinkle with chopped walnuts or pipe cream on top and decorate with walnut halves. Cut in wedges. (Serves 12 to 16.)

Fruit

JACK HORNER BAKED APPLES

4 baking apples
⅓ cup crushed graham
    wafers
2 tbsp. chopped walnuts
¼ cup chopped dates
1 tbsp. butter
½ cup brown sugar, packed
½ cup hot water

Heat oven to 350 degrees.

Wash and core apples. Peel ⅓ of the way down from the top. Put in deep 8-inch square baking dish.

Combine crumbs, walnuts and dates. Fill cavities in apples. Top each with a piece of butter and sprinkle with brown sugar.

Add water to pan, cover and bake 40 to 50 minutes, or until the apples are tender. (Serves 4.)

Note: The time of baking depends on the kind of apples used. Do not overbake.

BANANA DELIGHT

1 cup light cream
¼ tsp. anise seeds
¼ tsp. vanilla
1½ cups flaked coconut
6 bananas

Heat cream and anise seeds to scalding. Remove from heat. Stir in vanilla. Pour mixture over coconut. Press coconut down into liquid well. Cool, then chill at least 1 hour.

Spoon over sliced bananas at serving time. (Enough for 6 servings.)

BLUEBERRIES AND BANANA CREAM

2 cups blueberries
½ cup whipping cream
2 tbsp. sugar
1 ripe banana
½ tsp. grated lemon rind

Wash blueberries and put in 4 sherbet glasses.

Whip cream and sugar until they begin to thicken. Mash banana with a fork until smooth. Fold into cream mixture along with lemon rind.

Whip until blended and slightly thickened but still soft enough to pour. Pour over berries and serve. (Serves 4.)

CARAMEL PEACHES

3 tbsp. butter
1 cup brown sugar
½ tsp. mace
6 fresh peaches, peeled
½ cup cream

Melt butter in heavy frying pan. Add sugar and mace and stir well. Bring to simmering.

Add whole peaches and allow to simmer about 30 minutes over low heat, turning peaches often and basting with sauce. Be sure to keep heat low.

Place peaches in serving dishes. Add cream to sauce, stirring well and heating through. Spoon sauce over warm peaches. (Serves 6.)

Note: To peel peaches easily, dip them briefly into boiling water then their skins will just slip off.

HAWAIIAN POACHED PEARS

20-oz. can crushed pineapple
9-oz. jar red currant jelly
1 cup water
1 tbsp. lime juice
6 large fresh pears
3⅝-oz. pkg. instant vanilla
    pudding mix
1 tsp. vanilla
½ cup whipping cream
Slivered toasted almonds

Combine pineapple, jelly, water and lime juice in large heavy skillet with a tight lid. Heat gently until boiling and jelly is melted.

Cut pears in halves and peel and core them. Drop into pineapple mixture, turn heat to low, cover and simmer until pears are tender, about 10 minutes.

Lift out pears with a slotted spoon and put in bowl. Boil pineapple mixture hard until very thick and pour over pears. Cover and chill very well.

Prepare pudding mix as directed on package *except* use an extra ½ cup milk and add vanilla. Chill until serving time. Whip cream until soft peaks form at serving time and fold into pudding.

Spoon pears into serving dishes and top generously with pudding mixture. Sprinkle with almonds. (Serves 6.)

NEWFOUNDLAND STRAWBERRY SHORTCAKE

½ cup soft butter
1 cup sugar
1 pt. fresh strawberries
Shortcake Biscuits
    (recipe follows)

Cream butter thoroughly. Add sugar gradually, beating well after each addition, until light and fluffy.

Mash berries and add to creamed mixture. Chill.

Serve over split hot Shortcake Biscuits. (Serves 3 to 4.)

Shortcake Biscuits

2 cups sifted all-purpose flour
1 tbsp. sugar
3 tsp. baking powder
1 tsp. salt
6 tbsp. shortening
¾ cup milk

Heat oven to 450 degrees.

Sift flour, sugar, baking powder and salt into a bowl. Add shortening and cut in finely with a pastry blender or 2 knives. Add milk and stir just until blended (dough should be soft and puffy).

Round up dough and knead gently on a floured board about 6 times.

Roll out ½ inch thick and cut into six 4-inch biscuits.

Put on ungreased cookie sheet and bake 10 to 12 minutes or until golden.

HOT STRAWBERRIES

¼ cup butter
1 cup ½-inch white bread
    cubes (use day-old bread)
¼ cup brown sugar, packed
½ tsp. cinnamon
2 cups small strawberries,
    washed and hulled
Vanilla ice cream

Melt butter in heavy skillet. Add bread cubes and cook gently, stirring constantly, until cubes are golden. Add sugar and cinnamon and cook and stir until bread is crisp. Add berries and cook gently, stirring constantly, 2 minutes.

Spoon into serving dishes and serve topped with a spoonful of ice cream. (Serves 2 to 3.)

Add new Weekend Magazine Tested Recipes here

Add new Weekend Magazine Tested Recipes here

Add new Weekend Magazine Tested Recipes here

Add new Weekend Magazine Tested Recipes here

Add new Weekend Magazine Tested Recipes here

Add new Weekend Magazine Tested Recipes here

Bread and Batter Ideas

Some of the most popular recipes to appear in my articles have been the bread recipes. And why not? Bread, hot from the oven, is irresistible.

Besides, bread is part of our heritage. As far back as there are records, bread has been on the tables of rich and poor alike. There were times when the poor had only dark and heavy bread while the rich lived on white and light bread. But, except in times of famine, there has always been bread.

When our ancestors first came to this part of the world they made bread — good bread I'm sure. But because of limited supplies variety must have been limited too.

Today we're lucky. Because of the influence of other lands and the endless supply of good ingredients available, we don't have to settle for one or two kinds of bread. We can easily make any kind we prefer.

Perhaps you'd like a yeast bread. Whole wheat? Or French? Or is it a quick bread you want? How about muffins or a fruit loaf?

I have given a choice of recipes here I hope will cover almost any kind of bread you have in mind. The yeast recipes include loaves, buns, Danish pastries and coffee cakes. And there are muffins, scones, popovers, fruit breads, savory breads and coffee cakes among the quick bread recipes.

Waffles and pancakes are here too. And some suggestions for sauces and spreads to serve with them.

Flower Pot Bread — *recipe on page 146*

Yeast Breads

FLOWER POT BREAD

Any regular bread, either white or whole wheat, can be baked in clay flower pots for interesting shapes and special brown crusts.

Here is how to prepare pots for Flower Pot Bread:

1. Buy unpainted clay pots (be sure they are the good old-fashioned red clay kind, not some kind of plastic). You can choose from diameters of 3 inches (for individual loaves), 4 inches, 5 inches, 6 inches and 7 inches. If you want to buy just one size, the 5-inch pots make nice medium-sized loaves. Five this size should be enough for most bread recipes.

2. Scrub pots thoroughly in hot soapy water. I used a vegetable brush to scrub mine to be sure any powdery clay was washed away. Rinse very well under hot running water. Dry, then let stand several hours to be sure the water they have absorbed is completely dried out. (If you are in a hurry they can be dried in a slow oven.)

3. Oil pots very well on the inside, including the rim. Use vegetable oil and keep oiling until the pot will not absorb any more. You'll be surprised how much oil this will take.

4. Set the pots on a piece of heavy-duty aluminum foil in a cold oven. Turn thermostat to 400 degrees. When the temperature gets to 400 degrees, turn off the heat and leave the pots in the oven to cool. When completely cooled oil them again, return them to a cold oven and heat a second time, allowing them to cool in the oven. Now the pots are ready to use. Be sure to grease them well before each use, especially around the rim. Don't worry about the hole in the bottom of the pot. The bread dough will quickly seal the hole closed.

Try one of your favorite recipes or Egg Bread (recipe follows) baked this way.

Whatever recipe you use, let the dough rise as usual to the shaping stage. Then shape into balls just large enough to half-fill chosen pots. Put dough into prepared pots and let rise in a warm place until dough is level with tops of pots.

Baking time will vary with kind of bread and size of pots used. Bake until loaves sound hollow when tapped lightly on top. Use same temperature your recipe requires for these specially-shaped loaves.

Let loaves stand in pots about 5 minutes after baking before loosening carefully and turning out on racks to finish cooling.

Egg Bread

½ cup lukewarm water
1 tbsp. sugar
2 pkg. active dry yeast
1½ cups scalded milk, cooled to lukewarm
3 tbsp. sugar
1 tbsp. salt
3 eggs, lightly beaten
¼ cup soft shortening OR butter
7 to 7½ cups all-purpose flour
1 egg yolk
1 tbsp. cold water
Sesame seeds

Measure water, add 1 tbsp. sugar and stir until sugar dissolves. Sprinkle yeast over and let stand 10 minutes. **Put** scalded milk into large bowl. Add 3 tbsp. sugar, salt, eggs and shortening and beat together. Cool to lukewarm, stir in yeast. Add half of flour and beat thoroughly with wooden spoon. Add enough of remaining flour to make a fairly stiff dough that is easy to handle. Mix very well with hands.

Turn out on floured board and knead until dough is smooth and small bubbles appear under the surface (about 5 minutes). Round up and put in greased bowl. Grease top of dough, cover with a damp cloth and set in a warm place. Let rise until double in bulk (about 1½ hours).

Punch down and let rise again until nearly double (about 45 minutes). Punch down again.

Shape dough into balls (just as for dinner rolls), making them just large enough to half-fill your chosen flower pots (I used one 7-inch pot, one 6-inch pot and one 5-inch pot). Put balls in well-greased pots and set in a warm place. Let dough rise until level with the tops of the pots.

Heat oven to 375 degrees.

Beat egg yolk and cold water together lightly with a fork. Brush over tops of loaves and sprinkle generously with sesame seeds.

Bake about 1 hour or until loaves sound hollow when tapped lightly on top. Cover with aluminum foil if loaves start to brown too much on top.

Let stand in pots 5 minutes. Loosen carefully and turn out on racks to finish cooling.

Note: Bake dough in three 9 x 5 x 3-inch loaf pans if desired.

Slice home-made bread before freezing. This way you can use any part without having to defrost the whole loaf.

WHOLE WHEAT BREAD

½ cup milk
¼ cup molasses
½ cup shortening
1¾ cups lukewarm water
2 tsp. sugar
2 pkg. active dry yeast
4 tsp. salt
1½ cups all-purpose flour
4 cups whole wheat flour
½ cup all-purpose flour
Soft shortening

Combine milk, molasses and shortening in small saucepan and heat, stirring occasionally, until mixture is almost boiling and shortening is melted. Cool to lukewarm.

Measure water into large mixing bowl. Add 2 tsp. sugar and stir to dissolve. Sprinkle yeast over water and let stand 10 minutes. Stir well.

Add cooled milk mixture, salt, 1½ cups all-purpose flour and 1 cup of the whole wheat flour. Beat thoroughly with wooden spoon until mixture is smooth. Add remaining whole wheat flour and enough of remaining ½ cup all-purpose flour to make dough easy to handle but not stiff. Mix thoroughly with hand, squeezing the dough through fingers until it is well blended.

Turn out on floured board and knead until smooth and very elastic and small bubbles appear under the surface. Round up in large greased bowl, cover with a damp cloth, set in a warm place and let rise until double in bulk, about 1½ hours. Punch down and let rise again until nearly double, about 45 minutes.

Punch down again, divide dough in two and shape into loaves. Put in greased 9 x 5 x 3-inch loaf pans and let rise again until double, about 1 hour.

Heat oven to 375 degrees. Bake about 50 minutes or until well browned and loaves sound hollow when tapped on top.

Turn out on cake racks to cool and brush tops lightly with soft shortening. (Makes 2 loaves.)

FRENCH BREAD

1¼ cups lukewarm water
1 tsp. sugar
1 pkg. active dry yeast
1½ tsp. salt
3 tbsp. soft shortening
3½ cups all-purpose flour (approx.)
Cornmeal
1 egg white
2 tbsp. cold water

Combine lukewarm water and sugar in mixing bowl and stir to dissolve sugar. Sprinkle yeast over water and let stand 10 minutes. Stir well.

Add salt, shortening and about half of the flour. Beat well with a wooden spoon. Add remaining flour and mix with hand until dough is easy to handle (add a little more flour if necessary).

Turn out on floured board and knead until dough is very smooth and elastic and small bubbles appear under the surface. Round up in greased bowl and let rise in a warm place until double in bulk, about 1 hour. Punch down and let rise again until nearly double, about 30 minutes.

Punch dough down again and turn out on floured board or pastry cloth. Roll into an oblong 15 x 10 inches (if dough is so elastic it resists rolling let it rest about 15 minutes, then roll). Roll dough up tightly from one of wide sides, sealing firmly by pressing with the heel of the hand along the full length of the loaf at each full turn.

Put a hand on either end of the roll and roll it gently back and forth under the hands to lengthen the roll and taper the ends. Seal ends by pressing firmly against the board with side of hand and tucking under.

Grease a cookie sheet and sprinkle with cornmeal. Put loaf on sheet (diagonally if it is a small sheet), sealed edge down. Make slashes in top of loaf with a sharp knife. Have slashes 2 inches apart and about ¼ inch deep.

Brush top of loaf with cold water and let stand in a warm place until very light, about 1½ hours.

Heat oven to 375 degrees. Brush loaf with cold water again and bake 20 minutes.

Beat egg white and cold water together. Remove loaf from oven and brush top with egg white glaze. Return to oven and bake about 25 minutes more or until loaf is golden and sounds hollow when tapped lightly. (Makes 1 loaf.)

PUMPERNICKEL BREAD

1½ cups lukewarm water
1 tbsp. sugar
3 pkg. active dry yeast
½ cup molasses
4 tsp. salt
2 tbsp. caraway seeds
2¾ cups rye flour
2 tbsp. soft shortening
3½ cups sifted all-purpose flour
Cornmeal

Measure water into large mixing bowl. Add sugar and stir to dissolve. Sprinkle yeast over water and let stand 10 minutes. Stir well.

Stir in molasses, salt and caraway seeds.

Add rye flour and shortening and mix until smooth. Add all-purpose flour and mix thoroughly.

Turn out on lightly-floured board and knead until smooth and bubbles appear under surface.

Place in greased bowl and let rise in warm place until double in bulk (about 1½ hours).

Punch down and let rise again until almost double (about 30 minutes).

Shape dough into 2 round, slightly flattened loaves.

Sprinkle greased cookie sheet with cornmeal and place the two loaves on opposite corners. Cover with damp cloth and let rise about 1 hour.

Heat oven to 375 degrees, and bake 30 to 35 minutes or until loaves sound hollow when tapped on top. (Makes 2 loaves.)

RICH RAISIN BREAD

1 cup raisins
½ cup lukewarm water
1 tsp. sugar
1 pkg. active dry yeast
½ cup scalded milk
2 tbsp. sugar
1½ tsp. salt
1 tsp. cinnamon
2 eggs, lightly beaten
2 tbsp. soft butter
3½ cups all-purpose flour
   (approx.)
Melted butter
Sugar

Cover raisins with boiling water and let stand 5 minutes. Drain well and dry on paper towelling.

Measure lukewarm water into mixing bowl. Add 1 tsp. sugar and stir to dissolve. Sprinkle yeast over water and let stand 10 minutes. Stir well.

Cool scalded milk to lukewarm and add to yeast mixture along with 2 tbsp. sugar, salt, cinnamon, eggs and soft butter. Add half of flour and beat well with a wooden spoon.

Add raisins and enough of remaining flour to make the dough easy to handle. Mix thoroughly with hand. Turn out on floured board and knead until smooth and small bubbles appear under the surface.

Round up, put in greased bowl, cover with a damp cloth and let rise in a warm place until double in bulk, about 1½ hours. Punch down and let rise again until nearly double, about 30 minutes.

Shape into loaf and put in lightly-greased 9 x 5 x 3-inch loaf pan. Let rise until double in bulk, about 45 minutes.

Heat oven to 400 degrees. Brush loaf with melted butter and sprinkle generously with sugar. Bake 30 to 35 minutes or until loaf sounds hollow when tapped on top. Turn out of pan and cool on rack. (Makes 1 large loaf.)

HERB PAN BUNS

1 cup lukewarm water
2 tsp. sugar
2 pkg. active dry yeast
½ cup butter, melted
3 tbsp. sugar
3 tsp. salt
2 eggs, lightly beaten
2 cups lukewarm milk
8½ cups all-purpose flour
1 cup grated Parmesan cheese
1 tsp. oregano
½ tsp. marjoram
¼ tsp. sweet basil
Melted butter

Measure water, add 2 tsp. sugar and stir until dissolved. Sprinkle yeast over water and let stand 10 minutes. Stir well.

Combine butter, 3 tbsp. sugar, salt, eggs and milk and blend well. Stir in yeast mixture.

Add half of flour, cheese and herbs and beat with wooden spoon until smooth. Add enough of remaining flour to make a soft dough that is easy to handle. Blend well.

Turn out on lightly-floured board and knead several minutes until dough is smooth and elastic and small bubbles appear under the surface. Put in greased bowl, cover with damp cloth and let rise in warm place (85 degrees) until double in bulk, about 1 hour.

Punch down and shape into buns. Place them close together in two 13 x 9½ x 2-inch greased oblong pans. Brush tops with melted butter. Set in a warm place and let rise until double, about 1 hour.

Heat oven to 400 degrees. Bake about 15 minutes or until well browned. (Makes 6 dozen.)

PICNIC BUNS

½ cup lukewarm water
1 tsp. sugar
1 pkg. active dry yeast
¾ cup lukewarm milk
1 tbsp. sugar
1 tbsp. shortening
1½ tsp. salt
2½ to 3 cups all-purpose flour

Measure water into large mixing bowl. Add 1 tsp. sugar. Stir to dissolve. Sprinkle yeast over water and let stand 10 minutes. Stir well.

Stir in milk, 1 tbsp. sugar, shortening, salt and half the flour. Mix until smooth. Add enough of remaining flour to make dough easy to handle. Mix with hand.

Turn out on floured board and knead until smooth and elastic and small bubbles appear under the surface. Round up in greased bowl. Cover with damp cloth and let rise in warm place until double (about 1½ hours). Punch down; let rise until nearly double (about 30 minutes).

Divide dough in 2 parts. Roll each into 7½-inch square, ½ inch thick. Cut each square into 9 buns, each 2½ inches square. Place on greased cookie sheet. Cover with damp cloth and let rise until double (about 1 hour).

Heat oven to 400 degrees. Bake buns 12 to 15 minutes until brown. (Makes 1½ dozen.)

BUTTERHORNS

¼ cup lukewarm water
1 tsp. sugar
1 pkg. active dry yeast
¾ cup lukewarm milk
¼ cup sugar
1 tsp. salt
1 egg
¼ cup soft butter
3 to 3½ cups all-purpose flour
Soft butter
Poppy seeds and sesame seeds
   (optional)

Measure water into mixing bowl. Add 1 tsp. sugar and stir until dissolved. Sprinkle yeast on top of water and let stand 10 minutes. Stir until dissolved.

Add milk, sugar, salt, egg and ¼ cup soft butter. Add about half of the flour and beat thoroughly with a spoon. Add enough of remaining flour to make the dough easy to handle and mix in thoroughly with hand.

Turn out on floured board and knead until dough is smooth and small bubbles appear under the surface.

Put in greased bowl, cover with a damp cloth and set in a warm place (85 degrees) until double in bulk (about 1½ hours). Punch down and let rise again until near-

Yeast Breads

ly double (about ¹/₂ hour).

Roll dough out into a circle ¹/₄ inch thick. Spread with soft butter. Cut into 16 pie-shaped wedges. Roll each wedge up from the wide side and set on greased cookie sheet with the point underneath.

Brush with soft butter and sprinkle with poppy or sesame seeds, if desired. Set in warm place and let rise until double (about 1 hour).

Heat oven to 400 degrees.

Bake 12 to 15 minutes or until golden. (Makes 16.)

SESAME PUFFS

1 cup lukewarm water
1 tsp. sugar
1 pkg. active dry yeast
3 cups all-purpose flour
Melted butter
Sesame seeds
Salt

Measure water into mixing bowl, add sugar and stir to dissolve. Sprinkle yeast over water and let stand 10 minutes. Stir well. Add enough of flour to make a very stiff dough, working well with hand.

Turn out on floured board and knead until smooth.

Cover with a damp cloth and let rise in a warm place until double (about ³/₄ hour). Punch down.

Heat oven to 475 degrees.

Roll dough very thin (¹/₈ inch) on a floured board and cut in 2-inch rounds. Roll each round again to make almost paper-thin and put on greased cookie sheet. Brush each round with melted butter, sprinkle generously with sesame seeds and lightly with salt.

Bake about 5 minutes or until browned and puffed. Good served as snacks like potato chips or with soup or salad. (Makes 5 dozen.)

Bread Sticks

Use same dough as for Sesame Puffs and shape into sticks as shown in black and white photos.

Put on greased cookie sheet, brush with melted butter, sprinkle with salt and sesame, caraway or poppy seeds, if desired.

Bake at 475 degrees until golden, about 10 minutes. (Makes 32.)

DANISH PASTRIES

1 cup milk
¹/₂ cup lukewarm water
2 tsp. sugar
2 pkg. active dry yeast
¹/₂ cup soft butter
¹/₃ cup sugar
2 tsp. salt
2 eggs
2 tsp. almond extract
5¹/₂ cups all-purpose flour (approx.)
1¹/₂ cups cold butter
Egg Yolk Glaze (recipe follows)

Heat milk to scalding, remove from heat, cool and chill.

Measure water. Add 2 tsp. sugar and stir until dissolved. Sprinkle yeast over water and let stand 10 minutes. Stir well. Chill.

Cream ¹/₂ cup soft butter until fluffy. Add ¹/₃ cup sugar and salt and blend very well. Beat in eggs and almond extract. Stir in chilled milk and yeast mixture. (At this point the mixture will be *very* curdled.)

Add half the flour and beat well with a wooden spoon. Add enough of remaining flour to make a soft dough, mixing just enough to blend.

Turn out on floured board and pat with hand into a 10-inch square (do not knead). Fold all four sides into the centre and pat again with hand into a 10-inch square. Wrap in waxed paper and chill 15 minutes.

Roll dough into a rectangle 15 x 10 inches. With the long side of dough toward you, cover the centre ¹/₃ of dough with thin slices of the cold butter, using half of it. Fold left-hand ¹/₃ of dough over

Recipe continued on next page

TO SHAPE BREAD STICKS

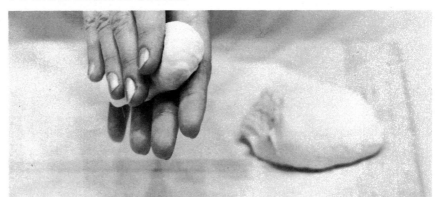

Roll small pieces of dough between palms until smooth and lengthened.

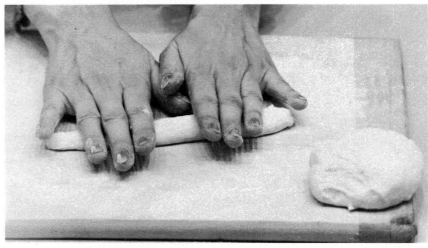

Put each piece of dough on a floured board and roll under palms of hand until it is long and about the thickness of a pencil.

butter. Seal edges around butter.

Cover left-hand ⅓ of dough (the ⅓ just folded over) with thin slices of butter in the same way, using the rest of the butter. Fold the right-hand ⅓ of dough over it and seal well around the edges.

Roll into a rectangle 20 x 12 inches. With the long side of dough toward you, fold into thirds again to make a rectangle approximately 12 x 7 inches. Wrap in waxed paper and chill 5 minutes.

Repeat this last rolling twice, *except* the last time chill dough 30 minutes.

Roll dough into a rectangle 12 x 8 inches. Cut in three sections each 8 x 4 inches. Wrap each piece of dough in waxed paper and chill at least 1 hour.

Remove pieces of dough one at a time from refrigerator and shape into pastries of any desired shape (see suggestions for Twists, Pockets and Butterflies).

Put on lightly-greased cookie sheets and brush with Egg Yolk Glaze. Let rise about 1 hour (pastries are better if they don't rise as much as double). Heat oven to 375 degrees. Bake 15 minutes or until lightly browned. Cool on racks. (Makes about 60.)

Egg Yolk Glaze

1 egg yolk
2 tbsp. cold water

Beat together well with a fork. Use to brush over pastries as directed.

TWISTS

Roll ⅓ of dough into a rectangle 12 x 7 inches. Cut in strips ¾ inch wide by 7 inches long. Twist ends of strips in opposite directions and shape into snails, knots

or figure 8s. Follow preceding directions for rising and baking except just before baking make a depression in the top of each pastry and fill with thick raspberry jam. Drizzle with Icing Sugar Glaze (recipe follows) while warm. (Makes 16.)

POCKETS

Roll ⅓ of dough into a rectangle 15 x 12 inches. Cut into twenty 3-inch squares. Put a spoonful of thick date or raisin filling or jam in the centre of each square and pinch two opposite corners together for some and all four corners together for the remaining. Follow preceding directions for rising and baking. Drizzle with Icing Sugar Glaze (recipe follows) while warm. (Makes 20.)

BUTTERFLIES

Roll ⅓ of dough into a rectangle 16 x 12 inches. Combine ½ cup thick apricot jam, ¼ cup finely-chopped almonds, 1 tsp. grated lemon rind and ⅛ tsp. cinnamon and spread this mixture thinly over dough. Roll dough up tightly from each 12-inch side, making the two rolls meet in the middle. Cut in ½-inch slices and lay, cut side down, on greased cookie sheets. Follow preceding directions for rising and baking. (Makes 16.)

Icing Sugar Glaze

2 cups sifted icing sugar
2 tbsp. water (approx.)
½ tsp. vanilla

Blend all ingredients until smooth, using enough water to make a fairly thin icing.

BRIOCHE

¼ cup lukewarm water
1 tsp. sugar
1 pkg. active dry yeast
⅔ cup scalded milk, cooled to lukewarm
1 tbsp. sugar
2 tsp. salt
4½ cups all-purpose flour
1 cup soft butter
5 eggs
1 egg yolk
1 tbsp. cold water

Measure lukewarm water into mixing bowl. Add 1 tsp. sugar and

stir to dissolve. Sprinkle yeast over water and let stand 10 minutes. Stir well.

Add milk, 1 tbsp. sugar and salt. Add 1 cup of the flour and beat hard until smooth. Add butter and beat thoroughly again.

Add remaining flour and eggs, one at a time, mixing well after each addition. (Dough will be very sticky at this point.)

Continue mixing, using hand and squeezing dough through fingers and picking it up and slapping it back down into the bowl occasionally. Handle the dough vigorously and continue mixing in this way until it stiffens and becomes very elastic, 10 to 15 minutes.

Cover with a damp cloth and set in a warm place until dough doubles in bulk. (Because dough is very rich this will take from 2 to 3 hours.) Stir well.

Cover again and chill overnight.

Grease 18 large muffin cups.

Pinch off dough in ¼ cup-size pieces (measure first one so you know size). Do only a few at a time and keep the remaining dough chilled so it is easy to handle.

Pinch a piece about the size of a small walnut from each piece of dough. Shape each large piece of dough into a smooth round ball and put in prepared muffin pan. Cut a cross in the top with a sharp pointed knife. Make each cut of the cross about ½ inch long and ½ inch deep. Press the points of the cross down with the tip of the knife to make a definite hole.

Shape each small piece of dough into a tear shape and drop the pointed end down into the hole in the top of the larger piece of dough. Settle this piece in firmly but don't flatten down. (It should look like a bubble on the top.)

Repeat this shaping until all the dough is used. Cover and let rise in a warm place until very light, about 2 hours.

Heat oven to 425 degrees.

Beat egg yolk and cold water together with a fork. Brush tops of buns with this glaze.

Bake about 15 minutes or until browned. Serve warm. (Makes 18.)

REFRIGERATOR ROLL DOUGH

1½ cups lukewarm water
2 tsp. sugar
2 pkg. active dry yeast
⅔ cup sugar
2 tsp. salt
⅔ cup soft shortening
    (part butter)
2 eggs
1 cup lukewarm unseasoned
    mashed potatoes (use instant
    if desired)
6½ to 7 cups all-purpose flour

Measure water into large mixing bowl. Add 2 tsp. sugar and stir to dissolve. Sprinkle yeast over water and let stand 10 minutes. Stir well.

Add ⅔ cup sugar, salt, shortening, eggs, mashed potatoes and half of flour. Beat thoroughly with a wooden spoon until well blended and smooth.

Add enough of the remaining flour to make a soft dough that is easy to handle. (It is important to keep dough soft for rolls that are tender and moist, so do not add any more flour than necessary.) Round up in greased bowl, cover with damp cloth and let rise until double in bulk. Punch down, grease top lightly with shortening and cover with waxed paper. Store in refrigerator until needed.

Use as required for coffee cakes, dinner rolls, cinnamon rolls, etc. (See following directions for some roll variations.) Since this dough keeps well in the refrigerator for a week, fresh breads can be baked several times from the same dough. Allow extra rising time since the dough will be cold when shaped (about 2 hours should be right). Half of the dough will make a large coffee cake or a large pan of cinnamon buns. The whole recipe makes about 4 dozen good-sized rolls.

Pan Buns

Shape dough into rounds one-third of the size you want for the finished buns. Put close together in greased layer-cake pans. Let rise until very light. Heat oven to 400 degrees. Bake about 15 minutes or until well browned. If desired shape into Parker House Rolls or Clover Leaf Rolls and let rise and bake as for Pan Buns.

Cinnamon Rolls

Use half of Refrigerator Roll Dough. Roll it into an oblong 15 x 9 inches. Spread with 2 tbsp. soft butter. Combine ⅔ cup sugar and 2 tsp. cinnamon and sprinkle over butter. Roll up tightly from one wide side and cut into 1-inch slices. Put, cut sides down, in greased 13 x 9½ x 2-inch baking pan. Let rise until very light. Heat oven to 375 degrees and bake 25 to 30 minutes or until well browned. While warm, drizzle with white icing made by combining 1 cup icing sugar with enough warm water to make a thin icing which will run off spoon.

COFFEE BUNS

¼ cup lukewarm water
1 tsp. sugar
1 pkg. active dry yeast
½ cup milk
¼ cup shortening
1 tbsp. sugar
¾ tsp. salt
2 eggs, lightly beaten
2 cups sifted all-purpose flour
½ cup melted butter
¾ cup sugar
2 tsp. instant coffee
½ tsp. cinnamon

Combine water and 1 tsp. sugar and stir until sugar dissolves. Sprinkle yeast over and let stand 10 minutes. Stir well.

Scald milk and pour into mixing bowl. Stir in shortening, 1 tbsp. sugar and salt and cool to lukewarm. Add yeast mixture, eggs and flour and beat very well.

Cover with a damp cloth and let rise in a warm place until double, about 1 hour. Stir well.

Grease sixteen 2½-inch muffin pans. Half fill pans with batter. Let rise in warm place until double, about 30 minutes.

Heat oven to 375 degrees. Bake buns about 20 minutes or until golden.

Roll hot buns quickly in melted butter, then in a mixture of ¾ cup sugar, coffee and cinnamon. Serve warm. (Makes 16.)

HOT CROSS BATTER BUNS

1 cup lukewarm water
1 tsp. sugar
1 pkg. active dry yeast
2 tbsp. sugar
2¼ cups sifted all-purpose flour
1 tsp. salt
1 tsp. cinnamon
¼ tsp. nutmeg
¼ tsp. lemon extract
1 egg
2 tbsp. soft shortening
½ cup currants
¾ cup sifted icing sugar
1 tbsp. cream (approx.)

Measure water into mixing bowl. Add 1 tsp. sugar and stir to dissolve. Sprinkle yeast over water and let stand 10 minutes. Stir to dissolve.

Add 2 tbsp. sugar, half of flour, salt, cinnamon, nutmeg and lemon extract and beat hard with a wooden spoon until smooth.

Add egg and shortening and beat again until blended.

Add remaining flour and currants and beat hard until smooth.

Scrape down sides of bowl, cover with damp cloth. Let rise in a warm place until double in bulk, 45 to 60 minutes.

Spoon into 12 large greased muffin cups, filling half full. Let rise until double, about 30 minutes.

Heat oven to 400 degrees. Bake 20 to 25 minutes or until well browned. Remove from pans and set on cake rack.

Combine icing sugar and about 1 tbsp. cream to make a thick icing and use to make a cross on top of each warm bun. Serve warm. (Makes 12.)

COFFEE CAKE

½ cup lukewarm water
1 tsp. sugar
1 pkg. active dry yeast
½ cup lukewarm milk
¼ cup sugar
1 tsp. salt
1 egg
¼ cup soft shortening
3¼ to 3½ cups all-purpose
    flour
2 tbsp. soft butter
½ cup sugar
2 tsp. cinnamon
½ cup seeded raisins
½ cup melted butter
¾ cup sugar
½ cup finely-chopped nuts

Measure water into mixing bowl. Sprinkle in 1 tsp. sugar and stir to dissolve. Sprinkle yeast over water and let stand 10 minutes. Stir well.

Stir in milk, ¼ cup sugar, salt, egg, shortening and half of flour, mixing thoroughly with a spoon. Add enough of remaining flour to make dough easy to handle. Mix with hand.

Turn out on lightly-floured board and knead until smooth and elastic and small bubbles appear under the surface. Round up in greased bowl and grease top of dough.

Let rise in a warm place (85 degrees) until double (1½ to 2 hours). Punch down and let rise again until nearly double (30 minutes).

Roll into an oblong 15 x 9 inches. Spread with 2 tbsp. butter. Sprinkle with a mixture of ½ cup sugar, cinnamon and raisins. Roll up tightly like a jelly roll from the wide side. Seal well.

Cut into 1-inch slices. Dip each slice in melted butter, then in a mixture of ¾ cup sugar and nuts.

Make a layer of slices in the bottom of greased 10-inch tube pan, putting cut side down with slices barely touching. Arrange rest of slices in layers on top, filling in spaces and overlapping slices, but avoid putting one slice directly on top of another. Press layers together gently.

Cover with a damp cloth and let rise until double (about 1 hour).

Heat oven to 375 degrees.

Bake 45 to 60 minutes until well browned and coffee cake sounds hollow when tapped on top. Invert on serving plate and leave pan over it for a few minutes to let all syrup from pan run down over cake. Serve warm.

ALMOND COFFEE RING

½ cup lukewarm water
2 tsp. sugar
2 pkg. active dry yeast
1 cup all-purpose flour
1½ cups milk
½ cup butter
3 eggs
⅔ cup sugar
½ tsp. crushed cardamom
2 tbsp. grated orange rind
6 to 6½ cups all-purpose
    flour
3 tbsp. melted butter
1 cup chopped blanched
    almonds
1 egg
1 tbsp. cold water
2 tbsp. sugar
¼ cup slivered blanched
    almonds

Measure ½ cup water into small bowl. Add 2 tsp. sugar and stir to dissolve. Sprinkle yeast over water and let stand 10 minutes. Stir well. Add 1 cup flour, blend well and let stand in warm place about 20 minutes or until spongy.

Heat milk to scalding. Add butter and stir until butter is melted. Cool to lukewarm.

Beat eggs well in large bowl. Add ⅔ cup sugar and beat again. Stir in lukewarm milk mixture, cardamom and orange rind. Add about half of the 6 cups flour and the yeast mixture and beat hard until smooth.

Add enough of remaining flour to make a soft dough that is easy to handle. Turn out on floured board and knead gently until smooth. Put in greased bowl, cover with damp cloth and set in warm place. Let the dough rise until double (1½ to 2 hours).

Turn out on floured board and knead again for about 5 minutes.

Cover with damp cloth and let rest 15 minutes. Divide dough into 2 pieces.

Roll one piece of dough into an oblong 16 x 9 inches. Brush with half of melted butter and sprinkle with half of chopped almonds. Roll up as for cinnamon rolls from one wide side. Put, sealed edge down, on greased cookie sheet, turn so roll forms a ring and pinch ends together. Make cuts two-thirds of the way through the ring at 1-inch intervals. Turn each of these cut pieces on its side (see black and white photo.)

Repeat this shaping with the second piece of dough.

Let rise until double in bulk (about 45 minutes).

Heat oven to 375 degrees.

Beat 1 egg and cold water together until blended. Brush this mixture all over tops of coffee cakes. Sprinkle 1 tbsp. sugar and 2 tbsp. slivered almonds over each cake.

Bake about 35 minutes or until well browned and coffee cakes sound hollow when tapped lightly on top. Serve warm or cold with butter. (Makes 2 large coffee cakes.)

JELLY BUSTERS

½ cup lukewarm water
2 tsp. sugar
2 pkg. active dry yeast
1½ cups lukewarm milk
½ cup sugar
2 tsp. salt
2 eggs, beaten
½ cup soft shortening
7 cups all-purpose flour
Fat for deep frying
Jelly
Sugar

Measure water into mixing bowl, add 2 tsp. sugar and stir to dissolve. Sprinkle yeast over water and let stand 10 minutes, then stir well.

Add milk, 1/2 cup sugar, salt, eggs, shortening and half of flour. Mix thoroughly with a spoon. Add enough of remaining flour to make a soft but not sticky dough. Mix with hand until well blended.

Turn out on floured board and knead until smooth and elastic, and small bubbles appear under the surface.

Put in greased bowl, cover with a damp cloth and let rise in a warm place (85 degrees) until double (about 1 1/2 hours). Punch down and let rise again until nearly double (30 to 45 minutes).

Turn dough out on to floured board and roll 1/2 inch thick. Cut with floured 3-inch cookie cutter. Let stand on board to rise until very light (30 to 45 minutes).

Heat deep fat to 375 degrees.

Drop rounds of dough into hot fat and fry until golden on both sides, turning once. Drain on absorbent paper.

Cut a short slit in the side of each when cool and spoon in some jelly. Close slits tightly and roll Jelly Busters in sugar. (Makes about 3 dozen.)

Crullers

Make dough as for Jelly Busters *except*, after second rising, roll dough 1/2 inch thick and cut in strips 3/4 inch wide and 10 inches long. Twist strips in opposite directions from each end to form twists and press ends together to fasten.

Let rise on board until very light and fry as for Jelly Busters. While still warm, dip in warm Glaze (recipe follows).

Glaze

1/3 cup boiling water
1 cup sifted icing sugar

Add water gradually to icing sugar, stirring until smooth.

Quick Breads

BACON MUFFINS

6 slices bacon
1 cup sifted all-purpose flour
¼ cup sugar
3 tsp. baking powder
½ tsp. nutmeg
½ tsp. salt
1 cup cornmeal
¼ cup bacon drippings
   OR melted butter
½ cup milk
½ cup thick applesauce
1 egg

Heat oven to 400 degrees. Grease 12 large muffin cups.

Fry bacon until very crisp. Lift out of pan and put on paper towelling to drain and cool.

Sift flour, sugar, baking powder, nutmeg and salt into mixing bowl. Crumble bacon finely and add to dry ingredients along with cornmeal. Mix lightly with a fork.

Combine bacon drippings or butter, milk, applesauce and egg and beat together with a fork. Add to dry ingredients and stir with fork *just* until dry ingredients are moistened, about 30 strokes.

Spoon into muffin cups, filling ⅔ full. Bake about 15 minutes or until browned and crusty. Serve warm. (Makes 12 large.)

BLUEBERRY MUFFINS

1 egg
¼ cup butter, melted
1 cup milk
½ tsp. vanilla
2¼ cups sifted all-purpose flour
¼ cup sugar
3 tsp. baking powder
1 tsp. salt
1 cup frozen blueberries
   (not thawed)
¼ cup sugar
1 tsp. grated lemon rind

Heat oven to 400 degrees. Grease 14 large muffin cups.

Beat egg. Add butter, milk and vanilla and beat thoroughly. Sift flour, ¼ cup sugar, baking powder and salt together into egg mixture and stir only until blended. Fold in blueberries, using as few strokes as possible.

Spoon into muffin cups, filling ⅔ full. Combine ¼ cup sugar and lemon rind and sprinkle a little of this mixture on each muffin.

Bake 25 to 30 minutes or until well browned. (Makes 14 large.)

BRAN MUFFINS

¼ cup cooking (salad) oil
½ cup brown sugar, packed
¼ cup molasses
2 eggs
1 cup milk
1½ cups natural bran
1 cup sifted all-purpose flour
1½ tsp. baking powder
½ tsp. soda
1 tsp. salt
½ cup chopped dates

Heat oven to 400 degrees. Grease 12 large muffin cups.

Combine oil, sugar, molasses, eggs and milk in bowl and beat together well with a fork.

Add bran and blend well.

Sift flour, baking powder, soda and salt together into first mixture. Stir just to blend, about 25 strokes. Stir in dates at end of mixing.

Spoon into muffin cups filling ⅔ full. Bake about 15 minutes. (Makes 12 large.)

BREAKFAST PUFFS

⅓ cup soft shortening
   (part butter)
½ cup sugar
1 egg
1½ cups sifted all-purpose flour
1½ tsp. baking powder
½ tsp. salt
¼ tsp. nutmeg
½ cup milk
6 tbsp. butter, melted
½ cup sugar
1 tsp. cinnamon

Heat oven to 350 degrees. Grease 8 large or 12 medium muffin cups.

Mix shortening, ½ cup sugar and egg together thoroughly.

Sift flour, baking powder, salt and nutmeg together. Add to first mixture alternately with milk.

Spoon into muffin cups, filling ⅔ full. Bake 20 to 25 minutes, until golden brown.

Roll immediately in melted butter and then in a mixture of ½ cup sugar and cinnamon. Serve hot. (Makes 8 large or 12 medium.)

CORN MUFFINS

2 eggs
⅔ cup milk
½ cup cooking (salad) oil
¼ tsp. anise seed
⅔ cup cornmeal
1⅓ cups sifted all-purpose flour
¼ cup sugar
3 tsp. baking powder
1 tsp. salt
1 cup well-drained whole-
   kernel corn

Heat oven to 400 degrees. Grease 12 large muffin cups.

Beat eggs with a fork. Add milk and oil and beat to blend. Stir in anise seed and cornmeal.

Sift flour, sugar, baking powder and salt together into mixture and stir just to blend. Fold in corn, using as few strokes as possible.

Spoon into muffin cups and bake 20 to 25 minutes or until well browned. (Makes 12 large.)

GINGER MUFFINS

½ cup soft shortening
   (part butter)
¼ cup brown sugar, packed
¼ cup sugar
1 egg
1 cup molasses
3 cups sifted all-purpose flour
1½ tsp. soda
1 tsp. cinnamon
1 tsp. ginger
½ tsp. cloves
¾ tsp. salt
1 cup hot water

Heat oven to 350 degrees. Grease 20 medium or 12 large muffin cups.

Cream shortening, brown sugar and sugar together well. Add egg and molasses and beat until well blended.

Sift flour, soda, cinnamon, ginger, cloves and salt together. Add to creamed mixture alternately with hot water.

Spoon into muffin cups, filling ⅔ full. Bake about 25 minutes or until tops spring back when touched lightly in centre. Serve warm with butter. (Makes 20 medium or 12 large.)

JELLY MUFFINS

1 egg
$\frac{1}{3}$ cup cooking (salad) oil
$\frac{1}{2}$ cup mashed very ripe banana
     (1 large)
$\frac{1}{4}$ cup milk
$\frac{1}{2}$ cup sugar
$1\frac{2}{3}$ cups sifted all-purpose flour
$\frac{3}{4}$ tsp. salt
2 tsp. baking powder
$\frac{1}{4}$ tsp. soda
$\frac{1}{4}$ cup red currant jelly

Heat oven to 375 degrees. Grease 12 medium muffin cups.

Beat egg, oil, banana and milk together lightly with a fork. Stir in sugar.

Sift dry ingredients together into first mixture and stir only until dry ingredients are moistened.

Spoon into muffin cups, filling $\frac{2}{3}$ full. Make a depression in the top of each muffin with the tip of a spoon and fill with 1 tsp. of jelly.

Bake 15 to 20 minutes. Serve warm or cold. (Makes 12 medium.)

ORANGE-DELIGHT MUFFINS

6 thin slices orange (do not peel)
12 tsp. liquid honey
6 tsp. melted butter
24 pecan halves
2 cups sifted all-purpose flour
3 tsp. baking powder
1 tsp. salt
3 tbsp. sugar
1 cup milk
1 egg
$\frac{1}{4}$ cup cooking (salad) oil

Heat oven to 425 degrees. Grease 12 medium muffin cups.

Cut orange slices into quarters.

Put 1 tsp. honey and $\frac{1}{2}$ tsp. melted butter in the bottom of each of prepared muffin cups. Put 2 pieces of orange and 2 pecan halves on top of honey and butter.

Sift flour, baking powder, salt and sugar together into mixing bowl.

Beat milk, egg and oil together with a fork. Add to dry ingredients and stir just to blend (batter should be lumpy).

Spoon into muffin cups, filling $\frac{2}{3}$ full. Bake 20 to 25 minutes.

Invert pan on rack and leave pan standing on top of muffins for 2 or 3 minutes so all honey mixture will run down. Remove pan and serve muffins warm, orange side up. (Makes 12 medium.)

OATMEAL SCONES

$1\frac{1}{4}$ cups sifted all-purpose flour
$2\frac{1}{2}$ tsp. baking powder
$\frac{1}{2}$ tsp. soda
$\frac{1}{2}$ tsp. salt
2 tbsp. sugar
$1\frac{1}{2}$ cups rolled oats
$\frac{1}{2}$ cup butter
$\frac{1}{2}$ cup cut-up dates
$\frac{3}{4}$ cup buttermilk
1 egg

Heat oven to 400 degrees. Grease a cookie sheet.

Sift flour, baking powder, soda, salt and sugar into bowl. Add rolled oats and blend lightly with a fork. Add butter and cut in finely. Stir in dates with a fork.

Beat buttermilk and egg together with fork and add, stirring until dough stiffens. Turn out on floured board and knead gently about 5 times to round up. Flatten with hand into a round 1 inch thick. Put on cookie sheet.

Mark round into 8 wedges with the floured tines of a fork. Bake about 25 minutes or until well browned. Serve warm with butter. (Makes 8.)

POPOVERS

1 cup sifted all-purpose flour
$\frac{1}{2}$ tsp. salt
2 eggs
1 cup milk

Heat oven to 425 degrees. Grease 6 deep (5-oz.) custard cups generously.

Mix flour and salt together lightly in a mixing bowl. Add eggs and milk and beat together with a rotary beater just until smooth.

Pour into prepared custard cups, filling about half full.

Bake until golden brown, 40 to 45 minutes. Serve immediately with butter and jam if desired. (Makes 6.)

Variation: Stir 1 tbsp. poppy seeds into batter just before pouring into custard cups.

BANANA BRAN BREAD

$1\frac{1}{2}$ cups sifted all-purpose flour
2 tsp. baking powder
$\frac{1}{2}$ tsp. soda
$\frac{1}{2}$ tsp. salt
$\frac{1}{2}$ tsp. nutmeg
$\frac{1}{4}$ cup shortening
1 cup sugar
1 egg
1 cup bran flakes (cereal)
$1\frac{1}{2}$ cups well-mashed ripe
     banana (about 3 large)
1 tbsp. grated orange rind
2 tbsp. water

Heat oven to 350 degrees. Grease a 9 x 5 x 3-inch loaf pan.

Sift flour, baking powder, soda, salt and nutmeg on to waxed paper.

Cream shortening and sugar together. Add egg and beat until fluffy. Stir in bran flakes, banana, orange rind and water.

Add dry ingredients and stir just to blend. Spoon into prepared pan and spread evenly.

Bake 50 to 60 minutes or until a toothpick stuck in the centre comes out clean. Turn out of pan and cool on cake rack.

HONEY-RAISIN BREAD

3 cups whole wheat flour
3 tsp. soda
1 tsp. salt
$\frac{1}{2}$ tsp. nutmeg
1 cup sultana raisins
$\frac{1}{2}$ cup chopped walnuts
2 cups buttermilk OR sour milk
$\frac{1}{2}$ cup liquid honey
Walnut halves
1 tbsp. liquid honey
1 tbsp. melted butter

Heat oven to 350 degrees. Grease a 9 x 5 x 3-inch loaf pan.

Mix flour, soda, salt and nutmeg thoroughly in mixing bowl. Blend in raisins and chopped nuts.

Combine buttermilk or sour milk and $\frac{1}{2}$ cup honey. Add to dry ingredients, stirring just enough to blend.

Spoon into prepared pan. Top with walnut halves. Bake 45 to 50 minutes or until toothpick stuck into centre comes out clean.

Blend 1 tbsp. honey and melted butter. Spread over hot bread. Return to oven for 5 minutes to glaze top of loaf. Cool before slicing.

ORANGE GRAHAM WAFER BREAD

$\frac{1}{2}$ cup soft shortening (half butter)
$\frac{1}{2}$ cup sugar
3 eggs
$2\frac{2}{3}$ cups fine graham wafer crumbs
1 cup coarsely-chopped pecans
$\frac{1}{2}$ tsp. soda
$\frac{1}{2}$ tsp. baking powder
$\frac{1}{2}$ tsp. salt
1 tbsp. grated orange rind
$\frac{1}{2}$ cup orange juice

Heat oven to 350 degrees. Grease a 9 x 5 x 3-inch loaf pan.

Cream shortening. Add sugar and beat until fluffy. Add eggs, one at a time, and beat well after each addition.

Combine graham wafer crumbs, pecans, soda, baking powder, salt and orange rind thoroughly.

Add graham wafer mixture and orange juice to creamed mixture and blend. Spoon into pan.

Bake 40 to 45 minutes or until a toothpick stuck in the centre comes out clean. Turn out on cake rack and cool before cutting.

WALNUT-RAISIN BREAD

1 cup boiling water
2 cups chopped seeded raisins
$\frac{1}{4}$ cup soft butter
$\frac{3}{4}$ cup brown sugar, packed
1 egg
1 tsp. soda
1 cup sifted all-purpose flour
$\frac{1}{2}$ tsp. salt
$\frac{1}{2}$ tsp. nutmeg
1 cup whole wheat flour
1 cup broken walnuts
Walnut halves

Pour boiling water over raisins and cool to lukewarm.

Heat oven to 350 degrees. Grease a 9 x 5 x 3-inch loaf pan.

Beat butter, sugar and egg together until fluffy. Add soda to cooled raisin mixture. Sift flour, salt and nutmeg together and stir in whole wheat flour.

Add flour mixture to butter mixture alternately with raisin mixture, beginning and ending with flour mixture. Stir just until blended. Stir in broken walnuts.

Spoon into prepared pan and decorate top with walnut halves. Bake about 50 minutes or until a toothpick stuck in the centre comes out clean. Cool before slicing.

CASSEROLE HERB BREAD

$\frac{1}{2}$ cup soft butter
2 eggs
$1\frac{1}{2}$ tsp. caraway seeds
$2\frac{1}{4}$ cups sifted all-purpose flour
3 tsp. baking powder
$1\frac{1}{2}$ tsp. salt
$\frac{1}{2}$ tsp. dry mustard
$\frac{3}{4}$ tsp. sage
$\frac{1}{8}$ tsp. nutmeg
$\frac{3}{4}$ cup milk
$\frac{1}{4}$ cup butter, melted
$\frac{1}{2}$ cup grated sharp Cheddar cheese
$\frac{1}{4}$ cup coarsely-crushed corn flakes

Heat oven to 350 degrees. Grease a $1\frac{1}{2}$-qt. casserole.

Recipe continued on page 158

Beat soft butter and eggs together well. Stir in caraway seeds.

Sift flour, baking powder, salt, mustard, sage and nutmeg together and add to butter mixture alternately with milk. Mix only until blended.

Spoon into casserole. Combine melted butter, cheese and corn flakes and spread over top of dough.

Bake 40 to 45 minutes or until a toothpick stuck in the centre of the loaf comes out clean. Serve warm or cold cut in thick slices.

STEAMED BROWN BREAD

2 cups whole wheat flour
1 cup cornmeal
2 tsp. salt
1 tsp. soda
2 cups buttermilk
¾ cup molasses
2 tbsp. grated orange rind
1 cup seedless raisins

Wash, dry and grease well three 20-oz. cans (fruit, vegetables, tomato juice, etc., come in this size).

Combine whole wheat flour, cornmeal, salt and soda in bowl.

Combine buttermilk and molasses and add to dry ingredients all at once along with orange rind and raisins. Stir only enough to moisten dry ingredients. Spoon into cans. Cover each can with aluminum foil.

Set cans on a rack in a kettle of boiling water (have water no more than half-way up the cans). Cover tightly and steam 2 hours or until tops spring back when touched lightly.

Loosen bread from sides of cans and turn out on racks to cool. Wrap in foil to store.

PARMESAN BUTTER STICKS

⅓ cup butter
2¼ cups sifted all-purpose flour
3½ tsp. baking powder
1½ tsp. salt
1¼ cups evaporated milk
½ cup grated Parmesan cheese

Heat oven to 450 degrees. Put butter in a 13 x 9½ x 2-inch pan. Set in oven just long enough for butter to melt.

Sift dry ingredients into bowl. Add milk and stir gently with fork until mixture leaves the sides of the bowl. Turn out on floured board and knead gently until dough gets rather firm, about 12 times.

Roll into an oblong 12 x 8 inches (½ inch thick) and cut into 32 strips (cut down the middle of the oblong lengthwise to make two pieces 12 inches long by 4 inches wide, then cut each of these pieces into 16 strips ¾ inch wide).

Drop strips into melted butter in the prepared pan and turn over. Sprinkle with half of the cheese. Turn strips again and sprinkle with remaining cheese.

Bake 15 to 20 minutes or until golden. Serve hot. (Makes 32.)

HAM CRESCENT ROLLS

8-oz. pkg. refrigerated crescent dinner rolls
Melted butter
4 thin slices cooked ham
Prepared mustard
¼ cup grated Parmesan cheese
2 tbsp. minced parsley

Heat oven to 375 degrees. Lightly grease a cookie sheet.

Open crescent roll package and unroll and separate pieces of dough as directed on the package. Brush each piece of dough lightly with melted butter.

Cut the slices of ham (the kind you buy from the butcher already thinly sliced) on the diagonal to form 8 triangles. Lay one of these triangles on each piece of dough, trimming to fit if necessary. Spread lightly with mustard.

Combine cheese and parsley and sprinkle some of mixture over each piece of ham. Roll dough up as directed on the package. Lay on cookie sheet, points down and turns ends slightly to form crescents.

Bake about 13 minutes or until well browned. Serve hot or cold. (Makes 8.)

BLUEBERRY COFFEE SQUARES

⅔ cup soft butter
1 cup sugar
3 egg yolks
3 cups sifted all-purpose flour
2 tsp. baking powder
½ tsp. salt
1 cup milk
3 egg whites
11-oz. pkg. frozen blueberries (not thawed)
⅓ cup lemon juice
1 tsp. grated lemon rind
¾ cup sifted icing sugar
¼ cup sugar

Heat oven to 375 degrees. Grease a 13 x 9½ x 2-inch oblong pan.

Cream butter and 1 cup sugar together well. Add egg yolks and beat until fluffy.

Sift flour, baking powder and salt together. Add to creamed mixture alternately with milk, stirring only until blended after each addition.

Beat egg whites until stiff but not dry and fold in.

Fold in berries, using as few strokes as possible.

Spoon into pan and bake 35 to 40 minutes or until top springs back when touched in centre.

Combine lemon juice, lemon rind and icing sugar in small bowl and set in warm place while cake is baking. Stir occasionally.

Pour lemon juice mixture over baked cake and spread it to cover top. Sprinkle with the 1/4 cup sugar. Slip under hot broiler for about 2 minutes until bubbling. Serve warm cut in large squares.

CRANBERRY-RAISIN COFFEE CAKE

1/2 cup soft butter
1 cup sugar
2 eggs
2 cups sifted all-purpose flour
2 tsp. baking powder
1/4 tsp. salt
1 cup milk
15-oz. can whole cranberry sauce, drained
1/4 cup chopped walnuts
1/4 cup raisins
2 tbsp. melted butter
2 tbsp. brown sugar
1 tsp. cinnamon
Glaze (recipe follows)

Heat oven to 350 degrees. Grease 13 x 9 1/2 x 2-inch oblong pan.

Cream butter and sugar. Add eggs and beat until light and fluffy.

Sift dry ingredients together and add to creamed mixture alternately with milk.

Combine drained cranberry sauce, walnuts and raisins. Spoon 2/3 of batter into prepared pan.

Drop teaspoonfuls of cranberry mixture over batter, using about 2/3 of mixture. Cover with remaining batter and top with cranberry mixture. Sprinkle with melted butter and a mixture of brown sugar and cinnamon.

Bake 30 to 35 minutes or until a toothpick stuck in centre comes out clean. Drizzle Glaze over top while warm.

Glaze

1 cup sifted icing sugar
1 to 1 1/2 tbsp. milk OR water

Blend together, adding enough liquid to make a glaze thin enough to run off spoon.

Waffles and Pancakes

To keep pancakes piping hot, try covering with a colander. The holes will let the steam out and pancakes will stay warm but won't become limp.

CRISP WAFFLES

2 egg whites
2 egg yolks
2 cups sifted cake flour
4 tsp. baking powder
1/2 tsp. salt
2 cups milk
1/2 cup butter, melted
Sugar
Cinnamon
Blueberry Sauce (recipe follows)

Beat egg whites stiff.

Beat egg yolks thoroughly. Sift flour, baking powder and salt together and add to egg yolks.

Add milk and butter and beat until smooth. Fold in stiffly-beaten egg whites. Batter will be thin.

Bake in hot waffle iron according to manufacturer's instructions.

Serve hot sprinkled with sugar and cinnamon and topped with Blueberry Sauce. (Makes 3 large waffles.)

Blueberry Sauce

11-oz. pkg. frozen blueberries
1/4 cup water
1/4 cup sugar
1 tsp. lemon juice

Combine all ingredients in saucepan.

Cover and cook over moderate heat 10 minutes, stirring and mashing berries occasionally. Serve hot.

BUTTERMILK WAFFLES

2 eggs
2 cups buttermilk OR sour milk
1 tsp. soda
2 cups sifted all-purpose flour
2 tsp. baking powder
1/2 tsp. salt
6 tbsp. soft shortening

Beat eggs well.

Add remaining ingredients and beat until batter is smooth. Bake in hot waffle iron.

Serve hot with syrup. (Makes 3 large.)

CORNMEAL WAFFLES

4 slices bacon
1 1/2 cups sifted all-purpose flour
1/2 cup cornmeal
1 tsp. salt
3 tsp. baking powder
1 1/3 cups milk
2 egg yolks
2 tbsp. bacon drippings
2 egg whites

Fry bacon until very crisp. Drain well on paper towelling and crumble. (Measure out and set aside 2 tbsp. bacon drippings.)

Heat waffle iron to temperature recommended by manufacturer.

Sift flour, cornmeal, salt and baking powder together into a bowl.

Beat milk and egg yolks together thoroughly with a fork. Add bacon drippings and blend well. Add to sifted dry ingredients and stir to blend.

Beat egg whites stiff. Add to first mixture and fold in along with crumbled bacon.

Bake according to directions given by manufacturer of waffle iron or until waffles stop steaming.

Serve very hot with syrup or with Maple Butter, for which recipe follows. (Makes 2 large — enough to serve 2 or 4.)

Maple Butter

1/2 cup butter
1/8 tsp. nutmeg
1/2 cup maple syrup
1/4 cup grated maple sugar (optional)

Beat butter and nutmeg until light. Gradually beat in syrup. Fold in maple sugar.

SCOTTISH PANCAKES

1 cup rolled oats
3/4 cup buttermilk OR sour milk
1 cup flour
1/2 tsp. salt
2 tbsp. sugar
1 tsp. soda
1 tbsp. cooking (salad) oil
2 tbsp. maple syrup
1/2 cup cold water
1 egg, slightly beaten
Butterscotch Sauce (recipe follows)

Soak rolled oats in buttermilk or sour milk, covered, several hours or overnight.

Sift flour, salt, sugar and soda together into rolled oats mixture.

Beat oil, maple syrup, water and egg together lightly and add. Beat well with a wooden spoon.

Fry on hot griddle. Serve hot with warm Butterscotch Sauce. (Makes 12.)

Butterscotch Sauce

1 cup brown sugar, packed
1 cup maple syrup
1 tsp. salt
1/4 cup butter
1 cup light cream OR top milk

Put sugar, syrup and salt in saucepan. Stir until sugar is dissolved.

Put over moderate heat and bring to a boil. Boil 2 minutes, stirring to keep from burning.

Remove from heat and add butter, stirring until melted. Stir in cream. Serve warm. (Makes 2 1/2 cups.)

WHOLE WHEAT PANCAKES

2 eggs
2 cups buttermilk OR sour milk
1 tsp. soda
1 cup sifted all-purpose flour
1 cup whole wheat flour
1 tbsp. molasses
1/4 cup soft butter
2 tsp. baking powder
1 tsp. salt
Honey-Orange Butter (recipe
  follows)

Beat eggs well. Beat in buttermilk or sour milk and soda.

Stir in remaining ingredients except Honey-Orange Butter and beat until smooth.

Bake on lightly-greased griddle until brown underneath and bubbles form on top. Turn and brown on other side.

Serve hot with Honey-Orange Butter. (Makes about 2 dozen.)

Honey-Orange Butter

1/2 cup soft butter
1/2 cup liquid honey
2 tbsp. orange juice
Grated rind of 1 orange

Beat butter until light. Add honey and orange juice gradually and continue beating until fluffy. Fold in orange rind.

THIN PANCAKES

3 eggs
1 1/2 tsp. sugar
1 tsp. salt
3/4 cup sifted all-purpose flour
2 cups milk
3 tbsp. melted butter
Butter

Beat eggs until light in a small bowl. Add sugar and salt, beating constantly. Continue beating and add flour alternately with milk and melted butter. Batter will be very thin.

Melt a little butter in a small heavy skillet (6 inches in diameter). Spoon 3 tbsp. of batter into pan and tip so batter runs to cover bottom of pan.

Cook over moderate heat until lightly browned, turn and bake on other side. Keep warm in low oven between the folds of a towel. (Makes 16 to 20.)

Note: Although it is usually recommended that thin pancakes be baked in a small pan as directed above, I have found it quite satisfactory to spoon the batter on to a well-greased griddle and spread it so it is very thin to make 6-inch cakes.

YEAST PANCAKES

1/4 cup lukewarm water
1 tsp. sugar
1 pkg. active dry yeast
2 eggs
1 1/4 cups sifted all-purpose flour
1/2 tsp. salt
1 cup lukewarm milk
2 tbsp. cooking (salad) oil

Measure water into cup. Add sugar and stir to dissolve. Sprinkle yeast over water and let stand 10 minutes. Stir well.

Beat eggs well. Stir in flour, salt, milk, oil and yeast. Beat thoroughly. Cover with a damp cloth and let stand in a warm place 1 hour.

Spoon on to lightly-greased hot griddle and bake until tops of pancakes are covered with bubbles and undersides are brown. Turn and brown other side.

Serve hot with butter and syrup. (Makes 16 large.)

Variation: Cook 1/2 lb. bulk sausage meat thoroughly and stir into batter just before baking.

YEAST WHOLE WHEAT PANCAKES

1/2 cup lukewarm water
1 tsp. sugar
1 pkg. active dry yeast
2 cups water
1 egg, beaten
1 cup sifted all-purpose flour
1 1/2 tsp. salt
2 cups whole wheat flour
1 tsp. soda
1/2 cup hot water
1 tbsp. molasses
1/4 cup butter, melted
1/2 cup chopped pecans
Maple syrup

Measure 1/2 cup water into large mixing bowl. Sprinkle in sugar and stir until dissolved. Sprinkle yeast over water and let stand 10 minutes. Stir well.

Stir in 2 cups water and egg.

Sift flour and salt together into the mixture, add whole wheat flour and beat well until smooth. Cover and let stand in refrigerator overnight.

Stir down batter in the morning. Dissolve soda in hot water and add to batter along with molasses and butter. Beat well. Stir in nuts. Let stand at room temperature 30 minutes.

Spoon on to hot griddle and bake until golden. Serve hot with maple syrup and bacon and sausages, if desired. (Makes about 36 four-inch pancakes.)

Ever wonder how to get your pancakes all the same size? Simply use a 1/4-cup measuring cup to dip out batter.

Add new Weekend Magazine Tested Recipes here

Add new Weekend Magazine Tested Recipes here

Add new Weekend Magazine Tested Recipes here

Add new Weekend Magazine Tested Recipes here

SECTION V

Christmas Trimmings

If there is any question about when the most baking and cooking is done I'm here to say, "At Christmas, of course." I know, because in November and December I get more requests for recipes than at any other time of the year.

But it's apparently also the time when most recipes are lost.

I couldn't finish this book without this section because as soon as the holidays are over each year I start getting requests for the recipes I gave just before the holidays started. The letters nearly always say the lost recipe was tried, was a favorite, but was somehow misplaced. And that's not too hard to understand — considering the confusion that Christmas brings.

So this section is dedicated to people who tell me they'd like, just once, to be able to have all their recipes together when the panic of Christmas preparations sets in.

Here are some of the most requested of my holiday entertaining recipes. They include cakes, cookies, breads, desserts, candies, beverages and hors-d'oeuvres.

Of course many of them can be used at other than the holiday season, but I hope they will be especially helpful when you do your Christmas planning each year.

Christmas Wreaths and Mincemeat-Almond Buns — *recipes on pages 171, 172*

Christmas Trimmings *

To keep fruit cake moist and prevent moulding, dip several thicknesses of cheesecloth in sherry or other spirits (not table wine), then squeeze out excess and wrap the cake in cloth then in heavy-duty aluminum foil.

BRAZIL FRUIT TREAT

2 lb. whole pitted dates
¼ cup slivered candied citron
¼ cup slivered candied orange peel
¼ cup slivered candied lemon peel
1 ring candied pineapple, cut in large pieces
1 cup well-drained whole maraschino cherries
1 lb. whole brazil nuts
1 cup sifted all-purpose flour
1 cup sugar
1 tsp. baking powder
½ tsp. salt
4 eggs, well beaten
1 tsp. vanilla

Heat oven to 300 degrees. Grease and line with heavy greased brown paper two 9 x 5 x 3-inch loaf pans (extend paper 1 inch above sides of pan).

Combine fruit and nuts in large bowl (dates, cherries and nuts are to be left whole). Sift flour, sugar, baking powder and salt together over fruit-nut mixture and mix.

Add eggs and vanilla and blend well. Spoon into prepared pans.

Bake about 1 hour and 40 minutes or until cake is firm to the touch. Let stand in pan 10 minutes, then loosen and lift out by paper. Peel off paper and cool. Wrap in foil to store.

Cut in very thin slices.

DATE-NUT CAKE

1 cup whole dates, packed
2 cups pecans (about ½ lb.)
⅓ cup orange juice
¾ cup sifted all-purpose flour
½ tsp. soda
½ tsp. cinnamon
¼ tsp. nutmeg
¼ tsp. salt
1 cup cut-up mixed candied peel
15-oz. can sweetened condensed milk
1 egg, beaten

Heat oven to 350 degrees. Line a greased 9 x 5 x 3-inch loaf pan with heavy brown paper.

Put dates and 1 cup of the pecans through the coarse blade of the food chopper (put a few dates and a few nuts in the chopper each time — the nuts will keep the dates from sticking in the chopper). Add orange juice to date-nut mixture.

Sift flour, soda, cinnamon, nutmeg and salt together on to waxed paper.

Combine date-nut mixture, remaining pecans, peel, milk and egg. Stir in flour mixture.

Spoon into prepared pan. Bake 60 to 70 minutes or until a toothpick inserted in centre comes out clean. Remove from pan and cool. Wrap in foil and let stand a day or so before slicing.

COCONUT FRUIT CAKE
(Light)

1 cup soft butter
2 cups brown sugar, packed
4 large eggs
3 cups sifted all-purpose flour
1 tsp. baking powder
½ tsp. salt
1½ cups candied cherries (½ lb.), cut in halves
1 cup sultana raisins
1½ cups candied pineapple (½ lb.), chopped
¾ cup citron (¼ lb.), shaved
1½ cups blanched almonds (½ lb.), slivered
3 cups shredded coconut (½ lb.)
1 cup orange juice

Heat oven to 275 degrees. Line a 10-inch tube pan or two 9 x 5 x 3-inch loaf pans with greased heavy brown paper.

Cream butter and sugar until light and fluffy. Add eggs, one at a time, beating well after each addition.

Sift together flour, baking powder and salt. Combine fruit, almonds and coconut in large bowl. Add flour mixture. Mix until all the fruit is coated with flour.

Blend fruit-flour mixture into creamed mixture alternately with orange juice, starting and ending with fruit-flour mixture.

Pour into prepared pan and bake 3 to 3½ hours for the tube or 2½ to 3 hours for the loaves. If cake begins to brown too much on top, cover loosely with aluminum foil.

LIGHT FRUIT CAKE

1 lb. blanched almonds, slivered
7-oz. pkg. flaked coconut
1 lb. sultana raisins
½ lb. citron, cut up
½ lb. candied orange peel, cut up
½ lb. red candied cherries, halved
½ lb. green candied cherries, halved
Grated rind of 1 lemon
4 cups sifted all-purpose flour
1 tsp. baking powder

½ tsp. soda
1 tsp. salt
1 cup soft butter
1½ cups sugar
1 tbsp. lemon juice
10 egg whites

Heat oven to 250 degrees. Grease a 10-inch tube pan and line bottom and sides with greased heavy brown paper.

Mix nuts, fruit and grated lemon rind in large bowl. Sift flour, baking powder, soda and salt together over fruit mixture and blend well until all fruit is coated with flour.

Cream butter. Add sugar gradually and continue creaming until light and fluffy. Add lemon juice and fruit-flour mixture and blend thoroughly.

Beat egg whites until stiff and fold in. Spoon into prepared pan, packing down lightly.

Bake at 250 degrees 2½ hours. Increase oven temperature to 300 degrees and bake until cake tests done when a toothpick is inserted in centre, about 30 minutes.

RICH DARK FRUIT CAKE

2 cups cut-up dates
½ lb. candied cherries, halved
1 lb. seeded raisins
1 lb. currants
2 slices candied pineapple, cut up
½ lb. chopped mixed peel
¼ cup finely-chopped candied ginger
⅓ cup strong cold coffee
1 cup soft butter
1 cup sugar
5 eggs
3 cups sifted all-purpose flour
1½ tsp. baking powder
1 tsp. salt
½ tsp. cinnamon
½ tsp. allspice
2 cups coarsely-chopped pecans
¼ cup red currant jelly, mashed with a fork

Combine fruit and ginger in large bowl. Pour coffee over and let stand 1 hour, stirring occasionally.

Heat oven to 300 degrees. Grease a 10-inch tube pan. Line

with greased heavy brown paper.

Cream butter well. Add sugar gradually, beating well after each addition. Add eggs, one at a time, beating well after each addition. Continue beating until very light and fluffy.

Sift flour, baking powder, salt and spices together into mixture and blend thoroughly. Add fruit mixture, pecans and jelly. Blend well.

Spoon into prepared pan. Bake 2 hours and 45 minutes to 3 hours, or until a toothpick inserted in centre comes out clean. Put a pan of water in oven during baking to keep cake moist. Cool, strip off paper, wrap in foil and let mellow several weeks.

ALMOND DROPS

1 cup soft butter
1 cup sugar
½ tsp. salt
2 egg yolks
1 tsp. almond extract
2⅔ cups sifted all-purpose flour
1 cup finely-ground almonds
2 egg whites
Whole blanched almonds
Candied cherries

Cream butter, sugar, salt, egg yolks and almond extract until fluffy. Add flour and ground almonds and blend well. Chill several hours.

Heat oven to 350 degrees.

Shape dough into small balls. Beat egg whites lightly and dip each ball into them, shaking to remove excess. Put on lightly-greased cookie sheet and top with an almond or half a candied cherry.

Bake 12 minutes or until lightly browned. (Makes about 6 dozen.)

CANDY CANES

⅓ cup soft shortening
⅓ cup sugar
1 egg
⅔ cup honey
1 tsp. vanilla
2¾ cups sifted all-purpose flour
1 tsp. soda
1 tsp. salt
Red food coloring

Mix shortening, sugar, egg, honey and vanilla well. Sift flour, soda and salt together and stir in, blending thoroughly.

Divide dough in two and color one half red with a few drops of red food coloring. Chill both halves of dough well.

Heat oven to 275 degrees.

Roll bits of each color of dough under hands to form long thin strips about the size of a pencil. Twist a red and a white strip together for each cane. Lay on a greased cookie sheet and turn end to form handle of cane.

Bake about 10 minutes or until cookies are set but only lightly browned. Cool on cake racks.

Ice with alternating thin lines of red and white icing on stripes if desired. (Makes about 3 dozen.)

Note: If preferred, omit coloring and roll dough ¼ inch thick after chilling and cut into desired shapes. Bake on greased cookie sheet at 375 degrees 8 to 10 minutes or until no imprint remains when they are touched lightly with finger.

CHERRY SNOWBALLS

1 cup soft butter
½ cup sifted icing sugar
1 tsp. vanilla
2¼ cups sifted all-purpose flour
¼ tsp. salt
¾ cup finely-chopped pecans
Maraschino cherries, well drained
Icing sugar

Blend butter, ½ cup icing sugar and vanilla thoroughly. Sift flour and salt together and stir in. Mix in nuts. Chill dough.

Heat oven to 400 degrees.

Wrap a heaping teaspoonful of dough completely around a cherry for each cookie. Be sure the cherries are dry.

Set cookies on ungreased cookie sheet. Bake 10 to 12 minutes. Cookies will be set but not brown. While warm, roll cookies in icing sugar. Cool and roll in sugar again. (Makes 4 dozen.)

SPICE-FRUIT DROPS

3 cups cut-up dates
1 cup coarsely-chopped
  candied cherries
1 cup chopped mixed peel
1 cup chopped pecans
½ cup soft butter
¾ cup sugar
1 egg
1¼ cups sifted all-purpose flour
½ tsp. soda
½ tsp. salt
½ tsp. cinnamon
¼ tsp. nutmeg
⅛ tsp. cloves
1½ tsp. cocoa
  Candied cherries

Heat oven to 375 degrees.

Combine fruit and nuts.

Cream butter, sugar and egg together until fluffy. Sift flour, soda, salt, spices and cocoa into creamed mixture, add fruit and nuts and blend thoroughly.

Drop by rounded teaspoonfuls on ungreased cookie sheet. Top each with a candied cherry half. Bake about 12 minutes or until set and browned. Cool before removing from pan. (Makes about 6 dozen.)

CHRISTMAS FRUIT DROPS

1 cup soft shortening
2 cups brown sugar, packed
2 eggs
½ cup sour milk
3½ cups sifted all-purpose flour
1 tsp. soda
1 tsp. salt
1½ cups coarsely-chopped
  pecans
1 cup mixed candied peel
1 cup halved candied cherries
2 cups cut-up dates

Mix shortening, sugar and eggs thoroughly. Stir in milk.

Sift flour, soda and salt together and blend into first mixture. Add nuts and fruit. Chill.

Heat oven to 400 degrees.

Drop by rounded teaspoonfuls 2 inches apart on lightly-greased cookie sheet.

Bake 8 to 10 minutes. (Makes 6 dozen.)

EASY RUM BALLS

**4-oz. pkg. chocolate pudding
    mix (type you cook)**
1 cup sugar
¹/₃ cup milk
1 tbsp. butter
¹/₂ cup finely-chopped dates
¹/₂ cup finely-chopped walnuts
¹/₂ tsp. vanilla
¹/₂ tsp. rum extract
  Chocolate shot

Blend pudding mix and sugar in saucepan. Stir in milk and butter. Set over moderate heat and cook, stirring constantly, until boiling. Turn heat to low and boil gently, stirring constantly, 3 minutes.

Remove from heat. Stir in dates, walnuts, vanilla and rum extract. Beat until mixture begins to thicken.

Drop by heaping teaspoonfuls into chocolate shot and roll each around to coat all sides with the shot. Set on waxed paper to cool and set. (Makes about 2 dozen.)

Note: Drop mixture into ground walnuts or tiny decorating candies if you prefer.

SHORTBREAD

1 lb. butter
**1 cup minus 2 tbsp. sifted icing
    sugar**
2 tbsp. light brown sugar
4 cups sifted all-purpose flour

Blend butter and sugar thoroughly. Stir in flour and mix thoroughly with hands. Chill.

Heat oven to 300 degrees. Roll out dough ¹/₃ to ¹/₂ inch thick. Cut into fancy shapes.

Decorate with red and green cherries, colored sugar or decorating candies.

Bake 20 to 25 minutes. Top of cookies should not be brown. (Makes about 4 dozen medium-sized cookies.)

OLD-TIME SHORTBREAD

3 cups sifted all-purpose flour
**¹/₂ cup plus 2 tbsp. sifted icing
    sugar**
2 tbsp. brown sugar
1¹/₄ cups sweet butter
  Milk
  Sugar

Heat oven to 300 degrees.

Sift flour and icing sugar into bowl. Add brown sugar and blend with fork. Add butter and mix, first with fork then with fingers, until blended. Knead gently in the bowl until smooth and velvety.

Divide dough into 2 and roll or pat each piece into an 8-inch round (they will be about ¹/₂ inch thick). Put on ungreased cookie sheets. Crimp edges. Mark each round into wedges with the tines of a fork.

Brush top of each round lightly with milk and sprinkle generously with sugar. Bake about 30 minutes or until delicately brown. Cool on pan. Store in a cookie tin with a tight lid for a week before using for best flavor. Break into wedges to serve.

Note: Recipe may be doubled if desired.

CHRISTMAS WREATHS

¹/₂ cup lukewarm water
2 tsp. sugar
2 pkg. active dry yeast
1¹/₂ cups milk
¹/₂ cup sugar
2 tsp. salt
**³/₄ tsp. finely-crushed cardamom
    seeds or ground cardamom**
2 eggs, beaten
¹/₂ cup soft butter
**7 cups all-purpose flour
    (approx.)**
1 egg yolk
2 tbsp. cold water
1 cup sifted icing sugar
1 tbsp. hot water
¹/₂ tsp. vanilla
  **Red and green candied
    cherries**
  Whole blanched almonds

Measure lukewarm water into mixing bowl. Add 2 tsp. sugar and stir until dissolved. Sprinkle yeast over water and let stand 10 minutes. Stir well.

Scald milk and cool to lukewarm. Add to yeast mixture along with ¹/₂ cup sugar, salt, cardamom, eggs, butter and half of flour. Beat with wooden spoon until smooth and blended.

Add enough of remaining flour to make a soft dough. Blend in with hand.

Turn dough out on floured board and knead until smooth and elastic and small bubbles appear under the surface. Round up and place in greased bowl. Brush top of dough lightly with shortening. Cover with a cloth wrung out in warm water and set in a warm place (85 degrees) to rise.

Let rise until double in bulk (about 1¹/₂ hours). Punch down and let rise again until nearly double, about 30 minutes.

Divide dough into 2 and each half into 3 equal parts. Shape each of these pieces of dough into a strand 24 inches long. (Put the dough on a lightly-floured board and roll under the hands until it is the right length.)

Lay the 3 strands parallel on board and cross them in the middle. Braid loosely in each direction from the middle. Shape braid into a ring, tucking one end under the other and sealing well by pinching together. Put on greased cookie sheet.

Repeat shaping with other half of dough.

Let rise until double (about 45 minutes).

Heat oven to 350 degrees.

Beat egg yolk and cold water together with a fork and brush over rings. Bake 30 to 40 minutes or until golden brown. (If tops begin to brown too much cover loosely with aluminum foil.) Cool on racks.

Combine icing sugar, hot water and vanilla and ice rings while still warm. Decorate with red and green cherries and whole almonds. (Makes 2 large wreaths.)

MINCEMEAT–ALMOND BUNS

1 cup canned mincemeat
1 cup slivered almonds
¹/₂ cup sweetened condensed milk
2 tbsp. soft butter
¹/₂ cup coarsely-chopped candied cherries
¹/₂ cup lukewarm water
1 tsp. sugar
1 pkg. active dry yeast
¹/₂ cup lukewarm milk
1 tsp. vanilla
2 tbsp. sugar
1¹/₂ tsp. salt
2 eggs, beaten
2 tbsp. soft butter
3¹/₂ cups all-purpose flour (approx.)
2 tbsp. soft butter
1 egg yolk
2 tbsp. cold water
²/₃ cup sifted icing sugar
2 tsp. hot water
¹/₄ tsp. grated lemon rind

Combine mincemeat, almonds, condensed milk and 2 tbsp. butter in saucepan. Bring to a boil over moderate heat, stirring constantly. Turn heat to low and cook gently, stirring, for 7 minutes. Remove from heat and stir in cherries. Cool.

Measure lukewarm water into bowl and add 1 tsp. sugar. Stir until sugar is dissolved. Sprinkle yeast on water and let stand 10 minutes. Stir well.

Add milk, vanilla, 2 tbsp. sugar, salt, eggs and 2 tbsp. butter. Stir in about half of the flour and beat mixture well with a wooden spoon. Add enough of remaining flour to make a soft dough, mixing it in with hand.

Turn dough out on floured board and knead lightly until smooth and small bubbles appear under the surface. Round up and put in greased bowl. Grease top of dough lightly. Cover with cloth which has been wrung out in warm water and set in a warm place (85 degrees) and let rise until double in bulk (about 1¹/₂ hours).

Punch down and let rise again until nearly double (about 30 minutes).

Roll out into an oblong 20 inches by 15 inches. Spread with 2 tbsp. soft butter. Spread cooled filling evenly over butter to within ¹/₂ inch of edges.

Roll up from wide side like a jelly roll. Seal well by pinching edges of roll together. Cut roll into 18 slices. Put, cut side down, in well-greased 13 x 9¹/₂ x 2-inch pan. Let rise until double (about 45 minutes).

Heat oven to 375 degrees.

Beat egg yolk and 2 tbsp. water together with a fork. Brush mixture over top of rolls. Bake about 30 minutes or until golden. Turn out on rack to cool.

Combine icing sugar, hot water and grated lemon rind and while rolls are still warm drizzle mixture over. (Makes 1¹/₂ dozen.)

Note: If you are freezing the rolls do not ice. Cool and wrap in foil. Reheat in same foil. Then ice.

STOLLEN

¹/₂ cup lukewarm water
2 tsp. sugar
2 pkg. active dry yeast
1¹/₂ cups milk, scalded and cooled to lukewarm
¹/₂ cup sugar
2 tsp. salt
2 eggs, beaten
¹/₂ cup soft butter
2 tsp. almond extract
7 cups all-purpose flour (approx.)
1 cup cut-up blanched almonds
¹/₂ cup cut-up citron
¹/₂ cup cut-up candied cherries
2 cups seedless raisins
2 tbsp. grated lemon rind
Soft butter
2 cups sifted icing sugar
¹/₂ tsp. almond extract
Cold water
Candied cherries
Citron
Toasted almonds

Measure water and 2 tsp. sugar into mixing bowl. Stir to dissolve sugar. Sprinkle yeast over water and let stand 10 minutes. Stir well.

Add milk, ¹/₂ cup sugar, salt, eggs, butter and 2 tsp. almond ex-

tract and stir to blend. Add half of flour and beat with wooden spoon until smooth and blended. Stir in cut-up almonds, citron, cherries, raisins and lemon rind.

Add enough of remaining flour to make a soft dough that is easy to handle. Mix with hand until smooth and blended.

Turn dough out on floured board and knead until smooth and elastic and small bubbles appear under the surface, about 5 minutes. Put in greased bowl, cover with a damp cloth and set in a warm place to rise. Let rise until double in bulk (1¹/₂ to 2 hours). Punch down and let rise again until nearly double in bulk (about 1 hour).

Divide dough in two. Shape each piece into an oval about 12 x 8 inches. Spread with soft butter. Fold over the long way, sealing the open edge by pressing lightly with the heel of the hand.

Set on greased cookie sheets and form into crescent shapes. Brush tops with soft butter.

Set in a warm place and let rise until double in bulk (about 1 hour).

Heat oven to 375 degrees. Bake loaves until they are golden brown and sound hollow when tapped on top, about 40 minutes. (If loaves begin to brown too much lay a piece of aluminum foil over them.)

Cool loaves to lukewarm. Combine icing sugar, ¹/₂ tsp. almond extract and enough cold water to make an icing of spreading consistency. Spread over slightly warm loaves and decorate with halves of cherries, strips of citron and toasted almonds.

SUGAR PLUM BRAID

¹/₄ cup lukewarm water
1 tsp. sugar
1 pkg. active dry yeast
³/₄ cup lukewarm milk
¹/₄ cup soft shortening
¹/₄ cup sugar
1 egg, beaten
1 tsp. salt
¹/₂ tsp. crushed cardamom seeds
¹/₂ cup seedless raisins
¹/₂ cup chopped walnuts
¹/₂ cup chopped citron
    OR mixed peel
¹/₂ cup chopped candied cherries
    Grated rind of 1 lemon
3¹/₂ to 4 cups all-purpose flour
    Quick Icing (recipe follows)
    Candied cherries
    Walnut halves

Measure water into mixing bowl. Add 1 tsp. sugar and stir until dissolved. Sprinkle yeast over water and let stand 10 minutes. Stir well.

Add milk, shortening, ¹/₄ cup sugar, egg, salt, cardamom seeds, raisins, walnuts, citron or peel, cherries, lemon rind and half of flour. Beat with spoon until well blended. Add enough of remaining flour to make dough easy to handle. Mix with hand.

Turn out on floured board and knead until smooth. Round up and place in greased bowl, cover with damp cloth and let rise in a warm place (85 degrees) until double (about 1¹/₂ hours). Punch down and let rise again until almost double (about 45 minutes).

Divide dough into 3 equal parts. Shape each part into a strand 14 inches long. Place on lightly-greased cookie sheet, and braid the 3 strands loosely so they have room to rise. Press the strands together at ends and tuck under the loaf.

Cover and let rise until double (about 45 minutes).

Heat oven to 350 degrees. Bake until golden brown, about 40 minutes. While slightly warm, drizzle Quick Icing over and decorate with candied cherries and walnut halves.

Quick Icing

1 cup sifted icing sugar
1¹/₂ to 2 tbsp. cream
    Blend ingredients together.

CHRISTMAS ICE CREAM

1 cup mincemeat
1 cup whole cranberry sauce
¹/₂ cup broken walnuts
1 qt. vanilla ice cream

Combine mincemeat, cranberry sauce and walnuts.

Put ice cream in chilled bowl and cream with wooden spoon until softened. Work quickly so it doesn't melt.

Add fruit and nut mixture and stir enough to give a marbled effect. Do not blend thoroughly. Freeze. (Serves 8.)

CHRISTMAS SNOWBALLS

Vanilla ice cream
Shredded coconut
Green crème de menthe
Milk Chocolate Sauce (recipe follows)

Scoop out as many balls of ice cream as there are guests (this step may be done several days ahead if you have plenty of freezer space). Roll each ball in shredded coconut and put on cookie sheet. Put in freezer and keep frozen until needed.

Put one snowball on each dessert plate at serving time. Spoon 2 tsp. crème de menthe over each. Pour warm Milk Chocolate Sauce around and serve immediately.

Milk Chocolate Sauce

1 lb. milk chocolate
2 cups light cream
¹/₂ tsp. vanilla

Combine chocolate and cream in saucepan and bring to a full rolling boil over moderate heat, stirring constantly. Remove from heat and stir in vanilla. (Makes 3 cups.)

FROZEN PLUM PUDDING

¹/₄ cup grated citron
12 maraschino cherries, chopped
¹/₄ cup slivered dates
¹/₄ cup chopped figs
¹/₂ cup maraschino cherry juice
¹/₄ cup currants
¹/₄ cup seedless raisins
¹/₄ cup toasted slivered almonds
1 qt. chocolate ice cream

Soak citron, cherries, dates and figs in cherry juice. Let stand overnight.

Put currants and raisins in a small saucepan and add a little water. Simmer 5 minutes, covered. Drain and cool. Add to other fruit along with almonds and mix well.

Soften ice cream by whipping it with electric mixer or a wooden spoon until soft and smooth. Work quickly so it doesn't melt. Stir in prepared fruit.

Pour immediately into 1¹/₂-qt. mould or individual moulds. Freeze until firm. (Serves 8.)

HOLIDAY ICE CREAM SAUCE

1 cup maraschino cherries, halved
1 cup cut-up dried figs
1 cup slivered dates
1 cup cut-up sliced canned pineapple
¹/₄ cup maraschino cherry juice
¹/₂ cup pineapple juice
¹/₂ cup sugar
¹/₂ cup slivered blanched almonds

Combine all fruit and cherry juice. (If figs and dates need softening, cover with boiling water, let stand 3 minutes, and then drain.)

Combine pineapple juice and sugar in small saucepan, bring to a boil and let boil 2 minutes.

Pour over fruit. Cool.

Add almonds and chill well before serving over vanilla ice cream. (Makes 12 servings.)

To protect cook book from flying batter during baking, cover with a sheet of transparent wrapping paper.

CHRISTMAS WREATH PIE

1 envelope (1 tbsp.) unflavored
   gelatin
¼ cup cold water
2¼ cups liquid (1 tall can
   evaporated milk plus water)
2 egg yolks
¼ cup sugar
Dash salt
2 egg whites
¼ cup sugar
1½ tsp. rum extract
½ tsp. vanilla
1 cup tiny cubes well-chilled
   jellied cranberry sauce
½ cup finely-cut mixed candied
   peel
Baked Nut Crust (recipe follows)
Nutmeg
Candied peel and cherries

Soak gelatin in cold water.

Scald liquid in top of double boiler over direct heat. Beat egg yolks, ¼ cup sugar and salt together lightly. Gradually stir in hot milk. Return mixture to top of double boiler, set over simmering water and cook until mixture coats a spoon like a thin custard, about 10 minutes.

Remove from heat, add gelatin and stir until dissolved. Set in ice water and chill until mixture mounds when dropped from a spoon.

Beat eggs whites until foamy. Add ¼ cup sugar gradually and beat until stiff and glossy. Fold into chilled mixture along with flavorings. Chill mixture again for a few minutes if it seems a little soft. Fold in cranberry sauce and finely-cut candied peel. Pour into pie shell and chill until set.

Sprinkle top of pie lightly with nutmeg and decorate outside edge with peel and cherries at serving time.

Baked Nut Crust

1 cup sifted all-purpose flour
½ tsp. salt
⅓ cup shortening
½ cup ground blanched almonds
2 tbsp. ice water

Heat oven to 475 degrees.

Combine flour and salt in mixing bowl. Add shortening and cut in finely. Add almonds and blend with fork. Add ice water gradually, mixing lightly with a fork. Shape into ball and roll between two sheets of waxed paper. Line 9-inch pie pan with pastry and make a high, fluted edge. Prick thoroughly with the tines of a fork.

Bake about 8 minutes or until nicely browned. Cool.

RICH PLUM PUDDING

1½ cups seedless raisins
1½ cups currants
1½ cups sultana raisins
1½ cups seeded raisins
1 cup cut-up cooked prunes
¼ lb. candied cherries, cut in
   halves
1 cup blanched almonds,
   chopped
3 cups ground suet
1 cup brown sugar, packed
4 cups soft bread crumbs
1 large apple, chopped fine
2 cups sifted all-purpose flour
1 tbsp. cornstarch
1½ tsp. baking powder
1 tsp. salt
2 tsp. allspice
½ tsp. nutmeg
⅓ cup brandy OR fruit juice
2 lemons, juice and grated rind
5 eggs, well beaten
Hard Sauce (recipe follows)

Mix thoroughly fruit, nuts, suet, brown sugar, bread crumbs and apple in a very large bowl.

Measure flour, cornstarch, baking powder, salt and spices into sifter, and sift together over fruit. Mix thoroughly so fruit is well coated with flour.

Add brandy or fruit juice, lemon juice and rind and eggs. Mix thoroughly again.

Pour into 2 well-greased 2-qt. moulds. Tie waxed paper loosely over moulds, and steam 6½ hours.

Serve very hot with Hard Sauce. (Each pudding will serve 12.)

Hard Sauce

½ cup butter
1 cup sifted icing sugar
1 unbeaten egg white
½ tsp. vanilla
Nutmeg

Cream butter until soft. Gradually blend in icing sugar.

Beat in egg white and stir in vanilla.

Put in serving dish, sprinkle with nutmeg, and chill well before serving.

YULE LOG

Jelly Roll (recipe p. 96)
Coffee Cream (recipe follows)
Chocolate Butter Icing
   (recipe follows)

Bake and cool Jelly Roll as directed in recipe, but unroll and spread with Coffee Cream (save ¼ cup Coffee Cream for icing), and roll up again.

Follow directions under black and white photos to finish the log.

Keep refrigerated until a few minutes before serving time.

Cut a diagonal slice from each end of roll to give it the shape of a log.

Stick cut pieces on top with icing to make knots. Ice tops of knots and ends of log with ¼ cup of coffee cream. Mark with fork to look like wood.

Ice the rest of the roll thickly with Chocolate Butter Icing. Put more icing in pastry tube and decorate log and knots to look like bark. If you have no pastry tube, run fork along sides of log.

Coffee Cream

¹/₃ cup water
¹/₂ cup sugar
5 egg yolks
1 cup soft butter
1 tbsp. instant coffee
1 tbsp. boiling water
¹/₄ tsp. vanilla

Combine water and sugar in a small saucepan. Heat, stirring until sugar is dissolved. Bring to a boil and boil, without stirring, to 238 degrees or until syrup falls in a 6-inch thread from the tines of a fork.

Beat egg yolks in a small bowl until thick and lemon-colored. Add sugar syrup gradually, beating constantly. Continue beating until lukewarm. Add butter in small pieces, beating at medium speed on mixer to blend after each addition.

Dissolve coffee in boiling water, cool and beat into mixture after butter has all been blended in. Blend in vanilla. If mixture is very soft, chill for a few minutes. Use to fill cake roll according to directions.

Chocolate Butter Icing

2 cups sifted icing sugar
¹/₄ cup soft butter
2 tbsp. cream
1 tsp. vanilla
2 squares (2 oz.) unsweetened chocolate, melted

Cream sugar and butter together. Add cream and stir to blend. Blend in vanilla and chocolate.

Use to ice outside of log according to directions.

BUTTER CRUNCH

1 lb. butter
¹/₂ cup boiling water
2 cups brown sugar, packed
2 cups toasted salted pecans, cashews OR almonds
1 tsp. soda
8 oz. milk chocolate
¹/₂ cup finely-chopped nuts

Melt butter in a heavy pan and let it bubble up. Remove from heat and add water. Return to heat and bring to a boil.

Add sugar and cook over moderate heat, stirring constantly, to 280 degrees (soft-crack stage).

Add 2 cups toasted salted nuts. Continue cooking, stirring constantly, to 300 degrees (hard-crack stage). Remove from heat and add soda and stir to blend.

Pour into large buttered flat pan so that it is about ¹/₄ inch thick. Cool. When hard remove from pan in one piece.

Half melt chocolate over hot (not boiling) water. Remove from heat and stir briskly until melted.

Spread half of it on one side of cooled crunch and sprinkle with half of finely-chopped nuts. When set, turn and coat other side with chocolate and nuts.

CANDIED ORANGE PEEL

Peel from 4 medium-sized oranges
Cold water
2 cups sugar
Granulated sugar

Remove peel from oranges in quarters. Put in small saucepan and cover with cold water. Simmer until tender (about 10 minutes). Drain, reserving 1 cup of the liquid.

Remove the inner white portion of the peel with a paring knife and discard. Cut the peel into ¹/₄-inch strips.

Combine the reserved 1 cup of liquid with the 2 cups sugar. Stir over low heat until the sugar dissolves then cook, without stirring, to 238 degrees (soft ball in cold water). Add strips of orange peel and simmer 10 minutes.

Set on cake rack to drain well. Place about ¹/₂ cup sugar in a small paper bag and add the strips of peel a few at a time, shaking to coat well. Cool.

CHOCOLATE-ALMOND BOUCHÉES

1¹/₄ cups sugar
1 cup blanched almonds
2 squares (2 oz.) semi-sweet baking chocolate
6 squares (6 oz.) semi-sweet baking chocolate

Put sugar and almonds in heavy skillet. Put over moderate heat and let sugar caramelize, stirring con-

stantly. When sugar and almonds are golden, pour mixture on to lightly-buttered cookie sheet. Let cool until brittle.

Break up brittle and put through coarse blade of food chopper. Cut up 2 squares of chocolate and add to almond mixture.

Put the whole mixture through the fine blade of the food chopper twice. (After the second grinding the mixture should change from a powdery texture to a rather oily one which will stick together to form balls. If it isn't moist enough, put through the food chopper again.)

Form into 1-inch balls and let stand to set for 2 hours.

Heat 6 squares chocolate over hot (not boiling) water until partly melted. Remove from heat and stir rapidly until melted and smooth. Be careful not to overheat chocolate.

Dip chocolate-almond balls in chocolate and return to waxed paper to harden. If desired, wrap each bouchée in a small square of foil. Store in a cool place. (Makes 2 dozen.)

CHOCOLATE ALMONDS

1 cup blanched almonds
6-oz. pkg. milk chocolate chips
2 tbsp. butter

Heat oven to 325 degrees. Sliver almonds and spread in a single layer on a shallow pan. Toast in oven about 20 minutes.

Combine chocolate and butter in top of double boiler over simmering water. Heat until melted. Stir in toasted slivered almonds.

Remove double boiler from heat but leave chocolate mixture over hot water. Drop chocolate mixture by teaspoonfuls on waxed paper. Chill until firm. (Makes about 2 dozen.)

CHOCOLATE BRITTLE

2 cups sugar
1 cup corn syrup
1/2 cup water
1 tsp. salt
6-oz. pkg. semi-sweet chocolate
    chips
2 tbsp. butter
8 oz. mixed salted nuts
1 tsp. vanilla
1/2 tsp. almond extract

Combine sugar, corn syrup, water and salt in saucepan. Set over moderate heat and cook, stirring constantly, until boiling. Cover and let boil 2 minutes. Uncover and continue boiling without stirring to 290 degrees (hard crack).

Remove from heat. Add remaining ingredients immediately, stirring in quickly. Pour out on large buttered cookie sheet and spread as thin as possible with 2 forks. Break into pieces when cold.

HOLIDAY CHOCOLATES

1 cup finely-ground toasted
    blanched almonds
1 cup sifted icing sugar
1 tsp. almond extract
1/2 tsp. vanilla
1 egg white
12 squares (12 oz.) semi-sweet
    baking chocolate
1/4 cup heavy cream
    Chocolate shot, sifted cocoa,
    red and green sugar, finely-
    ground almonds

Line a 9-inch square cake pan with waxed paper.

Mix 1 cup ground almonds, icing sugar, almond extract, vanilla and enough of the egg white to make a stiff paste.

Combine chocolate and cream in the top of double boiler. Set over simmering water and heat until chocolate is nearly melted. Remove from heat and stir until chocolate is melted and smooth. Add ground almond mixture and stir until well blended.

Pour mixture into prepared pan. Cool until firm. Cut into small squares and shape each square into a small roll or ball. Roll each in one of the remaining ingredients (use several or all of these coatings to make a nice variety). Store in a cool place.

GLAZED ALMONDS

Almond Paste (recipe follows)
Green food coloring (optional)
Toasted blanched almonds
2 cups sugar
2/3 cup water
1/4 tsp. cream of tartar

Tint almond paste a pale green with food coloring if desired. Make ovals of the paste slightly larger than whole toasted almonds. Press an almond into each oval of paste. Chill thoroughly.

Combine sugar and water in top of double boiler and stir until dis-

solved. Set over direct heat and bring to a boil. Add cream of tartar and cook, without stirring, to 300 degrees or until a few drops in cold water form brittle threads. Remove from heat and set over boiling water.

Pick up each chilled almond in almond paste with a fork or tongs and dip quickly into syrup. Lift out and shake off excess syrup (the coating should be thin). Put on buttered cookie sheet to set. Keep cool until used.

Almond Paste

1 3/4 cups almonds
1 cup sugar
1 3/4 cups icing sugar
1/2 tsp. almond extract
1/2 tsp. vanilla
4 egg yolks

Blanch almonds and spread out in a single layer on paper towelling to dry overnight. Grind them twice, using the fine blade of the food chopper. Add remaining ingredients and blend well with fingers. Let stand 1 day and knead well before using.

Note: You may put a bit of the almond paste between two walnut halves or top the paste with cherry halves for variations.

RICH TOFFEE

3 cups brown sugar, packed
1 cup butter
1 can sweetened condensed milk
1 cup corn syrup

Put all ingredients in a large heavy saucepan. Bring to a boil over moderate heat and cook to 290 degrees (hard-crack stage), stirring constantly. This will take a long time, probably about 45 minutes. Candy will turn dark brown during cooking. It will burn easily, especially at the end of the cooking time, so be sure to stir constantly.

Pour into large buttered pan in a thin layer. Cool. Break in pieces to serve.

Note: If you prefer your toffee chewy rather than brittle, cook to 245 degrees. This toffee may be flavored with rum extract or poured over nuts if desired.

Out-size ice cubes are nice in the punch bowl. To make them, freeze water in used frozen orange juice cans.

WHITE CHRISTMAS FUDGE

3 cups sugar
1/4 tsp. cream of tartar
1/4 tsp. salt
1 cup light cream
1 tbsp. butter
1 1/2 tsp. vanilla
1/2 cup chopped walnuts
1/4 cup finely-chopped dates
1/4 cup finely-chopped candied
   cherries

Combine sugar, cream of tartar, salt and cream in saucepan. Set over low heat and stir until sugar is dissolved. Increase heat to moderate, cover and heat to boiling, stirring occasionally. Uncover and cook to 236 degrees (soft ball in cold water), without stirring.

Remove from heat and add butter. Let stand until cool enough to put hand on bottom of pan. Stir in vanilla and beat until syrup begins to lose gloss. Quickly stir in nuts, dates and cherries and pour into buttered 8-inch square pan. Cool and cut into squares.

FLOATING ISLAND PUNCH

1/2 cup sugar
1 cup water
6-oz. can frozen lemonade
Three 6-oz. cans frozen orange
   juice
1 qt. ginger ale
1 qt. sparkling water
4-oz. bottle maraschino cherries
   and juice
1 orange, sliced thin
15-oz. pkg. frozen raspberries,
   thawed
1 pt. orange sherbet
Ice cubes

Heat sugar and water together until sugar is dissolved. Cool.

Combine fruit juice, ginger ale, sparkling water, cherries and orange slices.

Press thawed raspberries through a sieve to remove seeds and add.

Add sugar syrup. Pour into punch bowl and add ice cubes. Drop in sherbet by spoonfuls. (Serves 20 to 25.)

Note: If you can find bottled white grape juice use it in place of sparkling water. It gives a delicious and unusual flavor.

ORANGE EGGNOG

6 eggs
3/4 cup sugar
1/4 tsp. cinnamon
1/2 tsp. nutmeg
1 cup light cream
3 cups milk
1 cup chilled fresh orange juice
Grated orange rind
Freshly-grated nutmeg

Break eggs into a large bowl. Beat until light and fluffy. Beat in sugar, cinnamon and nutmeg. Stir in cream and milk.

Gradually stir in orange juice. Serve immediately in punch cups sprinkled with grated orange rind and freshly-grated nutmeg. (Makes 24 punch-cup servings.)

PINEAPPLE PUNCH

2 cups strong tea
3/4 cup lemon juice
1 1/3 cups orange juice
2 tbsp. lime juice
1 cup sugar
12 sprigs mint
2 cups fresh OR canned
   pineapple chunks
2 cups pineapple juice
2 qts. ginger ale
2 qts. soda water

Combine first six ingredients in large bowl. Chill well. Strain.

Add pineapple chunks and pineapple juice. Pour over crushed ice in punch bowl. Add ginger ale and soda water. (Serves 20.)

HOT WINE PUNCH

20-oz. can apple juice
2/3 cup sugar
2/3 cup almonds, blanched
2/3 cup seedless raisins
2 sticks cinnamon
24 whole cloves
2 bottles red burgundy

Combine apple juice, sugar, almonds and raisins in large saucepan. Tie cinnamon sticks and cloves loosely in cheesecloth. Add

to apple juice mixture. Boil 5 minutes. Remove spices. Add burgundy. Heat slowly just to boiling point. Serve in punch bowl. If using a glass punch bowl, put a metal spoon or ladle in bowl before pouring in hot liquid. (Makes 16 to 20 servings.)

HOT SPICED PUNCH

2 cups water
24 whole cloves
2 large sticks cinnamon,
   broken up
1 cup liquid honey
6 cups boiling water
1 cup lemon juice
10 thin strips lemon peel

Combine water, cloves and cinnamon in saucepan and bring to a boil. Turn down heat and simmer 10 minutes. Add honey and bring back to a boil. Add boiling water and lemon juice and keep hot until ready to serve.

Rub the rim of each of 10 mugs with a strip of lemon, then twist the strip and drop it into the mug. Pour in the hot spiced mixture. Serve at once. (Makes 10 servings.)

SPICED CRANBERRY PUNCH

1 cup apple juice
2 whole allspice
4 whole cloves
1 small piece cinnamon stick
1/4 cup sugar
2 tbsp. cider vinegar
1 pt. cranberry juice cocktail
1 cup orange juice
1/2 cup lemon juice
2 tbsp. rum OR rum extract

Combine apple juice, spices, sugar and vinegar in small saucepan. Bring to a boil and boil 5 minutes. Strain and cool.

Combine this spiced juice with all remaining ingredients and chill well. (Makes eight 1/2-cup servings.)

WASSAIL BOWL

3 oranges
3 dozen whole cloves
12 cups apple juice
2 sticks cinnamon
1/2 tsp. nutmeg
1/2 cup honey
1/3 cup lemon juice
2 tsp. grated lemon rind
Two 20-oz. cans pineapple juice
16-oz. bottle cranberry juice

Heat oven to 325 degrees.
Stud each orange with 12 cloves. Put in baking pan with a little water in bottom and heat in oven 30 minutes.
Combine apple juice and cinnamon sticks in large saucepan. Bring to boil, reduce heat, cover and simmer 5 minutes. Add remaining ingredients and simmer 5 minutes more.
Pour into punch bowl and float oranges in mixture. Use additional cinnamon sticks as stirrers in punch cups if desired. (Makes 40 punch cup servings.)

HOT BACON SQUARES

Pastry for 2-crust 9-inch pie
1 egg white, lightly beaten
8 slices bacon
2 tbsp. minced onion
1 cup finely-grated Swiss cheese
3 eggs
1 egg yolk
2 cups light cream
1/2 tsp. dry mustard
1/2 tsp. salt
1/8 tsp. pepper
Dash nutmeg
Dash cayenne
1/2 tsp. Worcestershire sauce

Heat oven to 350 degrees.
Roll pastry very thin into an oblong about 17 x 12 inches (make sides of oblong as straight as possible). Line a jelly roll pan 15 x 10 inches with the pastry, extending the pastry up the sides and fluting to make an edge at least 1/2 inch high to hold the filling. Brush pastry with egg white.
Fry bacon until lightly cooked (not crisp) and cut in small pieces.
Drain all but 1 tbsp. of bacon fat from the pan and add onion. Cook gently 2 minutes. Combine onion with bacon pieces and sprinkle over the pastry. Sprinkle with cheese.
Beat eggs and egg yolk lightly. Stir in cream, mustard, salt, pepper, nutmeg, cayenne and Worcestershire sauce. Pour this mixture over cheese carefully.
Bake 40 to 45 minutes or until filling is set and lightly browned.
Serve very hot cut in 1 1/2-inch squares. (Makes about 60.)

CHEESE TARTS

Pastry for 2-crust 9-inch pie
1 cup grated Swiss cheese
1 1/2 cups milk, scalded
3 eggs, beaten
1/2 tsp. salt
1/8 tsp. nutmeg
Dash pepper
Paprika

Heat oven to 375 degrees.
Roll out pastry and cut into 3-inch rounds. Line 36 tiny (2-inch) tart pans with pastry rounds. Sprinkle a generous teaspoonful of grated cheese into each tart.
Combine milk, eggs, salt, nutmeg and pepper and spoon this mixture into tarts over the cheese, filling each tart about 2/3 full. Sprinkle lightly with paprika.
Bake about 15 minutes or until pastry is well browned and filling is set. Serve warm. (Makes 36.)

DATE ROLLS

5-oz. can water chestnuts
20 pitted dates
1/4 cup bottled French dressing
1/2 tsp. curry powder
10 strips bacon, cut in halves

Drain water chestnuts and cut in halves (you should have about 20 pieces). Stuff dates with the pieces and put in a small bowl. Mix French dressing and curry powder and pour over. Let stand several hours, stirring often.
Drain dates and wrap each with half a strip of bacon. Fasten with toothpicks. Put on broiler pan and bake in 400-degree oven until bacon is browned, about 15 minutes. Serve hot. (Makes 20.)

HORS-D'OEUVRES PUFFS

Fat for deep frying
Cream Puffs (recipe p. 122)
1 tbsp. grated onion
1/2 tsp. paprika
1/4 cup grated Parmesan cheese

Heat fat to 375 degrees.
Make Cream Puffs dough as directed in recipe. After eggs have been added, put half of dough in another bowl. Add grated onion and paprika to one half and Parmesan cheese to other.
Drop batter by very small spoonfuls (about 1/2 tsp.) into hot fat and fry until golden. Serve hot.

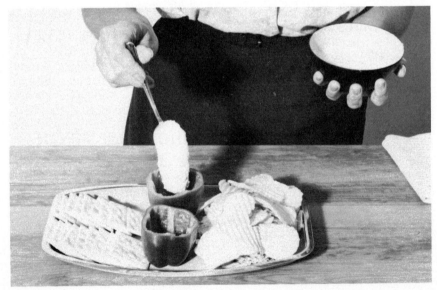

For extra and attractive dip containers during the holiday season, cut the tops off large green peppers and remove seeds. Peppers will add flavor to dips too.

LOBSTER ROLLS

Shell cooked lobster tails and claws. Cut meat into bite-sized pieces. Put in bowl and cover with a mixture of equal amounts of soy sauce and sherry. Let marinate several hours.

Drain lobster. Cut water chestnuts into thick slices. Wrap each piece of lobster and a slice of water chestnut with half a strip of bacon. Fasten with toothpicks. Put on broiler pan and bake in 400-degree oven until bacon is browned and crisp, about 15 minutes. Serve hot.

EASTERN MEAT BALLS

2 lb. ground beef
1/3 cup soy sauce
1/2 cup pineapple juice
2 tbsp. finely-minced candied ginger
1 clove garlic, crushed
2 tbsp. oil

Combine beef, soy sauce, pineapple juice, ginger and garlic, and shape into tiny (1-inch) meat balls (mixture will be fairly soft).

Heat oil in heavy skillet or electric fry pan and add meat balls. Cook gently turning often until browned on all sides. Serve hot on toothpicks. (Makes about 100.)

Note: These can be kept hot in a chafing dish.

Variation: For Olive Surprises wrap meat ball mixture around pitted ripe olives stuffed with toasted almonds. Brown as for meat balls.

STUFFED MUSHROOMS

30 large mushroom caps (about 1 1/4 inch)
1 tbsp. butter
3 tbsp. water
1 tbsp. sherry
1 chicken bouillon cube
1 tbsp. oil
1/2 lb. ground lean pork
1 tbsp. minced green onion
1/4 tsp. monosodium glutamate (optional)
1/4 cup minced water chestnuts
2 tsp. soy sauce
2 tbsp. melted butter
1/4 cup sesame seeds

Heat oven to 375 degrees.

Wash mushroom caps. Combine 1 tbsp. butter, water, sherry and bouillon cube in saucepan. Add mushroom caps and simmer 3 minutes. Lift out mushrooms with a slotted spoon and let drain and cool on paper towelling. Save liquid left in pan.

Heat oil in heavy skillet. Add ground pork and cook and stir until cooked through. Remove from heat. Combine with onion, monosodium glutamate, water chestnuts, soy sauce, 2 tbsp. butter and about 2 tbsp. of liquid mushrooms were cooked in (use just enough to moisten meat mixture). Stuff mushroom caps with meat mixture. Sprinkle tops with sesame seeds.

Put in single layer in shallow baking pan. Add remaining liquid left from cooking mushrooms. Bake about 20 minutes or until seeds are browned and mushrooms hot. Serve immediately. (Makes 30.)

APPETIZER CHEESE BALL

1/2 cup crumbled blue cheese
1/2 cup process cheese spread
8-oz. pkg. cream cheese
2 tsp. grated onion
1/4 tsp. monosodium glutamate (optional)
Dash Tabasco
1/2 tsp. Worcestershire sauce
1/4 cup finely-chopped celery leaves
1/4 cup finely-chopped salted toasted pecans
2 tbsp. finely-chopped parsley
1/2 cup chopped salted toasted pecans
Crackers

Let cheeses soften at room temperature and blend together thoroughly with onion, monosodium glutamate, Tabasco and Worcestershire sauce.

Stir in celery leaves, 1/4 cup pecans and parsley. Chill until beginning to get firm, then shape into a ball. Put in a covered bowl or wrap in waxed paper and chill several hours or until very firm.

Remove from refrigerator 1 hour before serving. Roll in remaining 1/2 cup pecans. Put in the centre of serving plate and surround with crackers and several small knives for spreading.

HAM AND CHEESE HOLIDAY SPREAD

4 1/2-oz. can devilled ham
8-oz. pkg. cream cheese
1/2 cup soft blue cheese
1/4 cup soft butter
1/4 cup chopped stuffed olives
1/4 cup chopped chives
1/4 cup chopped walnuts
Sprigs of parsley
Assorted crackers

Chill devilled ham very well. Open can and turn contents out on large serving plate.

Combine cream cheese, blue cheese, butter and olives and blend thoroughly.

Mould around devilled ham to form a ball.

Combine chives and walnuts and sprinkle over ball pressing into cheese so it is completely covered. Chill well.

Garnish with parsley sprigs and surround with crackers at serving time.

MARINATED SHRIMP

2 medium onions
2 lb. fresh shrimp, cooked, shelled, veins removed
1 cup cooking (salad) oil
2 cups wine vinegar
1/4 cup Worcestershire sauce
Dash Tabasco
1 tsp. dry mustard
2 tsp. paprika
1 tsp. salt
1/4 tsp. garlic salt

Slice onions very thin and separate into rings. Pack shrimp and onion rings in layers in a quart sealer.

Combine all remaining ingredients in a jar with a tight lid and shake until well blended. Pour over shrimp and onions. Store in refrigerator at least 24 hours before using. Serve as appetizers.

Roast Goose — *recipe on page 65*
Photo on next page

Add new Weekend Magazine Tested Recipes here

Add new Weekend Magazine Tested Recipes here

Add new Weekend Magazine Tested Recipes here

Index

Index

CINNAMON

Dried inner bark of evergreen of laurel family.

Available whole (in sticks) or ground.

Use whole in hot beverages including chocolate, fruit compotes, pickles, preserves, punches.

Use ground in breads, apple dishes, cakes, fruit cakes, cookies, puddings, pies, jams, preserves, lamb, ham, sweet potatoes, squash.

PEPPER

Dried berry of climbing vine. Black pepper berries are picked before ripe and darken as they dry. White pepper berries ripen before picked and outer shell is removed leaving light-colored kernel.

Available whole or ground including coarse ground black and cracked black.

Use whole in pepper mill, pickles, poached fish, stewed chicken, soups, sauces and stews.

Use ground in all dishes except sweets (occasionally used in pumpkin pie, spice cakes and cookies).

MACE

Part of fruit of nutmeg tree — skin covering the nutmeg. Flavor similar to nutmeg.

Usually purchased ground. Can be substituted for nutmeg.

Use in pound cakes, spice cakes, breads, cookies, muffins, puddings, apple dishes, fruit salad dressings, fish sauces and with pork, beef, lamb, chicken and vegetables.

MUSTARD

Small seed of herb plant. Two varieties of seeds, yellow and brown, combined to make dry mustard.

Available whole or ground.

Use whole in pickles, relishes, corned beef.

Use ground in egg and cheese dishes, sauces, salad dressings, meats.

PAPRIKA

Ground dried pod of sweet red pepper.

Available ground — mild or more pungent Hungarian.

Use in Hungarian goulash, paprika chicken, veal dishes, French dressings, mixed with flour for dredging chicken or meat, garnish for light-colored food.

GINGER

Dried and peeled root of lily-like ginger plant.

Available whole or ground.

Use whole in pickles, beverages, marinades for Oriental dishes.

Use ground in almost anything. Good baking spice. Also puddings, sauces, soups, Oriental dishes, vegetables, pickles, stewed fruit, chicken.